Teaching Adolescent English Language Learners

Essential Strategies for Middle and High School

Nancy Cloud

Judah Lakin

Erin Leininger

Laura Maxwell

With a Foreword by
Deborah Short

Caslon Publishing
Philadelphia

D1225639

We dedicate this book to all of our students at Hope High School who taught us much more than we ever taught them.

Cover and text photographs: Judah Lakin

Caslon, Inc.
P.O. Box 3248
Philadelphia, PA 19130

www.caslonpublishing.com

9 8 7 6 5 4 3 2 1

Library of Congress Cataloging-in-Publication Data

Teaching adolescent English language learners : essential strategies for middle and high school / by Nancy Cloud . . . [et al.] ; with a foreword by Deborah Short.
    p. cm.
Includes bibliographical references and index.
ISBN 978-1-934000-00-7 (soft cover)
1. English language—Study and teaching (Middle school)—Foreign speakers.
2. English language—Study and teaching (Secondary)—Foreign speakers.   3. Content area reading.   I. Cloud, Nancy.
PE1128.A2T387   2010
428.2'4—dc22   2009040268

Foreword

Teaching Adolescent English Language Learners: Essential Strategies for Middle and High School brings middle and high school English language learners alive. With evident respect and appreciation for these learners, the authors show teachers how to learn about their students and how to implement practical, effective instruction and program designs so the ELLs can be successful in school. The authors are bilingual and bicultural themselves and clearly demonstrate that they understand adolescents and schooling. The book is not just a guide for second-language acquisition and academic achievement—it is also about the social dimension of learning in secondary schools, of shaping one's identity, and of bridging boundaries between school and home, school and work, native languages and English, and in-school and out-of-school literacies.

This is a timely publication because many states and districts are currently seeking research-based methods for helping these learners stay in school, meet graduation requirements, and engage in productive postsecondary opportunities. Current estimates reveal that on average only 70 percent of *all* high schoolers graduate. As the Alliance for Excellent Education (2008) explains,

> Only about one third of the students who enter ninth grade each year graduate four years later with the knowledge and skills needed for postsecondary education. Another third graduate but . . . their diplomas do not mean they are academically prepared for the future. The final third simply drop out of high school before graduation day. Between the students who drop out and the students who receive a diploma, but lack critical skills, almost two thirds of each class of entering ninth graders leave high school unprepared for success in college or work. (p. 5)

The graduation percent for English language learners is significantly lower than the average in almost all states, according to the U.S. Department of Education. In cities with large populations of ELLs, such as New York and Houston, the differences are striking. In 2008, 56% of all students graduated, whereas only 36% of ELLs did. In Houston, the percent of all graduates was 68%, but for ELLs it was 23% (Zehr, 2009). This volume then is a welcome addition to the professional literature with its practitioner-based, classroom-tested material. The text goes beyond instructional techniques and lesson planning to a whole school approach with guidance for program design, professional development, and support services. It embodies the philosophy that every student can learn and, as the authors express it, "make it to graduation."

It is easy for some teachers, administrators, policymakers, and parents to discount English language learners. They may lump ELLs into one group, namely, students who do not know English; or they may decry the situation where they have to teach these students before they know English. They may complain that

ELLs bring down test scores rather than realize that No Child Left Behind requirements are inherently unfair when students are tested in English before they know English (Wright, 2006). The authors of *Teaching Adolescent English Language Learners* acknowledge these challenges, but they do not let the obstacles stop their efforts. They understand the pressures of middle and high school, particularly in this age of NCLB accountability, and they have taken positive steps toward creating a strong educational program for these learners.

The authors explain that in order to serve students, all students, well, teachers have to know them. This book provides reasonable goals for teachers to become familiar with their students, to understand their educational backgrounds, and to learn about their personal experiences and background knowledge. The authors carefully demonstrate how these students bring value to class and how the resources they hold can be tapped and further developed. Vignettes and interviews with real middle and high school students offer windows into their lives, their dreams, and their struggles in school and out. Samples of student work, from poems to journal entries, provide evidence that ELLs can attain high standards.

By showcasing the diversity among English language learners, the authors give teachers and administrators tools to plan better instruction and course scheduling. When teachers understand that some ELLs have been well educated in their countries, some have gaps in their school backgrounds, some have no literacy skills in any language, some are newcomers and others long-term ELLs, and still others have been in U.S. schools but never received ESL services because parents declined that option, the teachers can better differentiate instruction and design their lesson plans. Yes, they have standards and established curricula to address, but knowing more about the students sitting in the classroom can go a long way in providing quality instruction.

We know that quality of instruction is a key factor in learning a new language and learning content through that new language. *Teaching Adolescent English Language Learners* fortunately provides practical advice and field-tested strategies and techniques for the classroom. The authors have also drawn from the research literature on the transfer of skills from the first language to a second and competently explain how use of native language resources and respect for bilingualism can enhance student learning in Chapter 3. A plethora of instructional suggestions are included in Chapters 5–8 that apply to multiple subjects and types of learners, many with examples of student work, and all with steps for implementation. These ideas have been utilized in real-life classrooms so teachers can be assured that they work.

One topic not frequently discussed in the research literature is how to support ELLs in regular English language arts classes. Particularly at the middle and high school levels, these courses are quite different from the ESL *language* classes the students have had. On the one hand, ESL classes focus more widely on the four language domains of reading, writing, listening, and speaking and have a developmental goal. Students learn language frames to express themselves orally; they practice reading comprehension strategies; they learn how to write sentences, then paragraphs, then basic essays. On the other hand, ELA classes are the application of these learning objectives. Students are expected to know not just how to read but how to think critically about text and analyze literature. In addition, they must read faster and read more texts than most ESL classes require. Students in ELA classes are expected to know how to write, and efforts are placed on refining student writing. Yes, increasingly there are students who need help with these academic literacy skills, not just ELLs, but the authors rightly point out that there is an assumption in many ELA classes that the ELLs are former ELLs, meaning they know enough English now to be successful. It is not always the case, however. Many ELLs test out of the language-support program but struggle with general education classes. They in fact need additional support even after they have exited the ESL or bilingual program. Chapter 9 addresses this issue with concrete guidance for teachers of English language arts.

Moreover, this book is not just about who these learners are and how classroom instruction can improve. The book also addresses the broader programmatic issues. It tackles ELL scheduling, for example, which is often a conundrum for secondary schools. It gives tips for securing graduation credits for students who have been schooled in other countries or who can demonstrate proficiency in their native language. It discusses the professional development of guidance counselors, a necessary task but not one that many schools regularly undertake. Excellent guidelines for enhancing the knowledge base of counselors with regard to ELLs are offered along with practical advice for doing their job better—covering a wide range of issues from evaluating student transcripts to assigning ELLs to classes with highly trained teachers to putting the ELLs on a track to their postsecondary goals. Other support services, such as ways to extend learning time before and after school, as well as fostering more family involvement, are addressed as well. The authors recognize that schools need to identify and promote the "cultural brokers and language facilitators" among their staff.

A phrase in Chapter 9 sums up the perspective of the authors distinctly: "learning does not take place in a sociocultural vacuum." Indeed, that is a major strength of this book. The authors recognize that learning a second language and learning through a second language for secondary-level students is not just about rote memorization, grammar drills, learning 3,000 words per year, or mastering a five-paragraph essay. Learning a language—first or second or third—also involves social interaction, trial and error, motivation, and understanding of the cultural norms and nuances for using the language. For adolescents, identity is also wrapped up with learning. What language you speak says much about who you are and who you want to be. Students from linguistic and cultural backgrounds that are not prevalent in their schools need to negotiate the differences and find their place. Their teachers, guidance counselors, and administrators should help them and can do so successfully with the strategies and resources delineated in this book.

Deborah J. Short

References

Alliance for Excellent Education. (2008). *From No Child Left Behind to every child a graduate*. Washington, DC: Alliance for Excellent Education.

Wright, W. (2006). A catch-22 for language learners. *Educational Leadership, 64*(3).

Zehr, M. A. (2009, September 8). ELL graduation rates often a mystery. *Education Week, 29*(3). Retrieved online September 9, 2009, at www.edweek.org/ew/articles/2009/09/04/03ellgrads.h29.html.

Preface

Ivssara, Cape Verde

Teaching Adolescent English Language Learners grew from our discontent with the demands currently being imposed on secondary teachers with respect to educational reform initiatives prompted by No Child Left Behind and other federal and state mandates. For the most part, these mandates are constructed with little forethought about secondary students who are learning English or the teachers and programs that serve them. It also grew from our experience in secondary schools, both middle and high school, where we learned it takes the combined efforts of language and content teachers, as well as guidance counselors and families, to respond to the many demands and expectations secondary students are expected to meet to graduate from high school.

Unlike the elementary grades, in secondary schools there is no single teacher with full responsibility for the education of the English language learner (ELL). Instead, a number of teachers work with the student on a daily basis, and little time is provided for the teachers to coordinate their efforts with one another. From our firsthand experience in middle and high schools, we know that secondary educators want to meet the needs of their ELLs and are looking for strategies that can support them in their work, yet they find it hard to locate strategies that are realistic and proven to get results. This book is designed to offer some proven strategies to middle and high school teachers who work with ELLs, particularly with regard to the development of academic language in listening, speaking, reading, and writing. It is written by and for practitioners who work on a daily basis with a very diverse range of ELLs in urban secondary schools.

For many secondary teachers the pressure is great. Graduation seems a distant and unattainable goal for some of their ELLs—those who are just beginning to learn English in the later grades or those with limited formal schooling. We choose to focus on adolescents and secondary schools because of the intense needs of secondary ELLs and their teachers. At the same time, understanding the demands and time pressures placed on such teachers daily, we intend to make the book as practical and accessible as possible.

Research shows that more than two-thirds of new jobs require some form of postsecondary education (Barton, 2006), yet America has a steady high school dropout rate of nearly 30% (C. B. Swanson, 2008). Even worse for those working in urban schools, the rate is significantly higher for Latinos and African Americans (Barton, 2005; Menken, 2008; Thornburgh, 2006). In some urban school settings the dropout rate can reach as high as 60% of students (C. B. Swanson, 2008).

One source of high dropout rates is students' perception that they will never graduate. Experts like Richard Fry, senior research associate of the Pew Hispanic Center, document that ELLs are among the furthest behind on national standardized testing scores (Fry, 2007). In 2005 more than two-thirds (71%) scored below basic in mathematics, and the same percent scored below basic in reading on the National Assessment of Educational Progress (NAEP). The lack of proficiency among students in reading and math coupled with the high dropout rate has led to many reform initiatives for U.S. secondary schools. Most of the reform efforts focus on increased personalization of instruction, flexible use of time, educational structures, and professional development designed to support secondary teachers in meeting the seemingly impossible demands placed upon them (Association for Supervision and Curriculum Development [ASCD], 2006).

Fry (2007) also documented important changes in the composition of the ELL population between fourth and eighth grade where many students are moved out of that status as they acquire language skills, while many newly arrived immigrant children are added to the group. It is this pressure that middle and high school teachers of ELLs feel—the constant arrival of new students at all secondary grade levels with vastly different educational and proficiency profiles. Yet these students are expected to meet the same graduation requirements as every other student, despite the fact that they were educated outside of the United States for a significant portion of their schooling experience and are still learning English. Especially in urban secondary school settings, ELLs make up a sizable proportion of the secondary population, and this situation affects achievement and graduation rates. In fact, in New York City, ELLs are overrepresented in schools identified as failing (Menken, 2008).

But our purpose is not to sound alarm bells, as others have already done that. Nor is it to share ways to shelter instruction for secondary English language learners, as that has been well done by Echevarría, Vogt, and Short (2008) in their research-based SIOP approach. Instead, we focus on what is needed in order to program well for secondary ELLS; to create welcoming schools and classrooms where language and content teachers work together to actively develop their academic English across language and content classrooms. Teachers need proven strategies to advance students' English proficiency for academic purposes, and that is our primary reason for writing this book. We want middle and high school ELLs to make it to graduation.

At the same time we feel the pressures of secondary schooling environments; we know the joy of working with ELL young adults in middle and high schools. There is a satisfaction like no other in teaching in taking students who are in very formative years and aiding them in making a good transition to their adult lives, educations, and careers. We also hope we convey this joy in teaching in our writing, for it is this passion that can aid teachers in meeting the tremendous challenges involved in working with ELLs at the secondary level in the current climate of school reform and high standards.

Our Work in Schools

The authors met in an urban school in 2006 where we began a professional partnership focusing on a school-based professional development series designed to prepare content teachers to work more effectively with their ELLs and to obtain the ESL endorsement for their content-area teaching certificates. We were quite a diverse group of educators—ESL and bilingual teachers; English and public speaking teachers; foreign language educators; algebra, calculus, biology, chemistry, music, history, and technology teachers; and special educators—all focused on one thing: how to better serve ELLs in real-life secondary classrooms. Each classroom situation was unique and compelling, and one theme remained paramount in everyone's minds—how to help these kids make it. This experience help to clarify for us what secondary teachers need to advance the academic language of their learners—the essential teaching strategies that can promote language and literacy learning and the guidance and other support services that are needed to complement high-quality instruction and help the kids make it to graduation. It was because of this experience that some of us joined forces—a university professor, a seasoned ESL teacher, a bilingual content-area teacher (history), and an English teacher. We viewed ourselves as representative of the teachers that come into the lives of the students on a daily basis and try to do all they can to help them develop the skills they need to succeed. We have had many rich discussions since we first met, and these discussions finally culminated in this book.

We are first and foremost secondary educators by experience. We come from or still dwell in secondary classrooms. Our teaching experience is exclusive to adolescents, grades 6–12. These are "our kids," the kids we think about every day, the kids we worry about and carry in our hearts. We understand firsthand the high stakes our students face in U.S. secondary schools and are committed to making a difference for them and their teachers. We did this first and foremost for ourselves, but we also felt compelled to share with other secondary teachers the essential programming and language-development strategies we know work. So this book is fundamentally designed to share the highly practical strategies we know can make a difference for your kids.

Sharing Our Voices

I started my teaching career in San Francisco, where I lived and worked in the public schools for seven years. I taught in the early days of bilingual education, always in the middle grades, and I worked in schools with multiple bilingual programs and many levels of ESL. These were ethnically and linguistically rich schools, and I was hooked from the get-go, since Spanish language and literature were my areas of specialization and I had prepared to be a second-language teacher. I taught kids in grades 6–8 in both Spanish and English and networked with colleagues who taught in other high-incidence languages in bilingual programs in my school and across the city.

From the beginning, I felt the deep longing of the kids to be understood and respected, to learn English, and, almost without exception, to be successful at school and in life. No matter their motivation level or educational background, the road was not an easy one, and I admired their courage to face school each day in a second language with people unlike themselves, at times dealing with ugly incidents of prejudice and discrimination from not only other students but also some adults in the building and surrounding community.

In this environment, I learned very quickly the importance of having a strong native language and identity to get you through and help you succeed. I too was a learner and benefited greatly from the richness of my students' backgrounds and their life experiences.

The connection between these students and their teachers is very strong as teachers help them navigate a powerful life transition on many levels. I have always been aware of the depth of the relationships ESL and bilingual teachers experience with their students, and as a result, my work has always had power and purpose. Even on my worst days as a teacher in an urban school, I have known that what I did mattered and I felt tremendously inspired to continue, no matter the pressures.

Middle school is a demanding and at the same time wondrous place. When it goes right, teams of teachers collaborate to deliver integrated curricula to students and solve problems together to meet their students' needs. Urban schools pose special challenges yet offer unparalleled rewards. Most days I was running from the minute I arrived and often asked myself at the end of the day if I had ever eaten lunch. I had thousands of interactions, yet always felt the pain of knowing there were kids I didn't quite get to, despite my best intentions. Through it all, I loved it and still do. I am in urban schools as much as I can manage. ELL middle schoolers are going through a passage like no other. You are their witness and, if you are lucky, their navigator. It's a fantastic experience.

Ever since that time, my work has always focused on urban schools. I am completely committed to urban education and to improving urban public schools for ELLs. Now, as a teacher educator, I try to bring my passion for urban teaching to prospective and practicing teachers, especially secondary teachers. I want them to last. I want them to love it. I want them to know their kids and offer them everything they deserve. I want them to make sure their English language learners make it to graduation.

Nancy Cloud, Rhode Island College

I came to education through my work with children as an adolescent—volunteering in elementary schools, working with after-school programs, and working as a counselor at summer camps. I loved working with little kids—their enthusiasm, innocence, and wonder a constant source of motivation and inspiration for me.

After eight years of working with children, I decided to try my hand with adolescents. When I was 21 years old I worked as a residential advisor and teacher at a summer enrichment program for high school students. It was my first experience working with high school students and I was terrified—why would these students respect me, a young adult only a few years their senior? What I found was that I loved them and they loved me. My closeness in age allowed me to relate to them in ways that many other adults struggled to do. These young adults were yearning for instruction and guidance from somebody who could relate to them in a way that only I could, because I had recently gone through the struggles of adolescence myself.

Since then I have not looked back. I graduated from college with a B.A. in History and a state certificate to teach in the Rhode Island public school system. Now, I am in my fifth full year of teaching at the secondary level in an urban setting, and I have recently completed an M.Ed. in Teaching English as a Second Language. Over these five years, I have taught bilingual history, general education history, and ESL history, spanning all grades and all levels.

I have become inspired to specifically work with ELLs because of my own experience as a second-language learner in Ecuador. Although the process of learning a second language was a formative experience, it was actually living in a culture different from my own and connecting with people in that culture that was truly transformational and mind opening. My time in Ecuador changed who I am as a person and was one of the most difficult and rewarding times of my life. Being able to help others go through that process is an incredibly enriching experience, and my own struggles allow me to be both sympathetic and, more importantly, empathetic to my students' plight. Since my time in

Ecuador, I have also traveled to Argentina, the Dominican Republic, Ghana, and Guatemala—all in search of a better understanding of where my students come from and how I can help them. In the Dominican Republic, Ghana, and Guatemala, I spent time with family members of the very students I serve here in the United States, attempting to learn from them and understand them in a way that only being in their homeland can accomplish. I plan to continue these journeys around the world, as I continue to serve ELLs; they have been some of the most enriching and educational experiences of my life.

I am inspired to work in an urban setting because I consider myself to be both privileged and fortunate, and I think the only response for having been this lucky is to give back. In my opinion, there is no group more disenfranchised in the United States than ELLs and their families, and so it is them that I wish to serve. I believe that my experiences abroad in combination with my knowledge of a second language make me particularly adept at helping ELLs navigate the difficult world of U.S. secondary schools and come out successful; it is a challenge I thoroughly enjoy.

Judah Lakin, Bilingual Social Studies Teacher

I grew up and pursued my teacher education in Southern California, where there is an abundance of English language learners in the communities and the schools. Since I can remember, I have been intensely interested in both education and language. In fact, my "teacher education" began at a very early age, as I grew up hearing firsthand the educator view of school and school life. My dad was a high school administrator, my mom worked at the different schools I attended growing up, and I was always interested in their stories and conversations about education.

I was especially drawn to secondary education because of the amazing and inspirational secondary teachers I had in high school and the way in which I was challenged and motivated by them and by my high school experience in general. At the same time, my younger brother was often frustrated and unmotivated during his time in high school, and his experience has given me a broader view of what high school is and can be for different students. In turn, I am inspired by the challenges, views, and experiences high school students bring to the classroom, and how we can shape our shared experience to benefit all students.

I love and am fascinated by language, and how we communicate and relate to each other. Growing up in San Diego, I became aware at a young age of many immigrant issues, and was struck by how many of the prejudices, difficulties, and misunderstandings that revolved around immigrants and ELLs were the result of a communication barrier. I became committed to learning Spanish and studied in Spain for a year, experiencing firsthand what it is like to be a foreigner and language learner. In 2006, I traveled to the Dominican Republic for five weeks to visit and to learn how I can better serve my students and their families, both educationally and socially, as they make the transition to a new life in the United States. I engaged in a similar experience when I traveled to Guatemala in 2009 to visit the families of several of my current students. I believe that education is power, so I work hard to give my students the independence to make decisions and be successful on their own terms. I am committed to helping students and their families and communities gain access to education and opportunities to better themselves and their lives.

This is my fifth year of teaching ESL; and every year I feel I am equally learning about and refining my practice. I am endlessly energetic and relentlessly optimistic, and I use these characteristics to create a vibrant and dynamic classroom. I am inspired to work in urban settings with adolescent ELLs because I feel that this setting offers both the greatest challenge and the greatest need. I feel that my educational experiences, positive attitude, high energy, and bilingual perspective allow me to positively connect with kids, challenge them, and hopefully empower them to confront life with confidence and perseverance.

Erin Leininger, ESL Teacher

Working in an urban setting provides me with the cultural resources that a city has to offer as well as the cultural and language diversity and richness that immigrant populations bring. I'm also motivated to teach where I do because public schools are the frontlines of democracy. My work in the United States and in South Africa—through teaching and through work at several education reform initiatives—has convinced me that as our education system grows poorer or richer, weaker or stronger, so does our capacity to live out the promises of the U.S. Constitution and the Bill of Rights.

My commitment to adolescent ELLs and their families is as deep as my commitment to maintaining democracy: All residents of the United States need to have access to language support and civic education that will enable them to participate fully in the life of the country.

I have taught students from grades 8 to 12, and from at least 10 different language backgrounds. I love teaching adolescents because they are in the midst of developing a sense of their own identity; as such they are in desperate need—as desperate as the youngest children—of positive and powerful role models. They are also very curious and willing to question authority, traits that make them ripe for engaging in critical thinking and debate, the cornerstones of democracy.

Laura Maxwell, English Teacher

The Need for Specialized Strategies for Middle and High School Teachers of ELLs

Because we work in secondary schools, we understand the demands that are placed on teachers who serve as many as 120 students per day. We have written this book to try to offer specialized strategies for middle and high school teachers that respect their teaching roles and conditions.

Whether you serve as a language or content teacher, we take it as a given that you know your subject matter; therefore, our book does not pretend to tell you how to teach your subject. Rather, we share strategies for systematically developing the language and literacy skills of the students enrolled in your class for whom English is a new language. Our experience in secondary classrooms has taught us that teachers who know how to develop oral language and literacy skills, offer native language support to ELLs, and engage their learners in collaborative learning and meaningful, standards-based learning activities deliver powerful instruction to ELLs (DeCapua, Smathers, & Tang, 2007). English language learners excel most when enrolled in well-planned programs delivered by teachers who care and invest in them. Recent research on effective secondary schooling for ELLs affirms that caring teachers, culturally responsive pedagogy (Gay, 2000; Noddings, 1999), and effective second-language instruction motivate secondary ELLs and insure that they succeed academically (Travieso-Parker, 2006).

In the chapters that follow we first outline the challenges of secondary school as we see them and the critical role played by effective guidance services, particularly scheduling secondary ELLs into the appropriate classes. Then we describe how to make use of the learner's native language, even when the teacher does not know or speak the learner's language. The book then sets a framework for language and literacy development in secondary school to ground our work prior to sharing strategies for oral language, reading, listening and note taking, and writing that can be used with ELLs in language and content courses. Finally we describe the all-important topic of bridging to mainstream English classes, once ESL services are no longer required.

We conceptualize the book as a "how-to" guide, not a theoretical presentation or review of the literature. Instead, we present theory and educational frameworks only as needed to ground the practices suggested, with referrals to other sources for those who want to learn more. We offer as many concrete strategies, teaching tips, and resources as possible in the hopes that each teacher can select those he or she finds most useful for his or her particular teaching situation. Our goal is to show that we understand your world and its pressures and to offer you ideas that work—strategies, teaching tips, and concrete resources to aid you in your daily interactions with English language learners.

Contents

4 Language and Literacy Frameworks to Guide Teachers' Work with Secondary English Language Learners 75

5 Oral Language 94

6 Reading in a Second Language 119

CHAPTER 1

The Challenges of Secondary School for English Language Learners

Diego, Guatemala

Guiding Questions

- What are the primary challenges facing preadolescent and adolescent English language learners when they enter U.S. middle and high schools?
- What does the research say about these challenges?
- What are the needs that these challenges reveal to us—needs that, if addressed, can improve the educational experience of secondary English language learners?
- What broad approaches have been suggested to respond to these needs?

This chapter presents and discusses a number of major challenges English language learners (ELLs) face when enrolling for the first time in U.S. schools as adolescents.

Each of these challenges is an opportunity in disguise. They allow us to identify a need of our students that, if met, can help us design and deliver effective programs and instruction. This chapter is not written to dwell upon the challenges, but rather to show our awareness of the real-life schooling contexts in which middle and high school teachers work. The authors of this book are working in these settings as much as the teachers who read it. We empathize with the challenges faced by our readers because we live them daily. The essential strategies we offer in the rest of the book are designed to respond to the challenges to be outlined in this chapter.

In that spirit, at the end of the discussion regarding each challenge we will describe the needs of our students that the challenge implies—needs that we must meet if our learners are to be successful.

The Challenge of Graduation Requirements in the United States

The current emphasis on proficiency-based graduation has created a pressure-cooker situation for ELLs who enter U.S. schools as adolescents. If ELL adolescents have adequate schooling from their countries of origin and have developed high levels of literacy in their native language, they almost always succeed and graduate, provided they have sufficient time to do so. Yet even the best students face challenges in graduating from an American high school if they enter in the 10th, 11th, or 12th grade, given that they have to:

- Demonstrate a high school level of proficiency in English reading and writing on English Language Arts assessments,

- Amass the required number of Carnegie units in math, English, and other subject areas, and

- Demonstrate the same U.S.-valued content area knowledge and skills their counterparts have been acquiring since grade school.

English language learners who enter middle and high schools with weak literacy skills and interrupted or limited formal schooling will struggle. They may find it almost impossible to develop all the necessary language and literacy skills and take the required content courses to graduate in the time available. These students are most at risk of dropping out.

At the same time that states are raising their graduation requirements, more than two-thirds of eighth graders score below proficient on the National Assessment of Educational Progress (NAEP) reading and math tests (U.S. Department of Education, 2006). Those farthest behind are concentrated in high-poverty schools and districts (Achieve, Inc., 2007, p. 11). Nationally, 30 percent of high school students and nearly 50 percent of black and Latino students fail to earn a high school diploma (Achieve, Inc., 2007, p. 7). But the percentage is even higher among these special groups of secondary ELL learners. Secondary teachers feel all these pressures as they work with their students. They anguish over the many challenges they face in trying to help their ELLs make it to graduation.

Factors that can stand between learners and graduation include earning sufficient high school credits, passing high-stakes and end-of-course assessments, and completing other proficiency-based graduation requirements (e.g., generating portfolio-ready projects that meet high standards). Each of these challenges will be described in the sections that follow.

Earning High School Credits

The most commonly used criterion for awarding a high school diploma continues to be passing required courses (Achieve, Inc., 2007, p. 10). A survey of the courses required by each state for graduation (Achieve, Inc., 2004) found that

- Thirty-six states and the District of Columbia required all students to take at least four years of English to graduate, and six states required three years;

- Thirteen states required two years of mathematics, 24 states and the District of Columbia required three years, and five states required or in subsequent years were planning to require all students to complete four years of math for graduation.

- On average, states required three years of social studies. Thirty-four states and the District of Columbia require students to study U.S. history, 32 states and the District of Columbia require U.S. government, and seven states and the District of Columbia require state or local history or government.

- All 42 states with statewide graduation requirements and the District of Columbia required students to take science classes to graduate, although 20 states and the District of Columbia did not specify which science classes students must take. Of the states that do specify Carnegie units in science, 15 required biology and either an integrated physical science class or a separate chemistry and physics class; two require simply a unit of biology (Achieve, Inc., 2004).

By April 2007, Achieve documented that 13 states had raised graduation requirements to the levels recommended to insure college and workplace readiness, including courses in the humanities, math, science, and English (p. 13). For example, the survey documented that an additional five states had raised their graduation requirements to require three years of math (through at least Algebra II). Clearly, graduation requirements are becoming ever more demanding. A first challenge for our students is to somehow amass these credits, English credits often being the most difficult to attain.

Transfer of Credits upon Entry and Evaluation of Credits from Schools Outside the United States

In most states, when students arrive from other countries, their school transcripts are evaluated. Evaluation can be done locally or through established credential evaluation services such as the National Association of Credential Evaluation Services (NACES) (http://www.NACES.org). In some cases, state law specifically mandates that schools are responsible for doing the evaluation of the transcript (e.g., New York State Commissioner's Regulation 100.5), and mechanisms are established for doing this as uniformly as possible. In other cases, the student him- or herself may provide the original document with a transcript analysis done by a commercial service agency.

Either way, one constant concern in this endeavor is whether or not the credentials are being fairly evaluated based on an accurate understanding of the educational system from which the student has come, thus insuring that the appropriate number of credits be awarded for each course. In some cases, course work taken outside the United States may be more rigorous than that taken within the United States. It may include topics that are typical of more advanced courses in the United States, yet it may be considered equal to a lower-level course here because it carries a similar title. In other cases, courses may be taken that have no equivalents here and therefore can only count as "electives" when in fact they represent courses of equal rigor to courses in the humanities, math, and science that are typically awarded credits that count toward graduation in the United States.

Given the diversity of educational systems and countries from which adolescents come, the whole enterprise of transferring credits is tricky, and the potential exists that students may receive fewer credits than they should, thus making it harder for them to graduate. To get an idea of the complexity of educational systems involved, readers may want to review a document created for New York State Secondary Schools: *Evaluating Foreign Transcripts: The A-Z Manual* (no date, presumed published in 2006) available at http://www.nassauboces.org/cit/NCLB/LEP.htm#Resources. Beginning on page 16 with a country and/or regional index, this guide provides brief descriptions of more than 75 systems in terms of the length of the school year, the nature of the grading system, and the type of secondary schooling experience, as well as diplomas offered in some cases.

Earning Credits That Count Toward Graduation

Once in the United States, students may be awarded credits toward graduation, but how these credits are awarded varies greatly from district to district and state to state. For example, it is possible that one district may award English credit for an ESL course and another district may only count an ESL course as an elective or "foreign language" course for those learning English as an additional language. If the ESL courses they must take to acquire the English language are not awarded English credit (because they are not viewed as equal to the courses typically taken for English credit by native speakers of English), students may find it difficult—if not impossible—to have sufficient numbers of English credits to graduate by the time they reach the age of graduation. For this reason, we highly recommend that ESL courses and course projects be linked to state English standards, thus making it possible for them to be awarded English credit, at least beginning at the intermediate ESL level.

In terms of practices for granting credits for students' native language proficiency, some districts may grant foreign language credit to students who are proficient and literate in a language other than English (e.g., may count their native language proficiency as evidence of "foreign language" study), while other districts may require students to take additional modern language classes in order to receive such credit. In some cases students may be required to take "foreign language" course work in their own native language in order to receive credit—even though it is being taught as if it were a new language to them. In Connecticut and New Jersey, students may now receive foreign language credit for attending heritage-language schools, and credit by proficiency is becoming more popular, whereas in North Carolina and California, districts can determine their own policies for credit by proficiency (i.e., which tests to accept as evidence of proficiency) (Vu, 2008). Suffice it to say, there is great diversity in how students are awarded credits, and there is not always parity across districts and states. This situation creates inherent inequities for our students.

Taking the Right Courses at the Right Time

When students arrive, they need to receive timely guidance regarding the order in which courses must be taken so that they have the required prerequisite courses to be admitted into more advanced courses or to be considered ready for college. Most colleges have particular four-year course sequences that students must follow if they want to be admitted. Likewise, most advanced courses in math, science, and other subject areas have prerequisites that must be taken in order to qualify for enrollment. English language learners may be unfamiliar with these course sequences and requirements, and in cases where they do not take particular courses early enough or at all, they may find themselves excluded, for all practical purposes, from particular advanced course work or postsecondary options. Guidance strategies designed to avoid this situation are offered in Chapter 2.

Taking Tests; Passing High-Stakes Assessments

At the time of writing this book, statewide testing and accountability programs are a large part of what is currently going on in secondary schools due to No Child Left Behind (NCLB) and other education reform initiatives. According to Heubert (2002), about half of the states in the United States require students to pass graduation tests, and the number is expected to increase. Many set graduation-test standards at the tenth-grade level or higher (American Federation of Teachers, 1999). Despite the fact that ELLs are identified and qualify for special services by virtue of their inability to score at proficient levels on state language and reading tests and despite the fact that "common sense dictates that if you administer a test to students in a language they don't understand, they won't do well on it" (Wright, 2006, p. 22), still ELL secondary students are asked to take statewide reading tests in English after one year in the country. The students are also required to take their state's math test during their first year in the United States, even though performance on that test is also influenced by their limited proficiency in English (Wright, 2006). At the same time, we have ample evidence that students cannot learn enough English in one year to pass statewide reading tests given in English (Wright, 2006).

In addition to the statewide tests that are given, 29 states are pursuing end-of-course testing as a graduation requirement. Thirteen already have such tests in place, and 16 more plan to develop them (Achieve, Inc., 2007, p. 12). The purpose of these tests is to insure proficiency in a particular content area, not just "seat time" in a particular course. Taking end-of-course tests in English poses the same challenges as the statewide tests for students still in the process of learning the language. They may actually have the expected competencies in the content areas, yet not be able to demonstrate their competence because the test is administered in a language they are still learning.

In "Standard 9: Testing Individuals of Diverse Linguistic Backgrounds" of Standards for Educational and Psychological Testing (1999), the Joint Committee of the American Educational Research Association, the American Psychological Association, and the National Council on Measurement in Education states that "any test that employs language is, in part, a measure of (the test taker's) language skills. This is of particular concern for test takers whose first language is not the language of the test" (p. 91). Because of such concerns, various educational associations and agencies have issued position statements opposing the use of tests that are given in English to culturally and linguistically diverse learners in the process of learning English (Abedi, 2001; Coltrane, 2002; Del Rosario Basterra, 1998–1999; Teachers of English to Speakers of Other Languages [TESOL], 2003).

Given all the emphasis on tests and testing, it is clear that once ELLs make sufficient progress in learning English, they must be prepared to take and pass tests given in English if they are to succeed in the U.S. educational system. More will be said about this topic in the section that follows. Yet to protect our learners from the negative effects of premature testing in English, educators must work to insure that ELL adolescents are not administered assessments in English until such tests would reasonably yield valid results about their abilities, as urged by measurement specialists.

Learning How to Take Tests; Acquiring Test-Taking Skills for High-Stakes Assessments

Over time English language learners, like all students enrolled in U.S. schools, need to learn how to take tests; to acquire the test-taking skills needed to succeed on statewide and other high-stakes assessments. Coltrane (2002) advocates teaching ELLs the discourse of tests and test-taking skills. She feels it is beneficial to teach the typical discourse of standardized tests (predictable patterns and phrases) and their formats (layout, use of bubble sheets), as well as teach test-taking strategies (e.g., how to approach a multiple-choice question, how to locate the main idea of a reading passage), to help prepare ELLs for specific types of test items they may encounter. By doing this type of preparation on a regular basis as

ELLs learn English, they become empowered to demonstrate their knowledge on a test, rather than being intimidated by unfamiliar terms and formats.

Critics point out the drawbacks of narrowly focusing instruction on test preparation because of the detrimental "backwash" effects on the curriculum when test preparation becomes more important than true learning (Irujo, 2004). Still, some amount of instruction in test-taking skills and the discourse of tests—if well nested into high-quality language, literacy, and academic instruction—seems necessary to give ELLs with sufficient proficiency in English the same opportunity to pass the tests as their counterparts who have been prepared across the grades for test taking situations. For that reason, we recommend that these skills be taught, as students approach the requisite proficiency for tests in English, to yield meaningful results.

Filling in Gaps
in the Presumed Content Knowledge Assessed by High-Stakes Tests

When students take high-stakes tests, they may not have the foundational knowledge they need to do well on these exams. Often an assessment that is designed to measure one area (mathematical abilities) may involve other content areas (westward expansion) in the items or examples given. What is considered "common knowledge" by students who have been in U.S. schools since first grade may be completely unfamiliar content to those educated in other countries. Certainly, recently arrived students have not received the same curriculum to which their age mates were exposed prior to testing, and this fact is inherently unfair.

Rivera and Collum (2006) raise the additional concern that even ELLs who have been in the United States for some time might not have the knowledge of test topics because they have not participated in the same curriculum as their more English-proficient peers. They may have been excluded for lack of English proficiency from the curricula being taught in grade-level courses, or they may have been pulled out of particular core courses to receive ESL instruction (p. xxxiv).

Advocating for students to receive alternative assessments, time extensions, and other accommodations on all high-stakes assessments. The Joint Committee of the AERA, the APA, and the NCME (1999) advocate that, when test results are used to make significant decisions, alternative assessments be considered (e.g., additional tests, sources of observational information, modified forms of the chosen test) to ensure that the information obtained is adequate for the intended purpose. Likewise, Teachers of English to Speakers of Other Languages (2005) urges local districts to provide approved accommodations for ELLs when warranted. Specifically, TESOL calls for changing aspects of the test (administering only the parts of the test that are appropriate given the learner's proficiency and cultural background) or adapting administration procedures (individual administration, extended time, etc.). TESOL (2003) stresses the need for portfolios to demonstrate growth over time in content areas and English language proficiency, use of multiple assessments, and consideration of teacher judgment when making important decisions about students.

In addition to offering alternative assessments, districts need to identify accommodations that will be allowed for all ELLs when completing performance assessments, projects, and portfolios required for graduation and all timed and/or

---

What Kids Need: Appropriate Programming, Instruction, and Assessments

Our students need credits to graduate. They need to bring in the maximum number of credits from their prior educational system by having their courses fairly reviewed by knowledgeable reviewers. They need to earn credits for all the classes they are taking by having the classes aligned to state standards and proficiency-based graduation requirements, and they need to be advised to take the right classes in the right order so they have all the prerequisite classes needed to gain access to postsecondary programs. (See Chapter 2 for more information on providing quality guidance to ELLs.)

Our students need sufficient proficiency in English before they must take English-medium tests, especially for high-stakes decision-making purposes. They need test-taking skills for the test formats and protocols commonly used in the United States, and they need exposure to the fundamental knowledge (of U.S. history, geography, civics, and everyday community practices) that is assumed in formulating high-stakes test items.

Our students need appropriate assessment accommodations as well as alternative ways of evaluating their knowledge, skills, and abilities. They need a fair and equitable system to prove they have the requisite skills to be awarded a high school diploma in the United States. All secondary teachers must play a role in meeting these needs. (See Gottlieb & Nguyen, 2007, for more information on this topic.)

---

standardized assessments. These accommodations could include language simplification (reducing the number of words in a sentence, replacing complex phrases with simple, more direct language, using high-frequency words), use of glosses or glossaries, dividing tasks into smaller steps, adding visual support, allowing students to use graphic organizers to process questions and prepare responses, and providing extended time to take the test (Short, 2007). It is well documented that when individuals are working in a second language, it takes longer to process language because of the limitations imposed by working memory. This delay occurs because processing information in a second language is more demanding, and so working memory may be less efficient (Ardilla, 2003). In addition, words in a second language function as "low-frequency" words, and hence, semantic search takes longer when reading test questions.

The Challenge of Learning Academic English Sufficient for Success in Secondary School

As highlighted by Echevarría, Vogt, and Short (2008, p. 10), "the foundation of school success is academic literacy in English." Without proficiency in all English-language skills—listening, speaking, reading, and writing—students cannot acquire or demonstrate their knowledge of the subject matter taught in middle and high schools. "Language (and by extension, literacy) is a functional tool for learning academic subject matter" (Chamot & O'Malley, 1994, p. 11). Therefore, ELLs must learn the language of each subject area as they learn the most important concepts and skills of each discipline using academic language. They must use academic language to communicate in academic settings—to analyze, evaluate, justify, explain, and persuade others.

What We Know about Academic English

What Is Academic Literacy in English?

According to Short and Fitzsimmons (2007), in their crucial report on secondary ELLs, *Double the Work: Challenges and Solutions to Acquiring Language and Academic Literacy for Adolescent English Language Learners,* academic literacy

- Includes reading, writing, and oral discourse for school.
- Varies from subject to subject.
- Requires knowledge of multiple genres of text, purposes for text use, and text media.
- Is influenced by students' literacies in contexts outside of school.
- Is influenced by students' personal, social, and cultural experiences.

This report outlines the challenges that secondary ELLs face in trying to meet grade-level academic expectations while they are still in the process of acquiring the English language for social and academic purposes. The authors also reinforce the point that different ELLs are at different points on the continuum of development of academic language and literacy. Some have rich educational backgrounds and strong native language literacy, whereas others have rarely been to school and have never been taught to read and write in any language (Short & Fitzsimmons, 2007, pp. 11–12), a fact already noted in this chapter.

Why Is Academic Literacy in English So Important?

Short and Fitzsimmons (2007, p. 22) document the research literature showing a strong relationship between literacy level and academic achievement, a relationship that grows stronger as grade levels rise—irrespective of individual student characteristics. Developing academic literacy in English is important, yet it is complex because it involves all language skills (listening, speaking, reading, and writing), for varied and diverse school-related purposes. Students must listen in class and take notes (see Chapter 7 for teaching ideas and strategies), they must participate in literary and academic class discussions (see Chapter 5), they must read and process a variety of texts (see Chapter 6), and they must produce written products to show their comprehension of texts and knowledge of academic subjects (see Chapter 8).

The importance of the development of literacy that supports rigorous academic learning cannot be overstated. All the reports on adolescent literacy point to the need for school programs to support learners, both native and nonnative speakers of English, in their acquisition of advanced literacy skills. Because of the importance of this topic to secondary educators, Chapter 4 will describe and explore many of the important issues with respect to the development of academic literacy and expand on the discussion provided here. We will also introduce and describe in detail the stages of proficiency that ELLs go through on their way to being fully proficient in English, both for social and academic purposes.

Who Is Responsible for Teaching Academic English?

All teachers are responsible for teaching academic literacy, not just ESL and bilingual teachers. Adolescent ELLs need skillful teachers who can support literacy skill development for each content area. Yet, according to Short and Fitzsimmons (2007, p. 22), many of the educators working in middle and high schools have had little professional development for teaching literacy to adolescents let alone teaching second-language literacy to adolescent ELLs. Since the number of adolescent ELLs is growing in districts throughout the United States, it is clear that middle and high school teachers must learn how to promote second-language and literacy development at the same time they teach their subject matter. This book is designed to help them do just that.

The Role of ESL Teachers and Reading Teachers

There are many important roles that ESL and literacy specialists can play in their middle and high schools in terms of promoting academic language and literacy development (Short & Fitzsimmons, 2007, pp. 24–25). Of course, they can directly work with ELLs to advance their language and literacy skills. But they can also collaborate with content teachers to promote their use of best literacy practices with their second-language learners of English. Mentoring content teachers is a new role for many ESL teachers; to make it work, ESL and reading specialists need to acquire broad knowledge of and skills in using research-based strategies designed for ELLs. In order to help other teachers design instruction that improves ELLs' ability to read and understand content area information, they will need to identify teaching strategies that take into account ELLs' different proficiency levels while moving them toward grade-level literacy (Short & Fitzsimmons, 2007, p. 25).

Certainly we know that collaboration occurs at different levels in middle and high schools. Most middle schools foster teaming by giving common planning time to teachers working together to support the same group of students; in high schools, this practice is far less common. While the amount of coordination and mentoring will vary across schools, even in the least supportive situation, ESL and reading teachers can notice what students are doing in their content classes by looking through their notebooks or by observing their interactions with students in class or in after-school tutoring situations. Some high school ESL teachers may find it more workable to coordinate intensively with one or two teachers because of commonalities in their teaching schedules or physical proximity of their classrooms. Given that high school students of the same proficiency level may be taking different sets of content classes, this type of close coordination with all of a student's teachers may become less possible as the complexity of scheduling increases, but it is still worth finding those situations where coordination and mentoring can occur.

The Role of Content-Area Teachers

For ELLs to be successful in content-area classes, they must not only learn the specific content of courses, but they must also be able to handle the academic literacy demands of each subject area (i.e., reading, writing, listening and note taking, discussion skills). Academic literacy in each content area depends upon how knowledge is constructed and organized in that discipline. In order to fully engage in their subject-area classes, students must acquire the academic English of each subject area; the best person to define and support this learning is the subject-area teacher. While content-area teachers have been prepared to teach their subject matter, they may not have been prepared to teach the academic language associated with content learning. In content-area classes, reading and writing are intimately connected to the knowledge construction process. To gather information, students listen or read, take notes, make outlines, and create graphic organizers. To process or synthesize information, they take notes, write summaries of key ideas, prepare reports, and keep journals. To represent their knowledge, they make oral presentations in class, produce summaries on assessments, or create multimedia presentations. While doing all these things, learners acquire content area vocabulary so they can comprehend instruction, communicate in class, and represent their knowledge. This book will help subject-matter specialists work with their students to develop all of these language-related skills.

What Is the Role of the Native Language in the Development of Academic English?

There are two important findings about how the native language supports and contributes to the development of academic English (August & Shanahan, 2006a, 2006b). First, research shows that there are considerable cross-linguistic interactions between the native language and learning to read in English. One example that demonstrates this point is the way that bilingual learners use cognates—words that are identical or almost identical in the two languages and mean the same thing—to support comprehension in their new language (Nagy, García, Durgunoglu, & Hancin-Bhatt, 1993).

Second, a key finding of the National Literacy Panel on Language-Minority Children and Youth (August & Shanahan, 2006a, 2006b) is that first-language literacy is related in important ways to literacy development in English and that it affects word reading, reading comprehension, reading strategies, spelling, and writing. Those who are literate in their first language are likely to acquire literacy in English more efficiently and quickly than those who are not, because there are many skills that transfer directly. Studies show that language-minority students who are taught to read in their native language and then in English perform better, on average, on measures of English reading proficiency than those who are instructed only in English. This statement is true of elementary and secondary learners. It has also been demonstrated that when students have successful reading comprehension strategies in their native language, these strategies often transfer positively to English (Riches & Genesee, 2006).

Tapping the Knowledge Base Developed through L1 and Developing Knowledge through Use of the L1

The native language (L1) is often the language through which our secondary learners have acquired substantial amounts of content-area knowledge. Their native language is the language in which they have developed the specialized vocabulary of each content area and through which they can explain, in the clearest and most refined way, their most accurate understandings of phenomena. We definitely want to access the learning our students have accomplished in their primary languages and to help them acquire the academic language needed to express that existing knowledge in English.

> **What Kids Need: The Support of Content-Area Teachers for Developing Academic English**
>
> All secondary teachers can insure ELLs' success in school by helping them to develop academic English within their subject areas. To that end, the WIDA Consortium (2004) developed separate standards for the development of academic language in English language arts, science, social studies, and mathematics classes. The WIDA English language proficiency standards were used as the basis for the *PreK–12 English Language Proficiency Standards* (TESOL, 2006). Assessments that are based on these standards allow us to pinpoint ELLs' proficiency in academic English in each subject area, and then assist them to continue to progress in this area as rapidly and efficiently as possible. (More information will be given about English language proficiency standards and assessments in Chapter 4.) Every teacher has a role to play in promoting academic English. Reaching across disciplines is the best way to support learners. (See chapters 5–9 for strategies for accomplishing this purpose.)

Most English language learners have the skills and knowledge to complete classroom assignments and to engage in some classroom activities in their own language. It is important for teachers to learn as much as possible about students' existing knowledge, skills and interest, and to use this information as a foundation for teaching them English and other subjects. (Ontario Ministry of Education, 2005, p. 17)

ELL content teaching experts (Echevarría et al., 2008, p. 128) also recommend that students be given the opportunity to have concepts or assignments explained in their native language as needed during content classes delivered through the medium of English. This type of clarification provides important support for academic learning when students are not yet fully proficient in English. So the native language is an important learning tool that secondary teachers will want to honor and use. (See Chapter 3 for many more ideas on this topic.)

The Challenge of Being a New Arrival in a Complex Social Environment

When students move to a new school, they have to interact with a new peer group and new teachers and encounter a complex social organization (Berndt, Hawkins, & Ziao, 1999), all in a language they do not understand or are still learning. The changes in the school environment can be extreme for immigrant students coming from stable, self-contained social environments, such as rural schools with smaller numbers of students and teachers.

Changing schools disrupts ELL students' friendship groups and affects students' social networks in profound ways, particularly because they are crossing cultural and linguistic boundaries. Some may never have been to school with students unlike themselves, but in diverse urban schools, they will come into contact with many students and teachers unlike themselves.

Secondary School Is about More Than Academics

Middle and high school teachers are well aware that the secondary school experience is about much more than academics. Adolescents are developing in many ways; they are establishing friendship networks and building social skills that will support them in adulthood (Daniels, 2005). The social landscape of secondary schools is often of far greater importance to adolescents than the academic environment. Being successful in middle and high school is about much more than taking courses and getting good grades.

Clubs, Teams, After-School Activities, Special Events

American schools encourage extracurricular activities as a way of developing "well-rounded" individuals. These can include clubs, sports teams, bands and orchestras, choruses, dance groups, and other voluntary special interest activities. Postsecondary settings—college and employers—view students' extracurricular participation as evidence that students have initiative, leadership, and other personal qualities predictive of success in college or work settings. For these reasons, the secondary school experience of immigrant students must also include participation in the school's extracurricular life (Ruiz-de-Velasco & Fix, 2000, p. 83; Violand-Sánchez & Hainer-Violand, 2006).

When students have connections outside the classroom, it enhances their secondary school experience and contributes to their overall sense of efficacy.

> Newcomers from all backgrounds have a wide variety of interests and skills, and often can contribute a great deal to a school's co-curricular activities. Some may have highly developed skills in a sport that does not have a long history at the school. Others may want to form a language club. Many newcomers will have talents and stories to contribute to school concerts, special assemblies, and other events. All of these activities provide opportunities for English language learners to participate in school life. Getting them involved at all levels—from rookies to leaders—can go a long way towards building a genuinely inclusive school culture. (Ontario Ministry of Education, 2005, p. 41)

Cliques, Groups

To break down the complexity of the social environment of large urban high schools, students join smaller groups or cliques (Espejo, 2002). These smaller groups provide peer support—a network of friends who can lend social and academic support and help ELL teenagers establish a sense of identity and belonging (Espejo, 2002; Daniels, 2005). The creation of caring, inclusive, participatory communities for our students is very important because, when students' basic psychological needs are met, they become committed to the norms, values, and goals of schools (Blum, 2005; Schaps, 2003). Belonging has been associated with a host of positive effects, such as increase in motivation; display of prosocial behavior, altruistic behavior, and social-emotional competence; and increases in academic achievement (Blum, 2005; Schaps, 2003; Wentzel & Caldwell 1997). In contrast, socially rejected students show a higher incidence of behavioral problems and are at risk of dropping out of school and engaging in antisocial behaviors such as bullying, youth violence, and drug abuse (Blum, 2005; Cooper & Snell, 2003).

A painful truth about groups that exist in high schools is that some students are accepted into the high-status groups and feel like "insiders," while others are rejected and become "outsiders." Those without friendship networks feel marginalized and alone and do not integrate into the life of the middle or high school. In recent years, exclusion of marginalized students (sometimes including bullying and harassment) has led to extreme consequences such as school shootings and violence against self or others (Cooper & Snell, 2003, Espejo, 2002; National Middle School Association, 2006). Often, marginalized students join groups whose identities are in opposition to the school culture and engage in risky or violent behavior because of the hopelessness they feel for the future (Faltis & Coulter, 2008, p. 36).

Teachers must pay special attention to newly arrived ELLs who are not finding their own way. All school personnel must make concerted efforts to help ELLs fit in and feel comfortable in school—to support the social integration of students in classroom communities (Faltis & Coulter, 2008; Gibson, Gándara, & Koyama, 2004; Violand-Sánchez & Hainer-Violand, 2006; F. Williams, 2003). Friends make a huge difference in the adjustment and acculturation processes.

As shown below, newly arrived students go through a predictable sequence of stages in adjusting to their new life circumstances (Ontario Ministry of Education, 2005, p. 39; F. Williams, 2003).

Forming friendship networks in the new environment has stress-buffering effects that help students acculturate and progress to final stages of adjustment in the new culture, especially when the friends have a deep understanding of what it is like to be in a new school and a new country, speaking a new language (F. Williams, 2003).

Stages of Acculturation

1. Arrival and first impressions: Newcomers are excited to be in a new environment and optimistic about new opportunities. Everything seems new and exciting. Refugees are relieved to have arrived in a safe environment.

2. Culture shock: Newcomers are less optimistic as the challenges of resettlement become more evident. They find it difficult to make friends, and the challenge of learning in English may seem insurmountable. They miss friends, family, and everything that was familiar. Students may begin to wonder who they are. As a result, they may cling to their own language and culture or discard everything they feel marks them as different. Some children or other family members may get "stuck" at this stage, and even become clinically depressed. Students and their families need support and encouragement during this period, and special efforts must be made to help them feel part of the school community.

3. Recovery and optimism: A renewed optimism develops. For students, the new mood is often prompted by a success in school or by finding their first friend. Students who are well supported at school and whose linguistic and cultural backgrounds are valued by their teachers and classmates, begin to feel more confident about learning English and about fitting in without having to abandon their cultural identity.

4. Acculturation: Immigrants become comfortable with a new identity that balances their original culture with elements of the new culture. This balance is different for each person and depends on many factors. To help students achieve this balance, schools need to enable them to become bilingual and bicultural, able to move effectively between their old and new linguistic and cultural worlds.

(Ontario Ministry of Education, 2005, p. 39. © Queen's Printer for Ontario. Reproduced with permission.)

Within our schools, we also want to insure that ELLs are appreciated and understood by other students to avoid special forms of bullying and harassment that are only practiced against immigrants. Immigrant students may be taunted or teased about ways of dressing, food, legal status, or accents, and it has been documented that ELLs experience both physical and verbal bullying at higher levels than other teens because of these perceived differences (Ross, 2007). We must be vigilant for discrimination and make every effort to insure that ELL immigrants are respected and integrated into all aspects of school life (Faltis & Coulter, 2008; F. Williams, 2003).

Dress and Grooming

Students new to the United States may not understand the importance of clothing and grooming to "fitting in" in American secondary schools (Wilen, 2004). Some ELLs have culturally dictated dress codes that may clash with those established in U.S. schools (such as covering the head, face, legs—see Flaitz, 2006). Such students may find it hard to fit into U.S. schools because the traditional clothing they wear to school is quite different from that worn by U.S. teenagers. Conversely, they may find the American style of dress offensive or at least at odds with their own notions of modesty and appropriateness. As a part of their cultural orientation, they will need to have the predominant styles of dress explained so that they do not misjudge their peers or misinterpret the style of dress as provocative or shameful. In addition, the family may need support as parents see their children adopting American ways of dress and giving up more traditional clothing styles, especially in cases where parents do not want their children to emulate American norms. The same holds true with grooming, which may differ greatly in terms of bathing practices, use of perfumes and makeup, hairstyles and haircuts, or use of body painting or piercing. These are things that we do not often struggle with in the early grades, but in adolescent culture these things matter and take on special meanings that can even lead to conflict and violence between groups of students.

Maintaining a Positive Ethnic Identity

> Having a strong, positive ethnic identity is associated with high self-esteem, a commitment to doing well in school, a sense of purpose in life, confidence in one's own efficacy, and high academic achievement. (Violand-Sánchez & Hainer-Violand, 2006, p. 36)

Secondary educators are well aware that developing identity is one of the greatest psychosocial tasks of adolescence (F. Williams, 2003). Therefore, we need to insure that immigrant students feel that their language and culture are respected and that they belong without washing away their language or culture (Violand-Sánchez & Hainer-Violand, 2006). Teachers need to come to know and respect their learners, for helping students maintain a positive ethnic and linguistic identity leads to highly desirable outcomes. Supportive practices include honoring the native language in all aspects of school life (see Chapter 3) and demonstrating respect for the values, norms, and perspectives of diverse learners and their families (Violand-Sánchez & Hainer-Violand, 2006). Chapter 3 discusses many of these recommended practices and provides strategies to teachers that allow them to strengthen the linguistic and cultural identities of their learners to reap well-documented positive benefits.

Crossing Boundaries

The adjustment process our learners are going through as recent arrivals to middle and high schools is well documented (Coelho, 1994; Ontario Ministry of Education, 2005, p. 39). The students' adjustment is very much affected by

- Whether they had any choice in coming to the United States or whether their uprooting was forced;
- Whether they immigrated with their family intact or whether they experienced painful family separations;
- Their proficiency in English when they arrived;
- Their prior educational experiences;
- Their comfort or sense of isolation in the resettlement communities;
- Their loss of status;
- The degree of discrimination they have experienced;

and a host of other factors (Coelho, 1994; F. Williams, 2003). Certainly all newcomers show some effects of these powerful transitions that occur as they adjust to the culture of the school (Coelho, 1994; F. Williams, 2003).

Crossing Linguistic, Ethnic, and Gender Boundaries

Learning English is a huge challenge for middle and high school students, largely because the proficiency expectations are so high. They are not just expected to know English for everyday purposes, but as already noted, to handle the advanced literacy demands of secondary content-area course work and examinations, all conducted in English. This is a heavy demand. The rest of this book is designed to offer strategies to teachers so they can promote the language learning required to handle these demands.

English language learners are also crossing ethnic boundaries. Even students who share the same language may encounter varying levels of mutual understanding (Rosenbloom, 2004). Students want to be accurately identified ethnically, linguistically, and culturally. If students are referred to as Dominican, when in fact they are Guatemalan, they resent the misidentification. They speak the same language, but these students' experiences have been vastly different in terms of cultural orientations and life experiences. The cultural distance can be even greater when crossing linguistic and cultural backgrounds, say, having a student from Nigeria interact with students from Peru, the Philippines, and Cambodia. Such situations are commonplace in urban classrooms, but are teachers prepared to help students navigate these cultural boundaries? Improving intergroup relations and reducing intergroup tensions is a top priority in urban schools, and a variety of research-based educational strategies are recommended, such as cooperative learning, inclusion of multicultural adolescent literature, and the like (Romo, 1997).

Social integration of students in classrooms is seen as a major way to help students appreciate the diversity present in North American secondary schools. When students are encouraged to interact and have positive experiences with one another, they appreciate one another and form positive relationships with students unlike themselves (Faltis & Coulter, 2008; Romo, 1997). Teachers and counselors are responsible for encouraging good relationships and intervening when they go awry (F. Williams, 2003).

What Kids Need: Connection and a Sense of Belonging

Emotional and physical safety, close supportive relationships, and understanding are basic needs that secondary schools and teachers must meet for all of their learners (Blum, 2005; Schaps, 2003). Indeed this is a centerpiece of the reform initiatives going on in secondary schools—to create a sense of community and belonging for all learners (Committee on Increasing High School Students' Engagement and Motivation to Learn, National Research Council, 2003).

    We have to set up classrooms and school days that create a sense of belonging, connectedness, and mutual respect. We want to select teaching strategies and curricula that insure that these outcomes occur (see Chapters 3–9).

A final boundary is that of gender, because in many cultures gender roles are fixed, whereas people in the United States value egalitarianism and individualism. In some countries the schools are segregated by sex; boys and girls are not encouraged to work together; and in certain instances, girls may not attend school at all (See Flaitz, 2006; F. Williams, 2003). This is a huge boundary for ELL adolescents to cross if their cultural training has prepared them with particular expectations for classroom and school life that are at total odds with American schooling practices, values, and norms. Such transitions can be monumental for some learners, and teachers need to appreciate this problem and support their learners' gradual adjustment.

Helping Kids from Rural Backgrounds Adapt to Urban U.S. Environments

Students from rural backgrounds who are thrust into urban environments may experience a strong form of culture shock. Coelho (1994) points out that for many immigrants, the experience of being in an urban center may cause anxiety, stress, and depression to those from tight-knit, safe, and predictable rural environments. They may react negatively to the new climate, urban surroundings, and everyday routines of life (transportation, shopping). They may feel unsafe, especially when they do not speak the language or understand how to navigate a city or town. Such changes are indeed very stressful, and teachers may need to help their learners in making a successful transition in very concrete ways, such as helping them navigate the transportation system, learn to use 911, and the like. Chapter 2 provides some information about the types of support services schools might provide to aid students in making this transition.

The Challenge of Departmentalized Secondary Settings for ELLs

A central challenge faced by secondary ELLs is the organization of traditional middle and high schools. The fact that secondary schools, particularly high schools, are organized into departments (mathematics, sciences, social sciences) can make it more difficult for ELLs to integrate their language and content learning. Students may feel lost in some classes, as some subject-area teachers assume little responsibility for ELLs' linguistic and academic outcomes, instead feeling that these are the responsibility of language development specialists (ESL/bilingual teachers). Students do not receive the same level of support as at the elementary level because departmentalization restricts the opportunities for language and content teachers to collaborate in meaningful ways to improve immigrant student outcomes, particularly at the high school level. In addition, the structure of the typical secondary school day, typically divided into distinct class periods, often contributes to the discontinuities students feel as they go from class to class and teacher to teacher (Ruiz-de-Velasco & Fix, 2000, p. 14; Ruiz-de-Velasco & Fix, 2002).

Team Teaching in Middle Schools: How Does It Help? What Are the Challenges?

Not all secondary settings are departmentalized. Many middle schools and junior high schools promote the use of team teaching, thus making learning more connected for students. Team teaching is designed to organize schools so that a group of teachers share the same group of students; the responsibility for planning, teaching, and evaluating the curriculum and instruction that is offered; and the day's schedule and a space in a building. A key component of interdisciplinary team teaching is *common planning time* provided so that teachers can coordinate their efforts and discuss curricular and student issues together (Juvonen, Kaganoff, Augustine, & Constant, 2004, p. 21). The practice is widespread in middle schools. In a recent survey, 79% of responding middle school principals indicated that their school implements interdisciplinary teams (Juvonen et al., 2004, p. 22). It is widespread because empirical studies demonstrate positive achievement results for students when teams collaborate and plan together effectively. Such joint planning is positively associated with gains on eighth grade reading and mathematics scores (Juvonen et al., 2004, p. 22), and as a result, team teaching is labeled as a promising practice for improving student achievement in the middle grades.

Flowers, Mertens, and Mulhall (2000) report that there are other positive effects of teaming on teaching and learning: namely, improved work climate, more frequent contact with parents, and increased teacher job satisfaction. Teams with high common planning practices (more meetings per week) have even higher levels of these positive attributes. These authors report that teams with adequate common planning time, fewer of students assigned to the team (90 or less), and more years of working together attain the most improved student achievement (Flowers, Mertens, & Mulhall, 2000).

But there are challenges inherent in team teaching that may prevent these benefits from being realized for students. One of the biggest challenges in implementing team teaching is preparing teachers to collaborate effectively. Teachers from different disciplines must work closely together, yet some prefer the conventional structure because their disciplinary affiliation is more important to their professional identity than team membership. Others can view collaboration as an infringement on their independence. Some do not have the skills to collaborate effectively with teachers from other departments, largely because few preservice or in-service training programs focus on this aspect of pedagogy or develop the communication and other skills needed to be successful when working closely with others (Juvonen et al., 2004, p. 26).

How to Cope with More Departmentalized Settings: How to Build Bridges to Other Classrooms

As highlighted by Ruiz-de-Velasco and Fix (2000, 2002) and others (Center for School and District Improvement, 2004), a central challenge faced by secondary school students, particularly those in high schools, is the organization of secondary schools into subject-oriented departments and, within those, into particular classes and sections. This hampers teachers' efforts to collaborate with each other and isolates teachers into narrow disciplinary fields to attend to standards and assessments—standards and assessments that students experience as separate requirements and demands, rather than well-coordinated and integrated learning experiences. Ruiz-de-Valasco and Fix argue that when we free teachers to talk and work together and break down the organizational divisions between language and content instruction, a better-coordinated education is offered to ELL students (pp. 4–6).

Structures for Collaborating in Secondary Schools: Common Planning Time, Integrated Curricula, and Flexible Scheduling

Ruiz-de-Velasco and Fix (2000) suggest that as students' language and literacy backgrounds grow more diverse, increased flexibility is required of schools and teachers. Schools need to extend teacher planning and collaboration time and extend instructional time to meet student needs more effectively (p. 61). Juvonen and colleagues (2004) recommend flexible scheduling where blocks of time are allocated to allow students time to work on projects and to make connections across different disciplines (p. 23). Longer time frames allow more opportunities for interaction among students and between teachers and students, which have also been associated with improved affective climates for learning and relationship building (p. 24).

Some high schools create within-school groupings, *academies* for example, to try to encourage teachers to work together to support students they teach in common. But what can work against ESL teachers actively collaborating with content teachers is that the same group of students in a particular ESL class might be assigned to three or four different math classes—say, some to Algebra I, others to calculus, and a few to general math. This situation is multiplied by the fact that the same could be going on in student assignments to science and social studies courses. Despite such challenges, there are ways to build bridges. Some high schools agree to use standard formats for notebook organization and taking notes. Others use a common planner for assigning homework. When students struggle, some ESL teachers focus on working with the teachers to whom such students are assigned. Even if there is only one teacher that the struggling students all have in common, this approach gives the ESL teacher a partner to talk to and work with to help the students.

Working on academic vocabulary that cuts across academic subjects is another way to provide bridges. For example the *General Service List* (West, 1953;) and the *Academic Word List* (Coxhead, 2000) together help students recognize 85–90% of the words they will encounter in academic texts, irrespective of content area—words like *create, indicate, significant, consistent.* So if we all work on this type of academic vocabulary, students benefit.

> **What Kids Need: Personalization and Caring,**
> **Support, and Coherence in Curriculum and Instruction**
>
> Secondary school reform is currently highly focused on creating opportunities for rela-
> tionships among students and relationships among students and their teachers to
> flourish. Small schools and class sizes help. Larger blocks of time provide teachers
> more opportunity to interact with students for sustained periods of time, and advi-
> sory groups are another strategy used to ensure that each student has at least one
> close personal relationship with a caring adult in the school setting. These aspects
> play a crucial role in students' persistence and commitment to finishing school
> (Committee on Increasing, 2003; Stipek, 2006).
>
> Students also need curriculum coherence and the chance to see curricular con-
> nections. This purpose is easier to accomplish where teams of teachers work together
> with particular groups of students and collaborate to meet their academic and social
> needs. Schools organized into small learning communities in this way do a far better
> job with their students than large, disjointed, and impersonal secondary schools
> (Committee on Increasing, 2003), especially when teaching adolescent ELLs.

Offering after-school tutoring where you partner with other teachers allows teachers to see firsthand the work students bring to the center because they are having difficulty completing it. This can give teachers ideas as to how to work with students to help them succeed in their academic classes. By assigning ELL students to one or two guidance counselors, teachers can know whom to talk to when they see that ELL students need some extra support and follow-up. Another bridging strategy might be to assign particular ESL teachers to certain department's meet-ings, at least on occasion, so they can see what kinds of problems the ESL students are having in the various courses being offered in a particular discipline. The goal is to seek to build bridges wherever possible, especially in very complex secondary settings.

The Challenge of
Balancing School, Home, and Work Demands

Secondary Students Who Work

Based on our experience as secondary teachers of ELLs, we have witnessed first-hand students who are working significant numbers of hours per week at the same time they attend school. The working provides benefits (i.e., financial re-sources, a sense of responsibility), but it also presents challenges to students. The Bureau of Labor Statistics in its *American Time Use Survey* (2007) documents that U.S. high school students who work before or after school hours spend an average of 42 minutes a day less on educational activities than nonworking students. Those who work while attending high school also spent 42 fewer minutes doing leisure and sports activities and slept for 36 fewer minutes than high school stu-dents who did not hold jobs while attending school.

These findings show that students who work nights and weekends have less time to complete homework assignments. They have less time to rest, relax, and sleep. They have less time for sports and out-of-school recreation experiences. All these things can have a negative impact on students' school experience and academic success. Additionally, schedule conflicts can arise. For example, working students may find it hard to take advantage of after-school support programs designed to help them with their schoolwork and advance their language and literacy skills, because they have to report to work when the programs are offered.

Within the group of working students, there is a subgroup that for economic reasons must work full-time and try to go to school. These students are putting in workweeks of 40 or more hours to contribute to family income. As middle and high school teachers, each of us has had students who were working this way, despite the limits imposed by labor laws. They come to school exhausted. They arrive late. They sleep on their desks. They never have time for homework. They are functioning as adults; not as teenagers, and have many responsibilities well beyond their years that we have to understand in order to support them. In extreme cases, some of these students drop out, because they cannot make it all work and their priority has to be family survival.

Secondary Students with Heavy Family Responsibilities

As newcomers to the United States, they often acquire new responsibilities beyond the classroom. They may be called upon to work in order to help support their families, to translate for their parents or to care for younger siblings while their parents work. (Hood, 2003, p. 5)

As this quote shows, some students have heavy family responsibilities. These can include serving as the broker for all family business or, in some cases, serving as heads of households, caring for younger siblings, or taking care of their own children while attending high school.

Students Who Broker All Family Business or Serve as Heads of Households

Many middle and high school students report taking care of many functions for their families, such as apartment and employment searches, shopping, and interacting with authorities, because their parents do not speak English or do not read and write English well enough to perform these functions. Immigrant students of all ages experience unhealthy role reversals where they find themselves taking care of the adults in their family by providing translations, calling agencies, and interpreting situations (Gordon, 2007) because they speak more English than their parents. These demands affect students' attendance patterns and ability to complete schoolwork.

Students Who Provide Childcare So Parents Can Work

Some middle and high school students are responsible for childcare after school and evenings in order to allow parents to hold jobs. This duty affects their ability to participate in extracurricular activities and to study outside of school. ELL adolescents know that this responsibility supersedes their focus on school, because

> **What Kids Need: Flexibility, Options**
>
> Students who are faced with serious life commitments beyond school—responsibilities to work, to help their families in significant ways, or to raise children of their own—need flexible ways of meeting the academic demands of school. They need teachers to offer options in terms of how and when they can fulfill particular responsibilities. They need understanding when they find it hard to attend school and teachers who stay committed to them despite their absences. They need alternate ways to make up for time missed at school, to have their life experiences valued, and to receive credit for life experiences that merit recognition.

parents must work to provide for their families. Teachers must investigate their learner's lives outside the classroom so they can make needed accommodations to account for the entirety of responsibilities their students must handle.

Students with Children

A final reality of middle and high schoolers is that some of them have children of their own. While the incidence of teen pregnancy has been declining in the United States, we know that teen pregnancy is higher among students who live in poverty, and immigrants experience more poverty than other groups (Rhode Island Kids Count, 2007). In fact, in some states more than 80% of adolescents who give birth are from poor or low-income families, and children of color and of immigrants are more likely to grow up poor (RI Kids Count, 2007, p. 34). Given the additional facts that many teens drop out of school before they become pregnant and that nationally less than half of teen mothers graduate from high school (RI Kids Count, 2007, p. 76), and it is easy to see why we need to have increased levels of concern for ELLs who have children of their own, and we must have strategies for keeping them in school.

The Challenge of School Attendance

Appreciating the Meaning of a High School Education in The United States

Many immigrant parents find it hard to appreciate the meaning of a high school education in the United States because, in their countries of origin, high school was not universally accessible or having a high school education was not necessary to be successful in life (Wilen, 2004). Parents from countries with low levels of education may lack the perspective required to appropriately value having a minimum of a high school education to survive in the United States (Flaitz, 2006). Education in some countries is not compulsory as it is in the United States, and in nonindustrialized nations education may be restricted to the elite (ERIC Clearinghouse on Urban Education, 1997). In nations with significant disruption caused by war or famine, schooling is not a priority and access to schooling may be curtailed.

Helping Students and Families Appreciate the Importance of Regular School Attendance

In cases where we know families are not in a position to appreciate the importance of high school completion or the related importance of regular school attendance in insuring high school success, we must take steps to educate parents about these important differences between their country of origin and their new country (ERIC Clearinghouse, 1997).

Why Families May Not Appreciate the Importance of Regular Attendance

If parents come from countries where school was attended only when possible, the value of regular school attendance may not be appreciated. In addition, we know that immigrant families' immediate needs take precedence over long-term goals. This may be another reason why parents allow their children to be absent to take care of family business or accompany the family to appointments or trips to the homeland.

Things That Get in the Way of Regular Attendance

Many things can get in the way of regular attendance. First, immigrant families have less access to health care, and therefore they may be sick more frequently than other populations. Parents may need their children to accompany them when they have doctor appointments or go to community clinics. Older siblings may be asked to stay home to care for sick siblings or to babysit while parents take care of important family matters. Relatives may visit from home countries, and students may stay home to visit with them. There are many reasons why families may allow their children to miss school; all of which seem quite logical and reasonable to the parents, as they affect the well-being of the family (ERIC Clearinghouse, 1997).

Secondary Students Who Travel Back and Forth to the Home Country

A common practice of immigrant populations is to travel for extended periods (especially around the holidays) to the home country to visit with family members (Hetzner, 2007). It is not unusual for families to take their children out of school for more than a month at a time, either because they need to travel when fares are lower or because it is unreasonable and not cost-effective to travel long distances and stay for very short periods of time. Additionally, some families report that they have so many relatives and family friends to visit that they must stay for certain lengths of time in order to see all the people expecting them to visit. Thus traditional cultural norms and values may directly clash with American expectations that schooling take priority over what is seen through American eyes as "volitional" travel.

Students Who Move Back and Forth Frequently

For economic and emotional reasons, some families seem to move frequently back and forth between the place of origin and the United States. Often families are encouraged by family members to leave a location where they are not finding work, are finding it hard to support themselves, or are unhappy. Then when they move,

> **What Kids Need: Continuous Programming, Excellent Guidance, Flexible Options to Make Up for Missed Periods of Schooling during the Year**
>
> In order to address the challenges to regular school attendance that have been raised in this section, schools must create flexible options for students to attend school and to acquire the knowledge and skills missed when they do not. Excellent record must be kept as students weave in and out of a program, so that the content they miss is well documented whenever they are absent. This way, after-school, evening, summer, and tutoring programs (i.e., on-line, one-on-one service learning tutors) can help to fill in the gaps. Creating coordination among staff is critical, and having one person responsible for keeping track of kids with attendance problems is key. In some schools this may be done by the *advisory* class teacher; in other schools, it may be the guidance counselor who is charged with this critical responsibility. Once schools document the number of students who are finding it hard to attend school on a regular basis, they can create the necessary structures to respond to the challenge (ERIC Clearinghouse, 1997).

they may find that the other location does not provide any better circumstances, and they move back again. This back and forth movement is common among particular populations where travel costs are relatively low (say, between the Caribbean islands and the U.S. mainland, or between Mexico and the southwestern United States). In cases where students experience several moves a year, obviously their education is seriously interrupted and disjointed at best. This is a systemic problem that schools must work out with families. Chapter 2 indicates some ways that guidance counselors can address some of these challenges proactively and collaboratively with families.

Motivation and Secondary School Success

> When students have a secure relationship with their teachers, they are more comfortable taking risks that enhance learning—tackling challenging tasks, persisting when they run into difficulty, or asking questions when they are confused. Urban students claim that when a teacher shows genuine concern for them, they feel that they owe the teacher something in return. . . . Adolescents report that they work harder for teachers who treat them as individuals and express interest in their personal lives outside school. (Stipek, 2006, 46)

Why Adolescents May Lack Motivation Toward School

As alluded to in the preceding quote, when students feel they belong and are cared about, they feel motivated to invest in school. The social dimension appears to be of particular importance to at-risk youth. Researchers report that high school dropouts' most frequent explanation for leaving school was that no one cared. Conversely, those who remain in school credit meaningful relationships with adults who show an interest in them as people (Stipek, 2006).

For these students, caring teachers are defined as those who communicate directly and regularly with them about their academic progress and make sure they understand what has been taught (Stipek, 2006). This approach has been labeled *pedagogical caring* in the literature, referring to a teacher's expression of genuine concern about students and dedication to insuring that they are learning (Hult, 1979). This is one of the most important keys to motivating adolescents.

How Lack of English Proficiency Interacts with Motivation

Guadalupe Valdes (2001) documents the case of recently arrived immigrant students who began their schooling in the United States with optimistic expectations that they would learn English and succeed in school. But the school they attended failed to give them opportunities to acquire the academic English needed for school success. When students do not have the tools to succeed in American secondary schools, they often give up and opt out, either by not attending classes where they are unsuccessful or by sitting in silence, present but absent, disengaged in classrooms.

How Differentiating for Proficiency Level Affects Motivation

When students do not understand the language of instruction it is easy to imagine that this fact leads to lack of motivation. They are effectively shut out from participating. Motivation is intimately tied with learner engagement, and you cannot meaningfully engage with something you cannot comprehend. Middle and high school teachers who adapt instruction to the proficiency levels of their students increase their learners' motivation because they "have a way in." Teachers can modify the linguistic inputs they provide their students, enhance linguistic input with visual and hands-on learning supports, and create output demands that learners can meet with their current level of English proficiency. These are precisely the types of "scaffolds" that are urged in the literature on sheltered English instruction (Chamot & O'Malley, 1994; Echevarría, Vogt, & Short, 2008).

How Prior Schooling Interacts with Motivation

Students who have never or rarely been to school who enter American secondary schools as adolescents find it hard to sustain motivation, because the gap between their skill levels and the type of instruction taking place is so great (DeCapua, Smathers, & Tang, 2007; F. Williams, 2003). *Limited formal schooling* or *newcomer* students pose special challenges in secondary schools because they have limited experience with school and thus limited skills (Short & Fitzsimmons, 2007). Motivating these students to stay in school is a big part of what *newcomer programs* are designed to do, in addition to filling in significant gaps in schooling and providing social and emotional support (DeCapua et al., 2007; Faltis & Coulter, 2008; F. Williams, 2003).

Policies That Lead to "Pushouts" Increase Dropouts

No Child Left Behind and subsequent state high school reform policies can discourage kids from attending school regularly because students realistically assess that they will never graduate. A report of Advocates for Children of New York and the New York Immigration Coalition (2002) shows that, as a direct result of raising the graduation requirements, ELLs are dropping out at alarmingly high rates. The authors of this study believe this is the case largely because ELLs are required to pass an English language arts exam designed for native-born English-speaking children who have been learning English language arts since elementary school

(p. 1). Their data show that between 31% and 50% of high school ELLs drop out within four years. Directly contributing to this situation is the fact that middle school ELLs are not ready for the demands of high school (p. 3).

> The factors associated with increased academic risk for ELLs . . . include . . . the failure of too many schools to provide additional required English classes or to have trained and certified ESL and bilingual teachers; the lack of an ESL curriculum tied to the new standards; the lack of extended day, weekend and year round programs for late arriving ELLs and other at-risk ELLs; very high levels of dropouts in certain high schools; poor preparation for high school by many middle schools; and a "one size fits all" graduation standard which does not recognize the unique needs of late arriving and over-age ELLs. (Advocates for Children of New York and the New York Immigration Coalition, 2002, p. 4)

Short and Fitzsimmons (2007), in their recent report *Double the Work: Challenges and Solutions in Acquiring Language and Academic Literacy for Adolescent English Language Learners*, document that in 2005 a full 96% of eighth-grade limited-English-proficient (LEP) students scored below the basic level on the National Assessment of Educational Progress (NAEP) reading test, making it impossible for them to meet the literacy demands of grade-level classes. This study (Short & Fitzsimmons, 2007) also confirms that ELLs graduate from high school at far

---

What Kids Need: Personalization, Caring, Support, Methods with "Power"

Use of Advisory Periods to Support Students,
Personalize Instruction, and Motivate Students to Stay in School

In order to insure that all students have at least one adult who knows them well, advisory programs have been recommended as a structure for middle and high schools to provide students with mentoring, guidance, and support (Juvonen et al., 2004, p. 24). Hoffman and Levak (2003) affirm that advisory periods, interdisciplinary teaching teams, and interactive journals are among the strategies used in secondary schools to help teachers and other adults know their students better. Well-trained teachers who deliver a combination of sheltered and bilingual instruction, collaborative learning, and meaningful, standards-based learning activities add "power" to instruction for ELLs (DeCapua et al., 2007). Students need well-planned programs delivered by teachers who care about and invest in their learners. Caring teachers and effective second-language instruction motivate students to stay in school. For that reason, the remainder of this book will provide information about how to deliver native language support and effective second-language instruction to ELLs.

Personalization and Motivation in Secondary Schools: What We Know

According to Schaps (2003), "A growing body of research confirms the benefits of building a sense of community in school" (p. 31). We know that schools that cultivate supportive relationships among teachers and students, especially for students of diverse backgrounds, have higher attendance levels, help their students achieve at higher levels, experience fewer behavior problems, and have faculty who report a greater sense of satisfaction in their work (Schaps, 2003). Personalization is at the heart of secondary school reform for all these reasons.

lower rates than do their native English-speaking peers. According to the report, only 10% of young adults who speak English at home fail to complete high school, yet the percentage is three times higher for ELLs. They confirm that adolescent ELLs with limited formal schooling and below-grade-level literacy are most at risk of educational failure (pp. 15–16). These students are the ones most likely to give up and opt out when they assess that they are not likely to meet the requirements for graduation.

The Challenge of Receiving High-Quality Guidance in Secondary Settings and Assigning Students to the Right Classes

Ruiz-de-Velasco and Fix (2000) cite the importance of school counselors to school success for secondary students (p. 76). Throughout the discussion thus far, in order to respond to many of the challenges raised—meeting graduation requirements or being a new arrival in a complex environment or helping students appreciate the importance of regular attendance—the role of guidance counselors featured prominently in the discussion. Counselors need to identify the range of needs of each English language learner, place each one in appropriate classes and help him or her to receive needed services. School counselors can play a powerful "gatekeeping role" by assessing students as they arrive and placing them into classes (McCall-Perez, 2000). Teachers and counselors must work together to match students with appropriate services and to identify students with additional learning needs (newcomer students with limited formal schooling), as much as they identify those who are college-bound immigrants who can excel in advanced placement classes (McCall-Perez, 2000).

F. Williams (2003) notes that access to quality counseling and guidance are critical to immigrant students for many reasons. These students may experience posttraumatic stress disorder or suffer from inadequate social support networks, racial and ethnic stereotyping, and a host of adjustment issues. Counselors have to insure that students' full range of needs are met, not just their academic needs; although of course placement in the correct classes is paramount to their success in school (McCall-Perez, 2000). School counselors are in a pivotal position to ensure individualized attention for and service to newly arrived immigrant students in all these areas. McCall-Perez (2000) states: "These students are less likely than their native-born peers to have other means of gaining information essential to their schooling decisions" (p. 13) and as a result are much more dependent on counselors than their peers for success in, and beyond, high school.

Late Arrivals and Class-Space Considerations

One of the most difficult challenges faced by counselors is that students arrive all year long. Placing new arrivals in classes becomes a challenge if they enter school after most classes are full. Students may need particular classes, and yet guidance counselors may find that space considerations prevent placement of students into the classes they need.

When this problem becomes persistent, small class sizes may need to be established in classes that students typically enroll in all year long. Districts may be able to estimate this need based on past enrollment trends (McCall-Perez, 2000). Small class size is one of the education reforms suggested as a response to learner diversity. So small class size may be a good strategy for secondary schools, all the way around. When classes become full, guidance counselors must advocate for splitting classes, opening new classes, or hiring ancillary personnel to help teachers meet students' needs in classes that go over class-size limits.

Helping Students Understand the Importance of Good Guidance for Their Futures

Orienting Students

Immigrant students face many obstacles in completing high school successfully and need guidance to help them negotiate the system successfully (F. Williams, 2003). Guidance counselors can provide basic information about course sequences in the United States, graduation requirements, and preparing for, selecting, and applying to colleges (McCall-Perez, 2000). Counselors can assist ELLs in connecting with representatives of higher education institutions, signing up for college visits, and connecting with mentors who are college or university students (Lucas, 1996; McCall-Perez, 2000). Although academic support services are often available in schools, recent arrivals may not know of the offerings that could provide them with the support they need to graduate successfully (tutoring, summer schools, weekend programs, and academies). Counselors can definitely assist with all these functions. Yet many ELL students report not knowing their counselor or how and where to find the counselor (McCall-Perez, 2000), so a first step is to orient students to the importance of guidance and show them how to make maximal use of guidance services.

Orienting Families

As has been mentioned throughout this chapter, orienting families to secondary schools and graduation requirements in the United States is something both teachers and guidance counselors must actively address. School counselors can be instrumental in formulating family outreach programs that address the concerns and information needs of specific cultural and linguistic communities.

What Kids Need: Credits, Appropriate Programming, Long-Range Planning and Comprehensive Plans

English language learners need quality guidance counseling services that help them to amass the credits they will need to graduate (McCall-Perez, 2000). They need to receive the classes and services that will help them succeed in middle and high school. They need counselors who understand the unique needs of immigrant teens and their families (F. Williams, 2003) and have responsive ways of meeting those needs. They need counselors who care and who establish caring relationships with their advisees (Committee on Increasing, 2003). For all the reasons cited in this section, Chapter 2 will be dedicated to ways to provide effective guidance services to ELLs.

Identifying Students in Need of Support Services

Guidance counselors have another critical role to play: identifying students in need of support services and determining whether schools offer a wide enough range of services to meet the identified needs. They are best able to determine which students would benefit from counseling, tutoring, mentoring, and other commonly available services. They also know the community- and school-based resources and can help students and families access those resources. They will also know the barriers to use of particular services and strategies for overcoming these barriers (Pederson & Carey, 2002)

Summing Up

Without a doubt the challenges facing secondary teachers are great, from graduation requirements, to placing and serving students effectively, to the development of academic English as needed to succeed in secondary classrooms, to keeping kids in school despite the other demands they face.

In the chapters that follow, we address some of the broad issues of service delivery, particularly those that can be solved by quality counseling and program placement, but our focus will remain on the classroom and what classroom teachers can do to serve their ELLs more effectively. First we show how to use the native language as a support to learning, even when the teacher does not know the native language of the student. We outline important frameworks that must guide secondary language and literacy development. Then we turn our attention, one chapter at a time, to strategies to develop students' oral language, reading, academic listening and note taking, and writing abilities in a second language. In a final chapter, we discuss ways to integrate ELLs into the mainstream English class, when that time arrives, as it always does. The emphasis is on practical tactics teachers can use, with support for why the strategy is recommended so teachers can feel secure in the procedures they will use.

Checklist

Secondary Educators Serving ELLs: Identifying the Most Pressing Issues for Your School

Area I: Graduation Requirements

☐ Graduation rates for ELLs are a significant challenge for our school.

☐ Earning high school credits is a problem faced by our students

☐ Passing high-stakes tests is keeping our students from graduating

Area II: Learning Academic English

☐ Our teachers do not fully understand the challenges of academic English for ELLs

☐ Teachers are not completely clear about their role in facilitating the acquisition of academic English

☐ Teachers are not well informed about how the native language contributes to academic English

Area III: Being a New Student in a Complex Social Environment

☐ Our school does not have enough opportunities for ELLs to be a part of the school community (after-school clubs, etc.)

☐ There are recognizable "cliques" in our school that are unwelcoming to ELLs (marginalize ELLs/exclude ELLs)

☐ Teachers and guidance counselors are not familiar with the recognizable stages of acculturation of newly arriving students

☐ ELL Students have difficulty "fitting in," finding a place in the school because of cultural and linguistic barriers

Area IV: Departmentalized Secondary Environments

☐ Our school uses teams, but there are problems in the way ELLs are assigned to teams or the support given to ELLs placed on the teams (common planning time)

☐ Teachers at our school have little time to coordinate instruction for ELLs

☐ Our current weekly schedule is not working well for ELLs for a variety of reasons (alternate day, block, timing of class periods)

Area V: Balancing Home, School, and Work

☐ Many of our students work, and this fact is having an effect on their academic success

☐ Many of our students have heavy family responsibilities that compete with homework and reading outside of school

Area VI: The Challenge of School Attendance

☐ Regular school attendance is an issue for our students

☐ Students at our school regularly miss long periods of time because of travel to the home country

☐ We serve a highly mobile population of students that frequently move back and forth between districts and schools

☐ Inspiring student motivation toward school is a significant challenge in our school

☐ There are subgroups of ELLs at our school for whom motivation toward school is a significant issue impeding their academic success

Area VII: Quality Guidance for ELLs

☐ Placing students in the appropriate class as they arrive during the school year is a significant challenge at our school

☐ Orientation of students and families to the requirements of U.S. secondary schools is not being well done currently in our school

☐ Identifying students who need special support services to succeed is not systematic, or having available options for students in need of support services is problematic

Credits, Graduation, and Beyond: The Importance of Families, Teachers, and Guidance Counselors Working Together

Remny, Dominican Republic, with Ms. Harrigan

> One night in January I went to my school with my parents to fill out the financial aid forms for college. All the guidance counselors were there, along with many teachers and different community members who had volunteered as translators. Without all those people helping, I never would have filled out my forms successfully. I still go back to my high school every year to reapply for financial aid.
>
> Claudia, Age 20, Guatemalan

Guiding Questions

- Why are guidance services of paramount importance to English language learners at the secondary level?
- What different types of English language learners are there, and why is it important to understand the differences among ELLs as we assist them in navigating their secondary school experience?
- How can we, as teachers and guidance counselors, work together with parents to ensure the academic success and graduation of our English language learners at the secondary level?

The Importance of Guidance for English Language Learners

As discussed in Chapter 1, school counselors are an integral part of secondary school students' success, especially that of English language learners (ELLs). There are a whole host of reasons that ELLs are likely to have a critical need for excellent school counselors to help them navigate the confusing secondary school world. Some of these reasons include

- Newness to the United States
- Past, and possibly traumatic, experiences in their home country
- The language barrier
- Inadequate social networks
- Special problems they may face in secondary school settings, such as prejudice, discrimination, and bullying as directed against nonnative speakers of English

The purpose of this chapter is to provide practical solutions for school counselors, in consultation with teachers and families, to address the issues that many ELLs face when it comes to the issues of credits, graduation, and overall adjustment to secondary school.

Below are some helpful principles that can guide school counselors' work with ELLs at the secondary level.

Guiding Principles

- Because ELLs fall into different groups, each with unique educational characteristics and background experiences, it is necessary to learn the differences and needs of each group and plan accordingly when assisting them.

- Because appropriate programming for ELLs starts with understanding their unique academic backgrounds, it is necessary to seek out the appropriate resources to properly evaluate their transcripts and course work and give them the deserved number of credits.

- Because an ELL's placement should be guided by his or her English and native language oral language proficiency and literacy level, guidance counselors should check that their students are properly tested in both English and their native language whenever possible.

- Because ELLs defy the typical grade-level description, guidance counselors should schedule them first to ensure that they receive all the classes necessary to graduate. Unlike other, more stable, school-age populations, ELLs may be taking individual courses normally taken by freshman, sophomores, juniors, and seniors all at the same time in order to obtain the credits needed to graduate. Programming for ELLs is more challenging because their course work is not as standardized, and it is helpful if guidance counselors acknowledge this fact and respond by scheduling ELLs first.

- Because different teaching methods are required to effectively teach ELL students, guidance counselors and teachers need to work together to make sure that properly prepared or ESL-certified teachers are teaching all classes serving ELLs. Otherwise they may be programmed to classes in which they may not succeed because the required modifications for their English proficiency and cultural backgrounds will not be offered.

- Because ELLs face unique challenges when applying for postsecondary options, teachers and guidance counselors should familiarize themselves with immigrants' rights and responsibilities with respect to postsecondary options and financial aid, something that changes with time and can vary by locality.

- Because ELLs often experience severe homesickness and even a profound sense of loss, teacher and guidance counselors should actively create formal and informal opportunities for students to deal with and work through these expected emotions in systematic ways.

- Because secondary students' success is known to be linked to family involvement in the students' education, schools should actively work toward a more holistic approach to engage and support ELL families so they can become informed and involved in their children's education.

- Because data should drive instruction, schools serving ELLs should be diligent about collecting and analyzing data regarding their ELLs' performance on formal assessments, their graduation rates, and their success beyond high school.

Evaluating Guidance Services

The first step toward ensuring that your ELL students receive quality guidance is to evaluate the existing guidance services. Many schools have wonderful guidance counselors who successfully serve all of their students—including ELLs. Indeed, some schools have school counselors who are solely dedicated to ELLs and specialize in serving them. Other schools, however, are not fully responsive to the needs of ELLs, not out of malice or ill will, but simply out of not being entirely sure what to do or what is needed. This uncertainty can occur when school counselors do not speak the students' languages or when they are unfamiliar with their ELL students' educational and cultural backgrounds.

In attempting to assess how well your guidance department serves ELLs, consider asking the following questions:

- Who in your school's guidance department is most capable of assisting ELLs? When you ask this question, consider other personnel who may be able to contribute to the provision of responsive guidance services—family liaisons, lead teachers, and others.

- Does your guidance department have a counselor just for ELLs? If not, can they assign one?

- Does your guidance department ensure that they are serving *all* ELL students in a systematic fashion? In other words, are all ELLs receiving the same level and quality of guidance services? If so, how? If not, how can you improve the consistency of service to ELLs?

- Are your guidance counselors willing to provide the extra assistance and guidance that ELLs may need to graduate?

- Do your teachers, guidance counselors, parents, and administrators work together to collaboratively meet ELL needs?

Hopefully, the answers to these questions will lead your school toward creating quality guidance services for ELLs, if they do not already exist. This chapter will review the knowledge, skills, and orientations secondary guidance counselors can tap into to serve ELLs well. It will also review the features of quality guidance services for ELLs, since, as has been noted in Chapter 1, good support services are even more critical to the success of secondary school ELL students than to that of mainstream students. Certainly guidance counselors are a valued part of the school-based team that supports ELLs.

Understanding the Categories of ELLs and Their Needs

Perhaps the biggest challenge with respect to properly guiding ELLs is that guidance counselors embrace the idea that every learner is unique. English language learners, as a group, might be the most diverse and varied group of students that are classified under one label. To properly serve them it is important to understand all the different situations from which they might come. Broken down most simply, there are five categories that your ELL students will most likely fall into:

1. Immigrants who enter at, or close to, grade level in their native language and come from politically stable countries. An example would be a literate and well-educated student from Portugal or Brazil who performs on or above grade level in Portuguese and is now learning English.

2. Immigrants who enter significantly below grade level in their native language, but attended school, and come from politically stable countries. An example would be a student from rural Guatemala who, while he or she has attended school, is not on grade level in his or her native language for a host of different reasons.

3. Immigrants with limited formal schooling (LFS) or large gaps in their schooling who come from politically stable countries. An example would be a student who comes from an underdeveloped country where schooling is not commonly available and where literacy rates are low.

4. Refugees who come from politically tumultuous situations and usually have gaps in their schooling or would be defined as LFS. An example would be a student from war-torn environments such as Iraq, where war has interrupted schooling and where the student has been exposed to traumatic events.

5. Migrants who are constantly moving between places and generally work to assist their families economically. An example would be a student from Mexico who is in Ohio for the fall, working picking apples, and then moves with the change in season to another location for another seasonal agricultural job.

Each of these groups of ELLs carries with it challenges that teachers and guidance counselors will want to meet. It is the act of understanding the unique needs of the many types of ELLs that determines whether a school is living up to its role of *personalization*, a hallmark of school reform initiatives (Committee on Increasing, 2003; Stipek, 2006). See Table 2.1 for examples of the particular needs of each ELL group, as well as some needs they all share in common.

Now that we have defined the five categories of ELLs and noted some of their needs, we will briefly describe the types of programs that we find in secondary schools to address these needs.

Programs for ELLs

There is no one-size-fits-all approach to educating ELLs. Schools must determine what programs and services are appropriate for their ELLs given consideration of their target populations, goals, resources, and constraints. It is important to emphasize that all teachers who have ELLs in their classes share responsibility for ELL education, not just the ESL or bilingual teachers.

While there is considerable variation in the types of programs we find for ELLs in schools today, all programs for ELLs should meet the three-pronged Castañeda standard to determine whether school districts are taking "affirmative steps to overcome language barriers" as required by the Equal Educational Opportunity Act of 1974 (*Castañeda v. Pickard, 1981*).

TABLE 2.1 English Language Learner Groups and Their Needs

English Language Learner Group	Needs
Needs that are true of all ELL groups	• *To develop English proficiency*—This can be accomplished through either bilingual programming or sound sheltered programming. • *To achieve academically in all content area instruction* in bilingual or sheltered English content classes • *To have their credits appropriately evaluated toward graduation requirements* • *To construct a graduation plan* • *To receive postsecondary counseling, including career counseling* • *To receive assistance in finding work that may complement their academic training (e.g., internships)*
Unique needs of immigrants significantly below grade level in primary language	• *To develop native language proficiency*—This can be accomplished through a native language arts class where systematic instruction is provided in reading and writing in the primary language.
Unique needs of students with limited formal schooling or large gaps in their schooling	• *To acquire school habits*—Students often need instruction on basic procedures like sitting down, raising hands, holding a pencil, etc. • *To develop native language proficiency*—This can be accomplished through instruction in reading and writing in their primary language, in a native language arts class.
Unique needs of refugees	• *Social/emotional/mental health assistance*—Students have often experienced traumatic events including death, and are possibly separated from their families. They most likely need psychological services. • *To understand school routines; basic learning skills*—Students often need instruction on basic procedures like seating arrangements, raising hands, holding a pencil, etc. • *To develop native language proficiency*—This can be achieved through instruction in reading and writing in their primary language, through native language arts.
Unique needs of migrants	• *Immediate or functional skills development*—Students will often have gaps in their schooling due to constant mobility. Best to place them in classes where they can get functional math and literacy skills, as they will most likely be moving again. • *Flexible schooling*—Students will most likely have issues with absenteeism and tardiness due to their need to work. They need a more flexible academic plan. • *Obtaining/constructing portable academic records*—Because of their constant mobility these students will often not have academic records. It is necessary to attempt to locate the most accurate ones available by getting in touch with their previous school. • *Motivation and social reluctance*—Because of their constant movement and understanding that this is most likely their life, students will often struggle to grasp the purpose of education or make friends, as they will be leaving soon. • *To develop native language proficiency*—This can be offered through instruction in reading and writing in their primary language, in native language arts classes.

- Programs must be based on educational theory recognized as sound by experts.

- Resources, personnel, and practices must be reasonably calculated to implement the program effectively.

- Programs must be evaluated and restructured, if necessary, to ensure that language barriers are being overcome.

All programs for ELLs must ensure that ELLs can achieve academically in grade-level academic content area instruction (e.g., math, science, social studies, language arts) and that they can develop English proficiency for school success.

Complex grade level content area instruction can be made comprehensible to ELLs through bilingual programming or sound sheltered programming. Bilingual classes use two languages for instructional purposes, and sheltered instruction classes use sheltered instruction strategies to make complex content comprehensible to ELLs in English. Even where bilingual programming is not possible, schools are encouraged to draw on an ELL's native language to support their content area instruction (see Chapter 3 for details). In many contexts, neither bilingual programming nor comprehensive sheltered English programming taught by ESL specialists is possible. In these cases, all teachers who have ELLs in their classes use sheltered instruction strategies within the context of their general education classes to make the content they teach comprehensible to their ELLs.

All programs for ELLs (bilingual and English-medium) must include an English as a second language (ESL) or English language development (ELD) component so that ELLs can acquire the social, instructional, and academic English they need for school success. As we discuss in Chapter 9, English language arts is not ESL instruction. For a more detailed discussion of program models for ELLs, see *Program Alternatives for Linguistically Diverse Students* by Fred Genesee (1999).

Some schools have developed heritage language programs or native language arts classes (e.g., Spanish for Spanish speakers, Russian for Russian speakers) that enable students who speak a language other than English at home to maintain and develop their home language with attention to reading and writing in that language. These programs target ELLs as well as heritage language speakers. According to the Center for Applied Linguistics (2009), "Heritage language speakers are those whose home or ancestral language is a language other than English, including native Americans, immigrants, and those born in the U.S. whose family or ancestors come from another country, and speak a language other than English". In many communities in the United States there are heritage languages that are evident and continue to be used to establish personal and family connections. In many cases, these communities have institutions that maintain specific heritage languages (through clubs, churches, community centers). Schools can look for creative ways to link up with these community organizations to support the maintenance and development of heritage languages.

Some schools have developed newcomer programs for recent arrivals to the United States who have no or low English proficiency and often have limited literacy in their native language. The goal is to accelerate these students' acquisition of language and academic skills and to orient them to the United States and to U.S. schools. Some newcomer programs follow a bilingual approach and others use sheltered English strategies.

Equipped with an understanding of student needs and of types of programs for ELLs, we will now consider how to assign these students to guidance counselors and the skills guidance counselors will need to serve their ELLs well.

Assigning Students to Guidance Counselors

Necessary Skills

In some schools, one guidance counselor handles all of the incoming ELLs. In other schools, students are distributed among guidance counselors. Obviously either arrangement can work, provided assigned counselors understand how to interact effectively with students still in the process of learning English and understand best practices in programming and placement.

In order to serve ELLs well, guidance counselors will want to have:

- Knowledge of programs and services designed to serve ELLs of different language, literacy, and educational backgrounds (bilingual courses, native language arts (sometimes called heritage language classes), ESL classes, sheltered content courses, and newcomer programs)

- Understanding of the different levels of English language proficiency and the best placements for students at each proficiency level (McCall-Perez, 2000)

- Appreciation of the acculturation and resettlement processes and stress-buffering supports that aid in the adjustment process

- Ability to communicate directly with students and their families either through the native language, or by using translators and interpreters, or through second-language communication strategies (ESL communication approaches)

- Knowledge of the cultural values of the various ethnic and cultural groups served by the school and ability to communicate in culturally responsive ways with students and their families

- Knowledge of the services and supports available in the district and in the school, including all after-school, Saturday, and summer programs (for both academic and personal growth and development)

- Knowledge of community resources and other support services available to students outside of school, such as library- and community-center-based programs and services.

- Knowledge of culturally responsive counseling practices, cross-cultural counseling trends and methods

Many of these skills are suggested in *Ethical Standards for School Counselors*, adopted by the American School Counselor Association (ASCA) delegate assembly in 1984 and revised in 1992, 1998, and 2004 (available for download at http://www.schoolcounselor.org/files/ethical%20standards.pdf).

Ability to Communicate Using the Native Language

Guidance counselors often wonder if they need to speak their students' native languages to serve them well. It is obviously very helpful if guidance counselors speak the languages of their students, but even in cases where they do not, they can still be highly successful if they have the knowledge and skills listed previously.

In cases where they do not speak the languages of their students, it helps if counselors know how to work through cultural brokers and language facilitators (translators and interpreters) to strengthen their communication with students and their families (see Pedersen & Carey, 2002).

Skilled Placement Based on Student Proficiency Level and Literacy Characteristics

When students' proficiency in English is very limited, they need specialized classes or at least teachers with specialized training to meet their needs. As their proficiency increases, they are typically fully integrated into general education classes. In cases where bilingual classes are available, students with limited English proficiency and those with functional literacy in their native language should be primary candidates. Placing students in the appropriate classes—ESL/bilingual or general education—is always best done with a complete picture of the learner's language and literacy skills in both languages, level of academic preparation, and stage of acculturation. Counselors will want to have well-formulated criteria for placing students into programs and classes based on an understanding of each individual student's needs and strengths (McCall-Perez, 2000).

Now that we have provided a basic introduction of the types of ELLs as well as the knowledge and skills that help guidance counselors to properly serve ELLs, we will shift our attention to practical strategies for assisting ELL students with the challenges they face. Educators are very well aware that these strategies may need to be modified depending on the individual needs of their students.

The Guidance Services That ELLs Need

In the sections that follow we will share strategies for supporting ELLs in secondary school by considering five major categories of student support offered by guidance counselors and teachers:

- Educational guidance
- Personal and emotional guidance
- Before- and after-school support
- Family engagement and involvement
- Data collection to guide support efforts

Educational Guidance

Obtaining Needed Credits

English language learners usually bring with them transcripts or other academic records that need to be evaluated. Because of this, guidance counselors must be skilled in analyzing foreign transcripts or academic records in order to award ELLs with an accurate number of credits. This task can be challenging, since these transcripts come in all formats and languages. Beyond the language barrier, however, there are other issues you may face: varying schooling configurations/structures, different classes, semester versus whole-year classes, and different grading systems. For example, a transcript from Guatemala may show that a student took 10 courses during an academic year that lasted from January to October, with some of the courses only lasting a semester, and the grade referred to as "sixth." These credits need to be evaluated properly and understood so that students receive the maximum number of credits they are eligible for. Here are some resources that can help counselors accomplish this task fairly:

- Translators and interpreters

- Calls and correspondence to the previous school

- Internet research on the schooling system of the student's home country

- Guidebooks designed to explain the prior schooling experience of immigrants, such as *Understanding Your Refugee and Immigrant Students: An Educational, Cultural and Linguistic guide* and the companion volume *Understanding Your International Students* (Flaitz, 2003, 2006).

Translators and Interpreters

Monolingual guidance counselors, as well as any guidance counselor who does not speak the home language of a given student, will want to become adept at using translators for interactions with both their students and family members. According to the Office for Civil Rights, districts are to use procedures that ensure that the district's communication of information to national-origin-minority parents is as effective as its communication with parents who speak English. Specifically,

> Title VI of the Civil Rights Act of 1964, and its implementing regulation, at 34 C.F.R. § 100.3(a) and (b), which provides that recipients of Federal financial assistance may not, directly or through contractual or other arrangements, on the ground of race, color, or national origin, exclude persons from participating in its programs, deny them any service or the benefits of its programs, or subject them to separate treatment. With respect to the allegation involving effective notice to parents, a Department policy document, the May 25, 1970 memorandum to school districts, Identification of Discrimination and Denial of Services on the Basis of National Origin, 35 Fed. Reg. 11,595 provides that recipients have the responsibility to adequately notify national-origin minority group, limited-English proficient parents of school activities that are called to the attention of other parents, and that such notice in order to be adequate may have to be provided in a language other than English. (U.S. Office for Civil Rights, 2004)

These translation rights should be sufficient to provide basic access to information and participation in all school activities normally made available to other families. It is important to remember that families are guaranteed even further protection in certain situations—such as when a child is considered for special education and will require assessments to determine eligibility, and if found eligible, at subsequent IEP meetings [Individuals with Disabilities Education Act, November 2004, 20 U.S.C. §1415 (b) (4); 34 C.F.R. §300.503(c)(1)). Districts will usually provide translators or interpreters to meet this requirement, if they do not have certified staff who speak the parents' language. If for some reason your district does not provide translation services, your district office should have ideas on where you can go to get accurate translation services.

One way to effectively program for your secondary ELLs is to seek out community resources to help you in interpreting school records or speaking with parents to obtain needed educational information if you lack these services within the school or district. Depending on your purposes, these may include modern/ world language faculty members at local colleges or universities, bilingual personnel at local advocacy or community agencies, clergy, government officials at a consulate or embassy, or even bilingual representatives of the local chapter of the American Civil Liberties Union.

It is not okay to interact with a student, parent, or family member without an interpreter when it is clear that you cannot provide quality services that way. You have an obligation to gather information accurately from families as well as to communicate information relevant to the child's education in a language parents can fully comprehend. Remember, students' futures are at stake—you need to make every effort to support them and properly understand their past educational experience. In addition to providing the student with the deserved number of credits, your determination and willingness to seek outside resources to help them will not go unnoticed. This will be the building block for a relationship built on trust and understanding and will show the student and his or her family that you are committed to serving them.

It is very important to protect and preserve the confidentiality of the information that students and parents may provide you with. They may have experienced serious trauma, and rightfully fear government or school officials. As a result you should make clear that the information they are telling you or that you are reading in their documents is confidential and will only be used for the purpose of helping the student with his or her educational goals. For a review of confidentiality requirements, teachers and guidance counselors can refer to "Family Educational Rights and Privacy Act" (FERPA) produced by the U.S. Department of Education (2008). This document explains issues surrounding the privacy of educational documents and can be accessed at the following Web site: http://www.ed.gov/ policy/gen/guid/fpco/ferpa/index.html. Most guidance counselors are well aware of these provisions, but teachers may not be as familiar with the provisions of FERPA and may want to consult the document on line.

Phone Calls and Correspondence

Sometimes, even with the help of translation or interpretation services, there are still uncertainties about a student's transcript. In cases like these, an excellent strategy is to go straight to the source—the school from which the student has come. If you have a transcript there is likely a phone number either on the transcript or easily found through quick Google research. With the rise of Internet calling, specifically Skype™ (an Internet-based calling system that allows you to call anywhere in the world through your computer at very inexpensive rates), it is now both inexpensive and easy to make international phone calls. A short phone call, with the aid of an interpreter, can clear up a lot of potential misunderstandings.

Internet Research

Sometimes, no matter how hard you work to do things the right way, you end up in a situation where you simply cannot find the answers you need. Your interpreters are not from the same country as your student, the student's school is closed or the phone number is incorrect, and all of your attempts to access community resources have failed. In these cases, your last resort is to use the Internet to do simple searches to try and find some basic information on the schooling system in the country that your student comes from. At the very least, you should be able to find some generic information on the length of the school year and the structure of schooling that will help you in better evaluating the students' transcript.

Guidebooks

As has already been mentioned, there are guidebooks published for educators that provide detailed information on the school systems from which many immigrant students come. Two of these are

- *Jeffra Flaitz, Understanding Your Refugee and Immigrant Students: An Educational, Cultural, and Linguistic Guide.* Ann Arbor: University of Michigan Press, 2006.

    Provides information on countries that contribute a majority of refugees and immigrants to the United States: Afghanistan, Bosnia-Herzegovina, Croatia, the Dominican Republic, Ecuador, El Salvador, Ethiopia, Guatemala, Honduras, India, Iran, Laos, Liberia, Peru, Somalia, Sudan, and Ukraine.

    Each country profile features statistics about the country, a historical synopsis, an overview of the county's official education policy, cultural perspectives, and a problem-solution section containing classroom strategies. The linguistic systems of the languages featured are also included for teacher reference. This reference includes information about teacher-student relationships, discipline and class management, and appropriate nonverbal communication.

- *Jeffra Flaitz (Ed.), Understanding Your International Students: An Educational, Cultural and Linguistic Guide.* Ann Arbor: University of Michigan Press, 2003.

    Provides a table of information related to school calendars, curricula, exams, grades, homework, and classroom setup for Brazil, Colombia, Cote d'Ivoire, Cuba, Egypt, Haiti, Japan, Korea, Mexico, Morocco, People's Republic of China, Poland, Russia, Saudi Arabia, Taiwan, and Vietnam.

    These books can help counselors interpret the records they receive in order to award credits accurately and fairly.

Amassing the Right Credits

For ELLs who enter at the secondary level the issue of amassing the right credits is of paramount importance, as it will often determine which postsecondary options are actually viable. Guidance counselors will want to ensure that after evaluating their previous transcripts they place ELLs in the appropriate classes—meaning the ones that they need to graduate.

As you can see in the vignette, Yeni was fortunate that a guidance counselor caught her mistake before it was too late and that a history teacher was amenable to a special circumstance. Even so, a more careful review of her transcript at the beginning of the year could have avoided this situation entirely. Too often ELL students are placed in whatever classes are convenient, after their ESL class schedule has been figured out, with not enough attention paid to what they need to graduate and attend college. It is important to remember that these students often have no idea of what they need and too often have no adult who can help them navigate this world, so they rely on you, and mistakes can be costly.

Sadly, in some schools, counselors and teachers may just assume that their

Vignette: Proper Scheduling

Yeni entered high school from Guatemala in her sophomore year and spent that first year struggling to adjust to her new life in the United States and schooling in a completely new language. She was frustrated by her grades and anxious to pick up English. Her junior year then went fabulously well. She found her groove, improved her grades, and started to feel more confident in her academic English. During her senior year, she hoped to continue her success, gain more skills in academic English, and pursue higher education: first at a community college and then at a four-year college. She was determined and confident, and nothing could stop her.

In November of her senior year, Yeni received a note from her guidance counselor telling her that she had never passed U.S. History and could not graduate without it. She needed to either take an after-school course that would provide her with one year's worth of U.S. History or not graduate from high school. Yeni was enrolled in a history course for that year: Modern U.S. History, which was simply an elective.

Yeni had not passed her U.S. History course during her sophomore year because she had so much trouble adjusting and struggled with English. If Yeni needed U.S. History to graduate, you might ask why she was scheduled for an elective class she did not need instead of U.S. History, which was required for graduation. Now, Yeni, a good student determined to go to college, was faced with the difficult task of adding an extra after-school course to her already rigorous schedule. Luckily, a teacher of U.S. History at her school agreed to let her join late, make up the work, and she graduated on schedule.

Judah Lakin, Hope High School, Providence, RI

ELL students will not be attending college anyway, since they do not have enough English or the educational preparation and course work required, so they do not always analyze ELL students' schedules with enough care. Yet, when committed teachers, students, families, and counselors work together, not only can programming mistakes be avoided, but also a majority of ELL students can graduate from high school, and many can become prepared to attend and graduate from postsecondary institutions. They just need our guidance and support.

To help avoid harmful errors in scheduling, which can cost students the chance either to graduate or to continue to postsecondary options, we suggest that guidance counselors schedule ELLs first because doing so will guarantee them access into the classes that they need. Often guidance counselors use district-mandated grade-level requirements to schedule blocks of students, which work very well for mainstream students but tend not to work for ELLs. Because of their varying backgrounds and educational histories, students may need to fulfill graduation requirements that are often determined not by grade level but rather by gaps in the course work required to graduate. Often, the classes they need to graduate cause scheduling conflicts because they span grade levels. For example, they may need a world history class, which is normally a ninth-grade class, but also need precalculus, which is normally a senior course, and these two courses might be hard to schedule—there may be only one section of each that would allow you to give the student both. If guidance counselors schedule ELLs after all other students it may be impossible for them to obtain the two needed classes, as the sections that would work schedule-wise may be filled.

In short, our English language learners do not fit into standard grade-level profiles and need a more individualized approach to scheduling. When this is not provided, ELLs will sometimes be loaded up on electives and shut out of required courses they need to graduate.

Accurate Evaluations

In order to properly serve ELLs, guidance counselors and teachers can work together to ensure that they have accurate information on the proficiency level of the students. Too often, teachers and guidance counselors will hear a student speak for a few minutes and develop an informal assessment of that student's language abilities with which they determine the student's entire schedule. This approach is a problem because a student's conversational fluency in a social setting is distinct from their academic language proficiency, as will be explained in Chapter 5 (Cummins, 1981, 2006). When it comes to scheduling classes, it is students' academic language proficiency that matters—their ability to engage in academic listening, speaking, reading, and writing; not just their ability to engage in everyday conversations. Guidance counselors and teachers need to ensure that assessments are done that will accurately determine each student's academic language proficiency level, and students should be programmed based on that determination (see Chapter 4 of Gottlieb & Nguyen, 2007, for advice about student assessment, or see your local ELL assessment coordinator).

Qualified Teachers

In addition to being careful to accurately assess the students, guidance counselors need to ensure that students are placed with teachers who are prepared to teach ELLs. Unfortunately, ELLs are often taught by individuals without proper preparation. This deficiency may occur because content teachers have not been adequately prepared to serve ELLs, but it may also occur because of a scheduling mistake. Students, teachers, parents, and guidance counselors need to be vigilant in making sure that the appropriate teachers are instructing sheltered English classes. It is important to ensure that content teachers who are prepared to serve ELLs be given that teaching responsibility. Students will be better served and have more opportunities to succeed when they are instructed by teachers who are trained in pedagogical methods specific to ELLs. That said, it is also true that any content teacher with the desire to learn how to better serve ELLs can certainly do so through focused professional development such as that provided in this volume and highly useful guidebooks like *Making Content Comprehensible for English Learners: The SIOP Model* (Echevarría et al., 2008).

To insure the most responsive services, it is important that guidance counselors listen in for how ELL students are faring with the teachers who are educating them. Often students' reactions and academic progress can reveal which teachers are and are not well suited to work with ELLs. Teachers who serve ELLs need to both *want* to and *know how* to work with ELLs at the secondary level. ELL-friendly teachers ensure that their students are receiving the proper supports and scaffolds in the classroom to overcome the background knowledge and language barriers that can exist. When students do very poorly, the result may or may not have to do with their own efforts. It could also signal that the material is not being made accessible to them. When ELL student after student is doing well, however, this success is likely a sign that the teacher is skilled at assisting ELL learners. Neither a student doing well nor one doing poorly is enough to determine the efficacy of a teacher, so the guidance counselor will always want to pay close attention to the academic progress of, and feedback from, the students to evaluate the adequacy of their placement practices.

Abiding by Regulations

The last thing that guidance counselors need to do to ensure proper scheduling is confirm that their school is abiding by district, state, and federal guidelines regarding the scheduling of ELLs. Everyone who is working to ensure a quality education for ELLs should be familiar with their state's regulations and policies. If you are not, you can always go to the state education department Web site or contact the appropriate office in the state education department. English language learners are entitled to specific services, and counselors will want to be well versed in what state and federal regulations require.

Documentation

In the United States undocumented students have the right to complete a secondary education. According to the U.S. Supreme Court ruling in *Plyler v. Doe* (1982), schools cannot deny admission to students based on their undocumented status. The Court decided, "Denying enrollment in public school to children who are not 'legally admitted' into the United States violates the Equal Protection Clause of the Fourteenth Amendment." Although you might think that all your students are documented, the Urban Institute estimated in 2003 that some 65,000 undocumented students graduate from high school every year in the United States (Passel, 2003). Some of those students might be yours, so it is imperative that you understand their rights while in the United States.

After high school their access to education becomes more complicated, as they are no longer protected under *Plyler v. Doe*. The Federal Department of Homeland Security, in a letter, has clarified that they do not require reporting or inquiring into immigration status by institutions of higher learning. It also has stated, however, that the decision of whether to allow undocumented students to enroll should be left to the states. In the absence of state law the decision is up to specific institutions. Even so, they must use federal law to determine who is "undocumented," a requirement that means that this process may not be discriminatory. All of this information is available to see and explained thoroughly through a link provided for by the National Immigration Law Center at http://www.nilc .org/immlawpolicy/DREAM/Dream009.htm.

Because the prior discussion only refers to whether undocumented students should be admitted to colleges and universities, it is also the case that, even when admitted, undocumented students are not eligible for federal financial aid and will have to pay their own way. In addition, they will have very meager job opportunities if they manage to get a degree, given their lack of a social security number. Their plight is made even more difficult by the fact that our undocumented students are not eligible for in-state tuition and fees unless a state law permits. According to Carl Krueger (2006), thirty states had introduced legislation by 2006 to provide undocumented students with the ability to pay in-state tuition. These distinctions are constantly being created and challenged, so it is always important to check with National Immigration Law Center (http://www.nilc.org) to see which states currently have such laws on their books. While understanding the rights and regulations governing undocumented immigrants, we certainly want to encourage all of our students to further their education whenever possible.

Guidance counselors can assist ELLs in understanding their options based on their documentation status, and the earlier you start this process the better. If a student wants to go to college and cannot receive federal financial aid, then the student needs to look into private scholarships or part-time opportunities, and the guidance counselor should be equipped to help each student with this process. The best place to start would be with the financial aid offices of whatever universities your students hope to attend. They should be able to send you in the right direction. In addition, here are a few good places to start your search:

- The College Board (Web site, http://professionals.collegeboard.com/guidance/financial-aid/undocumented-students?vgnextfmt=default): This Web site is dedicated to helping professionals advise their undocumented students. It is replete with legal information, useful links, and downloads that can help you help your undocumented students weigh their options for higher education.

- Mexican American Legal Defense Fund (Web site, http://www.maldef.org/): This site has information on scholarships that are available to students regardless of immigration status.

- FinAid (Web site, http://www.finaid.org/): This site has information about many different types of aid for students seeking to go to college and has links explaining what students' options are if they are undocumented.

- Minnesota Office of Higher Education—Get Ready for College (Web site: http://www.getreadyforcollege.org/gpg.cfm?pageID=1586): This site has links to lists of national scholarships available to students irrespective of their documentation.

- ASPIRA—An Investment in Latino Youth (Web site: http://www.aspira.org/manuals/hispanic-scholarship-resources). This site has links to many scholarships, some of which are available to students who are undocumented.

Ultimately, in terms of understanding your students' rights, you should check with both your district and state governments to learn the specific requirements of your state. In addition, however, there are several national organizations that can help you in this process. The following organizations all have information on students' rights and are excellent jumping-off points for helping your students:

- National Immigration Law Center (NILC): You can find information on immigrant rights, benefits, and education.
  Web site: http://www.nilc.org/

- American Civil Liberties Union (ACLU): You can search for information on immigrants' rights and students' rights.
  Web site: http://www.aclu.org/index.html

- The National Lawyers Guild: A progressive organization set up to help change the structure of the political and economic system. You can search the Web site for local chapters and specific resources related to immigrants.
  Web site: http://www.nlg.org/

- The National Immigration Project (of the National Lawyers Guild): You can search through documents and recent cases, and even do a state-by-state search for immigration lawyers.
  Web site: http://www.nationalimmigrationproject.org/
- The Office for Civil Rights within the Department of Education: You can search this Web site for government initiatives, resources, and contacts on issues related to students' rights, immigration issues, and ELL issues. You can also access the Family Educational Rights and Privacy Act (FERPA) here.
  Web site: http://www.ed.gov/about/offices/list/ocr/index.html

Establishing Partnerships

Usually because of their late arrival or limited schooling background, some secondary ELLs will not graduate from high school with either the requisite English proficiency or academic abilities to immediately attend a four-year college or a university. These students may need to first enter other programs to help them acquire the skills they need to later successfully transition on to college. So guidance counselors will want to identify the preparatory programs that will eventually lead students toward successful college entry. Other ELLs are simply not interested in higher education and need help in finding postsecondary alternatives.

For the latter group of students, it is helpful if guidance counselors create partnerships with both continuing education programs and programs that serve as alternatives to higher education. Some options to consider include trade programs, outreach and lifelong learning centers, and apprenticeships. Many secondary schools establish productive partnerships with adult education and workplace training programs and guide their students toward these options when they are not interested in pursuing college preparation. The best starting place to investigate these options is with your state education department's adult education office or local community colleges and trade schools.

Personal and Emotional Guidance: Homesickness and the Importance of Family

One of the most important factors affecting ELLs is the aspect of homesickness. Many ELL secondary students leave their family behind when they come to the United States. For some of these students their homesickness prohibits them from functioning academically, leaving them constantly depressed about their separation from their place of origin, extended family, and friends. For others, they are okay most days, but may have bouts where they become upset or begin to cry. When teachers and guidance counselors understand the severity of homesickness, they can respond effectively. Most students, with assistance, can overcome the debilitating nature of these feelings, especially with the expressed compassion and concern on the part of adults. Students need to feel validated in their feelings but also find ways to deal with these naturally occurring feelings so they can take advantage of opportunities that their being in the United States has to offer.

In addition to being empathetic and listening to your students, guidance counselors and teachers can work together to create more formal opportunities for their students to deal with their emotions. Teachers can work with guidance counselors to identify students in need of more extensive support services. Guidance counselors and teachers can collaborate in the delivery of in-classroom activities that allow students to express their feelings. These activities may take the form of writing, acting, drawing, or any number of other expressive modes. In addition to in-class supports, guidance counselors and teachers may consider having personal meetings with their students or creating organized support groups. It is recommended that someone who speaks the native language of the students be present to help with the facilitation of these meetings or groups and that they occur either weekly or biweekly. Additionally, you should consider calling home at least once a month, and if possible visiting the home so that the school's efforts are connected to the family's. Last, teachers can keep tabs on students for whom they have any concern, through casual conversations in the hall or before and after school, to get an idea of how the student is doing. The important thing is that we be systematic in our efforts and provide services at the appropriate level to respond to the level of distress or depression often experienced by the uprooted student.

Before- and After-School Support

Given all the challenges that ELLs face, we will certainly want to insure that ELLs access meaningful before- and after-school opportunities to both assist with their academics and acclimate them to the United States and the daunting bureaucracy of secondary schools. It is important, when possible, to provide these opportunities both before and after school, as many ELLs will not be able to make one time or the other because of family or work obligations. The following paragraphs present ideas for the types of programs that we think are particularly useful.

One before- or after-school support option could center on orientation to life in their new community and useful knowledge and skills needed by young adults in the United States. Many of our students will have no idea how to do basic social tasks and because they are secondary school students may be too embarrassed to ask. It would be preferable to integrate such support into the ESL curriculum, but when it is not possible to do so, support should be offered in a structured way before or after school. One strategy is to run mini-workshops where you educate your students on things like "What Services Are Available at the Post Office?"; "Where Do You Go for Bus Passes?"; "How Do You Get a Lunch Number?"; "How Do You Set Up a Bank Account?" Sometimes students have other people who can help them with these types of activities, but often they do not, and providing them a safe and nonjudgmental place where they can learn is important. To help them be successful, we can make it our responsibility to give them not only academic skills but also life skills.

The second service that we suggest all schools serving ELLs have is a before- or after-school tutoring program. As secondary students are required to do "double the work"—learn English and content—it is often a daunting task to try and keep up with as many as eight subjects at a time (Short & Fitzsimmons, 2007). Many also face the challenge of working or family obligations that can consume many hours of their week as well. Although some of them actually want to do work at home, they simply may not have a space where they can quietly study because of small living quarters or large families. Additionally, they may also need access to a computer for much of their homework and not have one available to them at home. For all of these reasons, it is important to try to provide a well-structured before- and after-school tutoring program at your school that is developed not solely by teachers but by guidance counselors working in collaboration with teachers and families. Although every school and community is different, we have found that certain elements will help improve the efficacy of the program, and so we make the following practical suggestions.

Effective Elements of a Before- and After-School Tutoring Program

- *Staff and coordinate the program with ELL teachers and ELL guidance counselors*—English language learners will be more likely to come if their teachers and guidance counselors will be there because their presence will provide a certain level of comfort.

- *Properly train volunteers*—In addition to teachers, it is useful to have volunteers to provide students with more individualized instruction. It is important to remember, though, that these volunteers need to be equipped to properly assist the ELL students without simply giving them the answers. (You can get tutors from many sources, but college students in teacher preparation programs are good sources to tap, as their participation benefits them and your students.) Consider the following:
  - Explain your student's situation as background for the tutor.
  - Provide the tutor with a certain level of background information on how ELLs learn (conversational fluency versus academic language proficiency, L1 literacy and its connection to L2, etc.; these concepts will be explained more fully in the chapters that follow).
  - Give the tutor a specific task for the day and ask the tutor to report back at the end of the day on the progress made.
  - Allow the tutor time to simply get to know the student and form a relationship.
  - Provide the tutor with a white board and marker to give immediate explanations and work through problems that may arise during the tutoring session.

- *Provide computers and printers*—For many students this will be their only opportunity to work on a computer and be able to print material, so it is really important to try and provide these materials.

- *Provide incentives*—Students enjoy getting little gifts or prizes, or extra points, for attendance or hard work, and these show the program recognizes and values their hard work.

- *Contact parents*—Many parents of ELLs are very nervous about their students staying after school for a variety of reasons, and they are also often suspicious of why their students do not come home right away. As a result, it is a good idea to tell those parents that you will contact them at the beginning of tutoring to let them know that their child is there, and you will contact them when their child leaves, to let them know that their child is on their way home. This is only a slight inconvenience to you as a teacher or counselor, but it usually makes a world of difference for the parent or guardian, and allows students to get the extra help that they need.

- *Partner with classroom teachers*—It is important to try and be in touch with your students' other classroom teachers who do not participate in tutoring to tell them how their students are doing and find out if they think the tutoring is helping. They may also have suggestions on what they would like their students to be doing in tutoring. Such communication will also allow the students to see that you are in contact when their classroom teacher and will show that their work is being noticed by multiple adults and is paying off.

Family Engagement and Involvement

Administrators, guidance counselors, and teachers can work together to involve ELL students' families in the educational process. It is not enough, however, to simply provide interpreters and translators for these families. Schools need to consider a more holistic approach that both supports families and values their role in their students' education. In order to do so, many schools will need to appreciate the differences that exist between mainstream parents and parents who are culturally and linguistically diverse. Many ELLs went to small schools in their countries where families had constant contact with their teachers, and family involvement in the school was more organic and natural because the community was so small and tight. A more structured program including parent nights, PTAs, or even communicating through letters is often a foreign concept and will not engage families coming from more communal backgrounds. Specifically with letters and invitations, no matter how many times families receive them they may not respond because they have no relationship with the sender. These families are often reached through communication that is more personalized. Although there are many stories of successful family engagement at the elementary level in urban settings, they are few and far between at the secondary level in urban areas. High school and middle school settings bring with them unique challenges, including the fact that students themselves sometimes actively work to make sure their families do not get involved.

Even though it is a challenge, the situation is far from hopeless and there are many active steps we can take toward involving non-English-speaking parents. Our families willingly participate in school, and many of them actually long for the involvement they had in their hometowns. Some of the ways in which the school community can become more open and inviting of families of ELLs are through native language signage, multilingual staff, the use of students as translators and interpreters, culturally sensitive staff, stressing personal contact, expanding the role of the school, and actively seeking out and involving community partners. Following is a more detailed description of each of these strategies:

- *Native language signage:* For many families, American high schools are daunting and uninviting physical structures. Offices and teachers are usually difficult to find, and there is often little, if any, signage assisting parents and families—and if there is, it is usually only in English. Putting up multilingual directional signs as well as multilingual welcoming signs will make a huge difference when parents and families enter the building. They will feel welcomed and capable of finding what they need. These signs will also be a visible sign that your school values and affirms their language and culture.

- *Multilingual staff:* In the same way that multilingual signage is important, it is also important to try and have staff members that speak the languages of the

---

Vignette: Family Engagement Success

We had spent the summer traveling around the Dominican Republic, visiting the families of students we taught back at Hope High School in Providence, Rhode Island. It was an amazing experience, one filled with adventure and education. Although all the families were different, there was one constant—all the families yearned for more involvement in their children's education. They yearned for the days where they could walk down the street and talk to their child's teacher. Now their children were in another country, and they felt helpless. Upon hearing these families, we decided that if these parents, who did not even live in the same country as their children, wanted to be involved in their children's education, the same must be true of our ELL families in the United States. We always knew that we needed to do a better job of engaging our ELL families, and now we finally had the impetus to make that happen.

Upon coming back to Hope High School, we formed a new family engagement organization, and called it *Juntos (Together)*. We created multilingual signage for the entire building, identifying all rooms and teachers, so families could more easily navigate the building. We began calling all our parents, and ensured that every single family was called by someone who spoke their language. We wanted to make sure that families were called twice a month, so we held telethons at a local university where teams of teachers volunteered on Saturday to call all the families. We knew that if we began to personalize communication, we would have more success in engaging all families, especially ELL families. We planned a *Juntos* night to bring in all families to get to know teachers and Hope High. At this night we had music and food from our families' cultural traditions. We used local media, in multiple languages, to promote our event. We went into the community and asked for donations to support our work. We created a club of students who served as translators for parents who were not English dominant. In this way, all parents could communicate with teachers through translators. We had families fill out contact-information sheets. We sent home letters and fliers in multiple languages. We were beginning to shift the culture at our school. At our first night, more than 800 people came into our school. This was the most ever recorded for a family night at Hope High School. Teachers and families began the difficult but necessary process of creating relationships that would help our students succeed. This work was documented in three different newspapers. For more information on this work please see the following three links:

http://www.projo.com/ri/providence/content/mc_hope04_10–04–07_857CoMO.2f9134c.html

http://providenceenespanol.com/news.php?nid=1688&clave=a%3A1%3A%7Bi%3A0%3Bs%3A11%3A%22Judah+Lakin%22%3B%7D

http://www.browndailyherald.com/2.12232/hope-high-reaches-out-to-immigrant-parents-1.1672688

Erin Leininger and Judah Lakin, Hope High School, Providence, RI

---

school's families. Many times, this is not possible, but even if there is one staff member it makes a significant difference. The most important place for a multilingual staff member to be is in the front office, as many parents do not speak English and are very fearful of coming into school and not being able to communicate with anybody. Having a welcoming, encouraging person who also speaks the predominant native language(s) of the school community will make a huge difference in encouraging parents to visit the school.

- *Student translators and interpreters:* Tapping into the resources available within your student body is extremely important. Even at schools where the staff is primarily monolingual, there are certainly students that have some of level of bilingual proficiency. Creating a translating and interpreting club where these students can come and provide interpretation services at parent nights or PTA meetings is important. It shows the parents and family members that you are doing your best to provide them with interpretation and translation services, and it shows the students that their bilingualism is valued and important. At parent nights, you might consider providing them with signs in L1 that say, "I speak [insert language]," that they can wear around their neck identifying them as interpreters. Last, if available, it would be a good idea to bring in professional interpreters and translators to train these students. This will allow them to actually be better at what they are doing and show them that there are economic opportunities available to multilingual people.

- *Cultural sensitivity and awareness:* It is important when holding parent nights or official school activities that ELL families feel welcomed at these activities. Many times after-school activities involve music and food, but too often the music and food are not representative of the actual cultures of our students. If your students eat *arroz con pollo* (chicken and rice), then you might not want to have a parent night with spaghetti. Make sure you show them that you know about their culture and that you value it by creating events that include aspects of their culture—even if they seem trivial, such as music or food.

- *Personal contact:* Many schools today attempt to reach their parents through form letters and automated phone calls. Even when translated, these are generally ineffective ways to reach out to families of ELLs. A significant percentage of ELLs' families expect and prefer to be contacted in person, by their students' teachers. In our experience, this is the only way in fact that some families will become involved. After several personal communications, be it by phone or in person, parents will most likely also respond to written communication from that same person. It is important, therefore, that teachers of ELLs make sure that they attempt to contact their parents personally, through the use of an interpreter, if necessary. (Chavkin & Gonzalez, 1995; Espinosa, 1995; Scribner, Young, & Pedroza, 1999).

- *Expanding a school's role:* For many families their child's school is their only real connection to American society, because they often spend the majority of their time working and living in linguistically concentrated workplaces and ethnic communities. As a result, it is important for schools to become more expansive in the role they serve for their ELL families. Secondary schools should consider running workshops for ELL families on topics as diverse as "The American School System," "Standardized Testing," "How to Help Your Student with Homework," "Where Can You Learn English?" and "Health Care Options." Ideally schools would run monthly workshops to help families of ELLs deal with these issues. Such workshops would serve two purposes in that they would help families and also bring them into school and create multiple opportunities for them to become involved. If parents and families see that you are trying to help them, then you will begin to build up trust, which can be tapped into later when you need their assistance with their child.

- *Community partners:* It is important to remember that many families will not immediately trust the school for a variety of reasons. Therefore, it is important for the school to find community partners that are both better equipped to help the families of ELLs and more likely to be found trustworthy by the families as a result of being run by people in their own community. Many of the workshops just mentioned will require significant preparation and research, so it is always important to find people who can help you in these endeavors. More often than not there are already people engaging in these types of activities in your community, so it is important to try and partner with them to build up and enhance what they are already doing. The bottom line is that you want to help the families, so whether you provide the service, or whether you point them in the direction of somebody else who will, is unimportant. As long as they are receiving the assistance and they know that you are helping them, they will be more likely to trust in the school and become active partners in their children's education.

The information provided in this section was in no way comprehensive but merely meant to provide a framework through which to begin reenvisioning your school's approach toward family engagement combining the efforts of guidance counselors and teachers.

Creating Data and Using It to Monitor Your Effectiveness

Secondary School Success

Most schools monitor the progress of their students, and it is important to do the same with ELLs. Schools need to keep data on the academic progress of their ELLs and use it to help inform instruction (Gottlieb & Nguyen, 2007). It is important to use valid and fair assessments, such as the state's English Language Proficiency Assessment that accurately evaluates the student's level of English proficiency or authentic assessments like portfolios. Schools need to use well-thought-out procedures to create data specifically on their ELL population. If, as the years progress, ELLs are not making significant progress, then adjustments will need to be made. Data on ELLs must be disaggregated to get a good understanding of their achievement and rate of progress toward learning goals (see Gottlieb & Nguyen, 2007).

Graduation and Beyond

Most secondary schools keep track of their graduation rates, and many keep track of how many of their students go on to colleges and universities. Very few high schools, however, keep formal statistics on how many of their graduates actually matriculate at the universities where they were accepted and how many actually graduate. Many secondary schools think that these numbers are the sole responsibility of the college or university. The problem, however, is that the education a student received at his or her secondary school will clearly have an impact on that student's performance in postsecondary education. Therefore, it can be very helpful to track graduates for at least five years beyond graduation from high school, if at all possible. With these data available, you can also motivate other students in the future. This information is especially important for ELLs, as they tend to have higher dropout rates and more obstacles facing them when attempting to complete a postsecondary degree. Once armed with these data, you can see if you are succeeding with your ELLs, and the results can serve as a starting point to share best practices with other professionals in the field.

Often ELLs leave high school with the best of intentions. They get into a community college and say that they will learn English for two years, after which they will attend a four-year college for a bachelor's degree. Secondary teachers smile and pat themselves on the back because these are exactly the things we want them to do. Unfortunately, these students do not always match their words with actions. Some of them never even go to community college; they are too afraid, too in need of money, or simply lured away by the prospect of making money immediately and not having to struggle through English. Other students do attend but find it too difficult, or cannot keep up with the payments, and drop out. Another group of students completes community college but then is completely lost when it comes to four-year colleges, so gives up and moves into the workforce. It takes a great deal of strength, pride, and will, as an adult (which these students are, upon graduating from high school) to see the long road ahead and understand that it is worth the struggle. Many ELLs who enter high school in the middle of their secondary career leave high school still ELLs. As a result, they have to pursue their academic career elsewhere and improve their academic English before attending a four-year college, as already mentioned in this chapter.

It is important that your school develop a way to track its students and monitor their progress because it is very possible that your school might be able to modify what you do to better guarantee success after high school. For this reason, your school might want to dedicate one counselor to being the liaison for these students. If students do not feel academically prepared, perhaps you can ramp up your tutoring and class work. If students are simply intimidated or need extra support, perhaps you can meet them and help them through their transitional period. If financial aid is the issue, perhaps you can continue to help them apply or find private scholarships to assist with the money. The idea behind collecting data is to provide the opportunity to look at your practice and figure out what you can improve upon to better serve ELLs and guarantee their future success. By keeping track of them we can best ensure that they are continuing down multiple pathways toward success.

Conclusion

In reading this chapter, you might feel overwhelmed. That feeling is okay—English language learners and their families come to the United States with a whole host of needs and challenges, and in this chapter you might feel that we are asking you to meet all of them. Find hope in the fact that every time you help an ELL feel more comfortable in the United States, or complete an application for financial aid, or guide a student toward the right courses and instructors, you have done something valuable and highly significant to individual students and families.

You have already taken an important step—you are actually thinking about

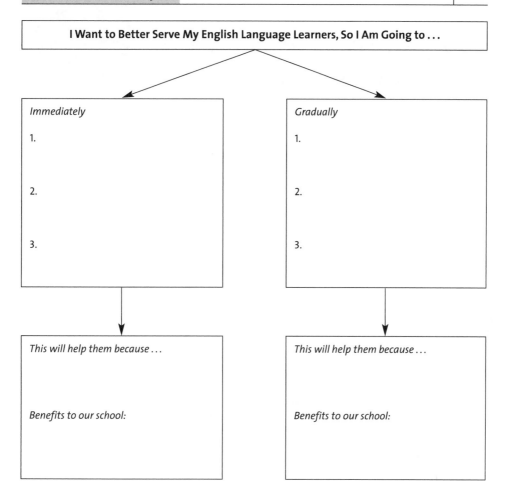

how to better serve your ELL population. It is also smart to focus on one or two initiatives a year in terms of large-scale objectives such as school data or signage. While initiating large-scale changes, you can immediately make smaller changes that you feel are possible like finding translators to interpret transcripts or scheduling an appointment with your ELLs once a week to check on their progress. Little by little it will all add up to quite a supportive array of services and tactics.

We have provided a graphic organizer to help you get started with this very important process. This chapter can be returned to again and again in search of additional practical ideas you can add to the work that you are already doing or to begin some new initiatives that will make a world of difference to secondary ELLs and their families.

CHAPTER 3

Using the Native Language to Support Secondary ELLs

Welcome sign, Hope High School

Every time I had my social studies class I felt scared. I hated this class at the beginning because the first time I went to this class everybody looked at me and laughed. Every time I talked the other students would laugh. Even my teacher could not understand me. One day my teacher came to school with a book that had Haitian Creole in it. Every time he wanted to tell me something, he opened the book and tried to read what he wanted to tell me in Creole. I will never forget that—he was the first person who helped me to speak English and my first teacher to be my friend. I trusted him because he showed me he cared about my culture and was willing to try and speak my language.

Oswalda, 18, Haitian

Guiding Questions

- Why is a student's primary language an important resource that should be effectively utilized to aid a student's acquisition of English?

- How can teachers incorporate classroom strategies that effectively utilize the primary language to support the acquisition of both content and English?

- How can teachers work together and with the community to create school environments where multilingualism and multiculturalism are encouraged and valued?

Imagine walking into a school in which, despite the fact that all of the teachers are very friendly, smiling and nodding, when they approach you to speak you do not understand them. Someone is asking you questions except that you have no idea what s/he is asking you. Now imagine having this feeling everywhere you go, and in everything you do, and not being able to leave. Everywhere you go people speak to you in a language you do not understand and look at you strangely when you stare back at them blankly. Now add the pressures of being a preteen or teenager—trying to figure out who you are and who you want to be—identity searching, while you struggle to understand the basics of what is going on around you. This is the experience of many secondary English language learners (ELLs)—a constant state of frustration, sometimes confusion, and in many cases yearning for the comfort of their old lives. They need ways to break in and to show their competence. Use of the native language is one of the most important tools for doing so when English is just beginning to be developed. For this essential reason, understanding how and when to use the native language effectively in both a school and classroom setting will be the focus of this chapter.

Teaching Principles

- Because ELLs are such a growing population, take the time to learn all the strategies effective in educating them, including use of their native language.

- Because there is ample research supporting the helpful role of a student's primary language in the acquisition of a second language, help your students pursue additive bilingualism by encouraging your students to maintain and nurture their primary language.

- Because a student's proficiency level in his or her primary language is important in determining the usefulness it will have in language and content classrooms, make sure to get as much information as you can about your students' abilities in their primary language.

- Because a school's implicit or explicit stance on the use of languages other than English within the school context will affect the access students, families, and community members are able to have (to policymakers, teachers, and services), evaluate your school's current uses of languages other than English and then work toward making it as inclusive and welcoming as possible to speakers of other languages who are still in the process of learning English.

- Because there are schools and people that are already leading the way on native language use in ELL education, avoid reinventing the wheel by seeking out models and advice from experienced colleagues and professionals in the field.

- Because it is impossible to know every language that your ELL students may speak, seek out the appropriate material and human resources to help you in supporting all your ELL students through use of their home languages.

- Because the Internet has expanded the access to dual-language dictionaries and translation services, actively use these services to support the learning of content and the development of English proficiency in your classroom.

- Because secondary ELL students often feel lost and out of place, whenever possible use your knowledge of a second language to get to know students on a more personal level—beyond academics.

Changing Demographics

According to the U.S. Census Bureau, between 1995 and 2005 the number of foreign-born people in the United States went from 24.5 million to 35.7 million. During that same period, according to the National Clearinghouse for English Language Acquisition, the number of English-language learners in K–12 education in the United States went from 3.2 million to 5.1 million, growing about 57%. Additionally, in 20 states, the number of ELLs doubled in that same ten-year period (Maxwell, 2009).

What makes these statistics even more significant is the fact that the overall K–12 population has remained stagnant, meaning that our ELL population has begun to represent a more significant percentage of our school-age children. In terms of immigration patterns, the United States is also seeing a demographic shift away from the European immigration of the past and more toward Latin America, Africa, and Asia (Maxwell, 2009), thus enhancing the ethnic as well as the linguistic diversity of the nation. This significant shift in the demographics of the United States has brought the issue of educating ELLs to the forefront of the discussion on K–12 public education in the United States (Maxwell, 2009).

As Deborah Short and Shannon Fitzsimmons write in *Double the Work: Challenges and Solutions to Acquiring Language and Academic Literacy for Adolescent English Language Learners,*

> In virtually every part of the country, middle and high schools are now seeing expanding enrollments of students whose primary language is not English. Rising numbers of immigrants, other demographic trends, and the demands of an increasingly global economy make it clear that the nation can no longer afford to ignore the pressing needs of the ELLs in its middle and high schools who are struggling with reading, writing, and oral discourse in a new language. (Short & Fitzsimmons, 2007, p. 1)

The face of America is forever changing, and it is becoming increasingly important that teachers find ways to effectively communicate with their ELL students in a language they understand. According to the EPE Research Center (2009), 75% of ELLs in the United States speak Spanish as their first language (Maxwell, 2009), so Spanish will most likely be one of the languages that will need to be accommodated.

Too often, students, families, and teachers see the native language as an obstacle to English fluency. Those who do not understand language acquisition often believe that to gain proficiency in English students must stop using their native language. As you will see in this chapter, students can maintain proficiency in their native language while acquiring English proficiency. When schools operate under a philosophy of additive bilingualism in which the student's comprehension of two languages is understood as an advantage and not a disadvantage, ELL learners and their families reap the benefits. As Table 3.1 shows, there are many professional organizations that promote the use and maintenance of the native language, for the reasons we will outline.

Additive versus Subtractive Bilingualism

An important distinction to understand when discussing bilingualism is the difference between additive and subtractive bilingualism. Too often, without careful consideration of the language acquisition research, schools support subtractive bilingualism. This is a process by which schools encourage non-English-speaking children not to use the native language; rather, to function solely in English. Whether the native language is used in instruction or not, subtractive bilingualism most often occurs when students are given the message that it is only their achievements in English that matter (Faltis & Hudelson, 1998). Unfortunately, what this does is encourage ELLs to lose their native language and replace it with English, instead of seeing English as a language and set of skills that they can add to their already existing skills in their primary language (Faltis & Hudelson, 1998). Certainly no one denies the importance of students learning English. But it should also be important to us as educators that they maintain their native language. This chapter will outline the important reasons why.

We recommend that teachers and schools emphasize the importance of both languages and explain that they both carry currency in different contexts. We believe that when ELLs engage in additive bilingualism and see their native language as an asset for academic learning and English fluency, they win on every level, including their acquisition of English. The way to understand how a native language

TABLE 3.1 Professional Organizations That Endorse the Use of the Native Language

Professional Organization	Name of Position Statement
Teaching English to Speakers of Other Languages (TESOL) www.tesol.org/s tesol/seccss.asp?CID=95&DID=1565	Conceptual Framework Pre K-12 English Language Proficiency Standards (2006)
National Council of Teachers of English (NTCE) www.ncte.org/ell	*English Language Learners: An NCTE Policy Research Brief*
National Education Association (NEA) www.eagleforum.org/educate/2007/aug07/NEA-Convention07.html	*Resolution B26—Educational Programs for English Language Learners*
English Plus Information Clearinghouse http://www.idra .org/IDRA Newsletter/January 1996 English Plus Not English Only/English Plus Information Clearinghouse/	*Resolution on English Plus*
The National Association for the Education of Young Children (NAEYC) www.naeyc.org/positionstatements/linguistic	*Responding to Linguistic and Cultural Diversity— Recommendations for Effective Early Childhood Education*
International Reading Association www.reading.org/General/AboutIRA/PositionStatements/ChildrensRightsPosition.aspx	*Making a Difference Means Making It Different: Honoring Children's Right to Excellent Reading Instruction*

can assist students in becoming fluent in English is made evident in Jim Cummins' (1981) common underlying proficiency (CUP) theory of language acquisition.

Common Underlying Proficiency (CUP) versus Separate Underlying Proficiency (SUP)

Too often people assume that the acquisition of a second language is completely independent of one's skills in a first language. They think that each language comprises its own compartment in people's brains. Jim Cummins (1981), a renowned educational psychologist, has described this concept of understanding bilingualism as the separate underlying proficiency (SUP) model. Anyone who holds this understanding does not think that there is any interaction between an individual's primary language and his or her secondary language (Cummins, 1981). As a result of this belief, some educators then assume that providing materials or assistance in a student's native language is not advisable, since the only way to develop English is to expose ELLs to as much English as possible and cease to offer the native language (Faltis & Hudelson, 1998).

Fortunately, both Cummins (1981; 1991) and Krashen (1996) have shown educators that the two languages of a bilingual person are actually highly interrelated. One's knowledge and skills in one language, from literacy (Edelsky, 1982; Faltis, 1986; Hudelson & Serna, 1994; Krashen, 1996) to other academic concepts (Henderson & Landesman 1992; Minicucci, 1996) can and do transfer to a second language. Cummins has developed a theory to explain how this process works.

Essentially, Cummins (1981) posits that all academic abilities, regardless of whether they are in the primary language or the secondary language, operate within a single cognitive system. As Christian Faltis and Sarah J. Hudelson (1998) explain of Cummins' (1981) theory in their book *Bilingual Education in Elementary and Secondary School Communities: Toward Understanding and Caring,* "This operating system connects the two languages of a bilingual so that what an individual knows and is able to do academically through one language readily applies to situations carried out in the other language. Cummins refers to this view of bilingualism as the Common Underlying Proficiency (CUP) Model" (p. 18)—a model which asserts that the two languages are mutually supportive of one another.

As Faltis and Hudelson (1998) explain, "The CUP model took educational psychologists interested in bilingualism many years of research and writing to construct" (p. 18). Faltis and Hudelson argue that, in addition to the cognitive functioning of the individual, bilingualism is also a matter of socially shared interaction. There is now general agreement that an individual's capabilities in a second language are directly linked to that same individual's capabilities in his or her primary language and benefit from the proficiency in and content knowledge established through the primary language. The implications for teaching are that there is clearly value in teaching in a student's primary language, providing resources in that language, and promoting its continued development, because it supports both academic achievement and English language learning.

Evaluating and Understanding Our Students' L1 (Native Language)

As we discuss the relevancy and possible uses of L1, it is important to remember that, just as a student's strong foundation in L1 could prove extremely useful in supporting the learner, it is conversely true that if students have not had the opportunity to develop their L1 to functional levels, then the L1 will not be useful as a support. For example, if you have a student who is not literate in his or her primary language, there is little purpose in providing texts in the primary language to assist them in learning content topics. So, teachers will want to begin by inquiring as to which of your students could make good use of the native language in the classroom, and which ones probably could not.

In all cases, the strategies we offer are largely independent of your proficiency in your students' languages. So whether or not you speak or read the languages of your students, this chapter is written for you. The first section of this chapter outlined some of the research that supports the use of students' native language in their schooling, and the remainder of the chapter will focus on specific strategies you can use to help you make good use of your students' primary languages in both the school and classroom environment.

First, we will focus on how to evaluate the context in which you work, by analyzing your school's implicit or explicit stance with respect to use of students' native languages. Second, we will focus on different initiatives your school can take while it works toward being more open and inclusive of multilingualism. Last, we offer a range of strategies that you can implement in your language or content classroom to promote the native language as a resource for learning.

Clarifying Your School's Stance on Primary Language

There are six steps to follow when clarifying what your school's implicit or explicit position is on native language use, as well as what you can do to change that position if you think it needs changing.

Step 1: Ask Questions

It is important to remember that many districts and schools do not have an official written position with respect to the use of native languages by students, teachers, faculty, or staff. They do, however, have de facto stances evident in the way that the school is set up and activities operate. If your school does not have an official position ask yourself, "What is the de facto position on use of languages other than English?"

Before answering this question you might want to first consider the following: What community does my school serve? What languages are spoken inside and outside of school? What signs are posted in the community in languages other than English? What languages are routinely used in other community-based institutions, such as banks, post offices, and other public places?

Then consider the following questions:

- What, if any, evidence is there in the building that shows and supports the community we serve?
- Do we have any signs in languages other than English?
- Do we have any faculty or staff that speak languages other than English?
- Do we translate documents that are sent home into the languages of the community we serve?
- Do we have interpreters to make phone calls? If so, for which languages?
- Do we provide interpreters at meetings? If so, for which languages?
- What attempts do we make to recognize and promote cross-cultural understanding?
- When students are speaking a language other than English, how do teachers react? How do other kids react?

In answering these questions, you will start to see your school's stance regarding use of languages other than English at school. Unfortunately, some schools that serve large populations of ELLs often make no attempt to support or use any other language aside from English. Moreover, these same schools often do not provide services for parents or community members who might want to participate in the life of the school but cannot, because of language barriers.

The important thing is that we take note of the implicit or explicit views that currently exist about use of languages other than English in our schools. This step allows us to take the necessary steps to create a more welcoming and supportive learning climate for students and their families.

Step 2: Assess the Language Needs of Your School

The second step toward clarifying your school's position is to assess the language needs of your community. The reality for most ELL students is that they need their native language to survive outside of school. American society is increasingly multilingual. Businesses and media sources almost always provide written, visual, and oral material in languages other than English. When schools do not encourage students to use their native language, they are essentially hindering their ability to fully participate, not just at school, but also in the wider society. For example, in Providence, Rhode Island, big businesses like Cardi's Furniture are constantly running advertisements in Spanish, and the *Providence Journal* (the main daily newspaper) has also created print materials in Spanish. Several television stations also broadcast their secondary audio program in Spanish. When we see that languages other than English are part of the linguistic landscape of our communities at large, we will want to insure that our students are ready for this reality by developing high levels of biliteracy

Step 3: Look for Models

The third step toward establishing a responsive stance toward languages other than English is to seek out existing schools and districts that might have more formalized positions. Too often teachers spend time inventing things that already exist. With a little research you might very well find a school or district that you can use as a model because it is doing work very similar to the work that you wish to do. The following subsections describe four districts that you might want to learn about to give yourself an idea of how other districts have responded to the linguistic diversity of their communities.

Denver Public Schools

The Denver public school district provides 11 strategies for effectively instructing all students, including ELLs. They adapted these strategies from *Educating Everybody's Children: Diverse Teaching Strategies for Diverse Learners* (Cole, 1995). This book was the culmination of work by the Association for Supervision and Curriculum Development's (ASCD) Urban Middle Grades Network, the special Advisory Panel on Improving Student Achievement, and the Improving Student Achievement Research Panel. The document is titled "Strategies to Support Culturally Competent Instruction" (see http://curriculum.dpsk12.org/Planning_guides/Literacy/Secondary_Culturally_Competent_Strategies.pdf). Some of these strategies include: teachers' learning about the students' home culture, teachers' using students' previous experiences as a place from which to start their learning, teachers' respecting community language norms, and dispelling stereotypes. Their document specifically says, in Strategy 10, "Teachers demonstrate respect for each student's language and do not prevent bilingual students from alternating between English and their native language (code switching) while they work together" (Denver Public Schools, 2006, p. 4).

Houston Independent School District

The first thing you will notice about the Houston Independent School District (2008) is that its Web site is available in three languages: English, Vietnamese, and Spanish (see http://www.houstonisd.org). Additionally, they have a document entitled "How Can We Help You?" that contains important information about school and district policies and is available in eight languages: English, Spanish, Vietnamese, French, Farsi, Mandarin Chinese, Arabic, and Urdu. It is also made clear, through their Multilingual Bilingual/ESL Programs Web site, that they believe in bilingualism and only offer ESL because they have a shortage of teachers.

> In bilingual programs, the function of the native language is to provide access to the curriculum while the student is acquiring English; instruction in the native language assures that students attain grade level cognitive skills without lagging behind. Due to the critical shortage of bilingual certified teachers at the elementary level, schools

are unable to offer bilingual education to all LEP students. These schools that cannot offer bilingual programs, even after team teaching possibilities have been exhausted, must then offer an ESL program (under exception) as an alternative to bilingual education. (Houston Independent School District's Multilingual Bilingual/ESL Program's Web site, 2008)

It is clear that they believe in the importance of bilingualism both through their written positions and the fact that their Web site is trilingual.

Berkeley Unified School District

The Berkeley Unified School District (2008) in California provides a mission statement that focuses on preparing its students to be life-long learners who are capable of succeeding in a changing society by "offering alternative learning experiences in a racially integrated, multilingual environment" (see http://www .berkeley.net/index.php?page=our-mission-and-vision). This school district makes it clear that it sees that promoting a multilingual environment will ultimately give its students the tools they will need to succeed in the outside world.

Fairfax County Public Schools

The Fairfax County school district provides information on its Web site in seven languages besides English: Arabic, Chinese, Farsi, Korean, Spanish, Urdu, and Vietnamese (see http://www.fcps.edu/index.shtml). This fact makes clear that the schools value these communities, their languages, and their ability to be partners with the school district. Additionally, on their Web site dedicated to teaching English to speakers of other languages (ESOL), they state that it is their mission to develop English proficiency among their students by creating "supportive learning environments which value and build on students' academic, linguistic, and cultural backgrounds" (Fairfax County Public Schools, 2008). Fairfax is making clear that they value what their students bring to the school and see their students' linguistic backgrounds as jumping-off points from which to learn English.

These four school districts provide different examples of how a school and district can begin to promote and support using the native language. All four of these districts have evidence on their Web sites demonstrating that they have started acknowledging the importance of use of the native language in schools. Clearly, other schools and districts are thinking about how students and families can appropriately use their native language and how schools can support students and families in doing so.

Step 4: Assess Existing Positions

The fourth step toward clarifying your school's stance on the use of native language is assessing what already exists and then figuring out what you still need to create to respond to needs that are unique to your school and community. Only you, in conjunction with your colleagues, can determine what is needed to be fully responsive to the communities you serve. When doing so, though, you should consider posing some of the following questions:

- What do we like about model districts we have looked at?
- What do we think is relevant to our situation? What is not viable for our situation?

- Should we, as a school, specifically say when the native language can and cannot be used? Should we differentiate between the proficiency levels of students when doing so?
- Should we mandate when documents and or signage need to be translated and into how many languages?
- Do we have the resources to support the practices we advocate?
- Should we mandate heritage language classes? If so, in which languages?
- What can we as a school do that fits well with other existing district policies?

The answers to these questions will help guide you through your process. The most important thing in assessing schoolwide positions that deal with the use of languages other than English is to understand what you may want to change, which leads us to our fifth step.

Step 5: Making Changes and Monitoring Them

The most important step in the process is actually attempting to create some change based on what you find. This change will vary from school to school and teacher to teacher. Some schools and teachers might want to try to create a written document that outlines certain guidelines that all staff should follow when dealing with students' native languages. Other schools and teachers might want to focus their energy on one initiative such as signage or parent outreach. But once you decide on a needed change, you will want to work toward it consistently and comprehensively. It is important to establish committees that can oversee the implementation of proposed initiatives to make it possible to assess their impact.

While all this important work is going on regarding school- and districtwide policies, teachers still have to teach. So it is important that, in addition to the larger scale schoolwide work taking place, teachers have strategies that they can use immediately in their classroom to promote the use of students' native languages. So, after offering schoolwide strategies, we will then offer classroom-based strategies.

The following section presents three schoolwide initiatives that you might want to try. While in no way comprehensive, it will provide ideas on how to think about responsive solutions for the entire school.

Schoolwide Strategies

All staff can contribute on a schoolwide level to making their school more multilingually friendly and to ensuring that both students and families feel welcome and supported so that they can pursue additive bilingualism. By all means we encourage you to pursue other ideas (such as those provided by Coelho in 2006), as we know that initiatives always work best when there are passionate teachers behind them. But these strategies may give you a few ideas to get started in your school.

Strategy 1: Creating Visible Signs of Students' L1s in the Life of the School

One of the simplest ways that you can incorporate the native language into your school's environment is through a schoolwide effort to increase native language signage in your school. First, it is a good idea to have welcome signs posted outside all classrooms in all the languages that your students speak. Second, it is helpful to provide classroom rules, procedures, and routines written out and posted in all the classrooms in as many languages as you can. This strategy keeps students from being confused about these important aspects, and it also allows all new students to have immediate access to that information, regardless of their English proficiency. English language learners tend to be a highly mobile group, so it is not uncommon for teachers of ELLs to receive new students throughout the year. With multilingual signage, teachers can direct students to the signs to familiarize them with the important rules and procedures, no matter at what point during the academic year they enter the school environment.

In addition to signage, all teachers in the building can actively seek out other printed materials to put around the classroom that reflect the languages and cultures of the students. Teachers can easily find materials online, or perhaps a better way to access this material is to ask students to bring it in. Students are usually more than willing to bring in posters, maps of their native countries, photographs of people they care about, and other material in their primary language to share with the class. This is something that can be done during the first couple weeks of school. Teachers can dedicate a section of the room to multilingual signs and have students share what they brought in and why. By allowing students to bring in their own materials to put around the classroom and permitting these materials to be in a language other than English, teachers allow the classroom and the school to move beyond *their* space and become a more communal space that welcomes and includes the students. In addition, it shows that you value where your students come from, who they are, and the experiences that they bring with them.

Strategy 2: After-School Opportunities to Maintain Heritage Languages and Promote Languages Other Than English

One powerful way that teachers and schools can show that they value students' native languages and believe in the importance of bilingualism is to create extracurricular opportunities for students to use their native language. Teachers can create and promote native language conversational groups, classes that continue education in the native language (e.g., Spanish for Spanish speakers), heritage language preservation groups, interpretation and translation classes, native language book clubs, or really any groups and clubs that would encourage and promote the use of students' native language. In doing so, teachers and schools allow students to embrace their roots and continue to educate themselves through their primary language. Sometimes teachers are not aware of the value of students' accessing and developing their native language. They may even question why students are placed in native language classes. For example, they may ask, "Why is Julio in Spanish class? He already speaks Spanish." If this question were reasonable, why would we require native English speakers to take English throughout high school? The important distinction still remains. Native English speakers take English language arts, not English as a foreign language—and native speakers of other languages should take equivalent courses in their primary language. With just a little reflection, all teachers can come to appreciate the value of students' continuing to develop their native languages at school, especially those who still need help and support in becoming biliterate adults with full academic language abilities in their mother tongue.

Students might receive help in the form of heritage language classes where students can develop their primary language reading and writing (native language arts), instead of within the context of "foreign language" classrooms that were not designed to fill their needs. In addition, they certainly would benefit from opportunities to read and appreciate the literature produced in their native language and to learn about the lives and work of the major authors that span the cultural groups who share their native language. After all, native English speakers do exactly the same thing in English class; so this practice is certainly easy to justify and support in bilingual or multilingual communities. It is worth mentioning that heritage language classes are often for-credit courses, not simply extracurricular courses. For more information on heritage language courses offered in schools and in the wider community, visit the Heritage Language in America Web site at www.cal.org/heritage.

Strategy 3: Native Language as Outreach

Chapter 2 focused largely on how to properly engage and support family involvement in the education of ELLs, but this topic is worth mentioning here briefly in relation to the use of students' primary languages. It is important to understand that many parents and family members are not able to access classes to learn English, despite their desire to do so. Some do not have the time because of their demanding work schedules (e.g., some newly arrived immigrants are working multiple jobs just to live), or they may lack the resources to learn English (access to spots in English classes, money to fund classes at a community college). For this reason, we always want to try our hardest to reach our families through their native languages, because we know that even if they are studying English, learning a language takes time.

Teachers can make really meaningful contributions by finding interpreters to speak with parents, even if such persons may not be professionals. We can also work hard to seek out people who can translate documents we wish to send home. Finding someone to help you when placing phone calls or during parent meetings is also a real gift to recently arrived families. Since we know the power of strong parental involvement, use of the native language is a critical strategy to employ so that parents and guardians of ELLs can become full participants and lend their support to our in-school efforts. Chapter 2 has already explored the strategies mentioned here as well as other strategies to reach out and support parents and families. These are key tactics to review and employ.

Using the Native Language in the Classroom

Now that we have spent some time talking about ways in which you can help bring the languages of your school community into your school, we are going to focus on specific strategies you can use in your classroom to help students maintain their bilingualism and access their native language as a way to enhance content learning and as a means to increase their proficiency in English. Even language teachers (English language arts, English as a second language, and reading teachers) can make effective use of the native language—for example, when noting cognates, allowing students to check on the meaning of difficult words through the native language, explaining complicated grammar rules, or clarifying an author's purpose or point of view (Cook, 2001). Language teachers are also finding it effective to encourage emergent bilingual writers to write text in their two languages (see Cummins et al., 2005) to encourage them to write and to affirm the value of multilingualism. To view middle school students' bilingual texts in a variety of languages, see www.multiliteracies.ca.

As a teacher, if you speak the primary language of any of your students, you are at a distinct advantage when it comes to using that language in the classroom. If you are monolingual, you might be asking yourself, "How could I possibly use the native language of my students in the classroom?" But, with a little creativity, all teachers can do so. Each set of teachers—bilingual and monolingual—can actively use the native language of their students in the classroom, just in a different way. The goal is the same—to access resources to help you utilize the native language in a meaningful way. Trying to find useful and trustworthy materials in a language other than English can often seem a bit daunting, so the following lists present places and people that can help you—starting points toward your goal.

Where Can I Go to Find Resources in Languages Other Than English?

- *Local colleges' or universities' resource centers or curriculum libraries:* These centers and libraries are often rich places with many sources of materials, including multimedia. Borrowing the materials you need obviously gets them into the classroom much faster than having to find funding to purchase the material for the school.

- *Local libraries with native language collections:* More and more local public libraries are reaching out and stocking non-English materials for the various ethnic communities of their patrons. These are another key place to search.

- *Cultural and linguistic clubs or organizations:* As mentioned previously, in communities with long-standing immigrant communities, there are most likely organizations set up to preserve their heritage. They will often be quite welcoming if you are taking an interest in their language and culture and may help you on your quest to find and fund the materials you need.

- *The English language learner office at your school district:* If there are ELLs in your district, someone is in charge that can assist you. Ask if the office has a collection of native language resources that you can access for use in your classroom.

Who Can I Go To for Native Language Resources?

- *Your students' families:* In addition to basic material like music, periodicals, or novels, you may find that your students' families have access to academic materials because they attended school outside the United States or because they were teachers and other related professionals in the country of origin.

- *Bilingual or native-language-speaking teachers:* In your school there may be teachers who teach bilingually or whose primary language is one other than English who can provide you with materials, or at least ideas on where you might be able to find them. These teachers are a key resource to tap.

- *Modern and world language teachers:* Teachers of modern and world languages are often wonderfully resourceful in figuring out how to find authentic materials in languages other than English. They not only know publishing houses, but may also have small collections of interest that you can access.

- *Paraprofessionals:* Some schools may have bilingual paraprofessionals for classes designated as serving ELLs, and these individuals are often wonderful resources with good access to native language materials.

Now that we have identified some people and places that might able to help you locate useful native language resources, we will focus on strategies that teachers can use to make excellent use of the native language as a scaffold. Classroom strategies are divided into three different sections. First, we will focus on translation strategies. Second, we will discuss strategies that support the content. Last, we will talk about strategies that help support your students in social situations.

Classroom Strategies

Translation Strategies

Strategy 1: Making Use of Bilingual Dictionaries

Dual-language dictionaries are very useful tools for ELLs. Teachers can suggest to all their students that they carry with them a personal bilingual dictionary, so that they can look up new words whenever they choose. In addition to print dictionaries, students might consider purchasing a Franklin electronic bilingual dictionary (http://www.franklin.com/handhelds/bilingual_dictionaries/) in which they can type words in their native language and receive translations instantly, or vice versa. Additionally, teachers may want to provide classroom sets of bilingual dictionaries for students who may not have the economic means to provide their own. Show them how to keep a section in their notebook where they can list words that they know they will need again. In other words, teach them how to learn new words on their own and also how to use a bilingual dictionary just for on-the-spot "repairs" so they can capture the meaning of what is going on at the time.

Teachers may also want to have their own set of bilingual dictionaries in every language that their students speak, or at least as many as possible. When teachers look up key words for their students in an attempt to help them, the students really appreciate it. This might take place on the spot when a student is struggling with a particular word that is essential to the activity. Although sometimes the students will look up these words, it is important to model this activity for them. In addition to showing them that you too, as a teacher, will use the dictionary, it also gives them an opportunity to be the expert as they support and guide you. If you look up the word and then attempt to pronounce it, the result can often lead to a mispronunciation or misuse, unless you are familiar with the language in question. Although it may seem insignificant, this struggle with language almost always endears you to your students. It shows humility and allows the students to feel like the expert, as opposed to the rest of the time when they are constantly unsure and attempting to navigate a system foreign to them.

Although in-class assignments and homework are wonderful opportunities to use a bilingual dictionary, a less obvious opportunity might be found in exams and quizzes. As teachers, our tendency is to not allow anything that might aid a student and thus not reveal an "accurate" portrait of the student's ability. The problem is that there are often aspects of tests or exams that create problems for ELL students that have nothing to do with what you are hoping to test them on.

For example, if you are a social studies teacher and you are testing your students on important vocabulary terms related to a unit on European exploration, you probably want them to know important words like *New World, exploration, settlements,* and *trade routes.* In an exam on these words you might have a section where you have sentences that they have to complete using a word blank. On the test you might have the sentence "People from England, France, Holland, Portugal, and Spain all came to the New World, claimed lands, and created _____ where they could live." A beginner ELL student might very well have studied and understood the word *settlement,* but still not put the right word in that section because he or she will be confused by other words liked *claimed* or *could.* Allowing students to look up words in the dictionary would allow them to understand the sentence and then make the right choice. If they did not study and do not understand the word *settlement,* then these other translations will not help them, so we can be sure that we are still accurately testing what we want to know—comprehension of the terms that are important to our unit.

This use of the native language to support learning is recommended by second-language experts like Jana Echevarría, MaryEllen Vogt, and Deborah J. Short (2008) as a very helpful way to make content area comprehensible. In their Sheltered Instruction Observation Protocol (SIOP) model, they show the value of and recommend the use of students' native languages as a scaffold or bridge to content learning and to English development. Certainly, we want to use L1 as a bridge for adolescents whom we know to have functional literacy in their native language, as it is a very viable tool to support learning of rigorous subject matter.

Strategy 2: Bringing Cognates into the Classroom

One of the easiest ways to access the primary language is through the use of cognates. Cognates are words that are identical or almost identical in the two languages and carry the same meaning—for example, *conclusion/conclusión* (Spanish), *telephone/teléfono* (Spanish). Cognates are an extremely useful vehicle through which students can use their primary language to build vocabulary in English (Nagy et al., 1993) and are the reason that the SIOP model (Echevarría et al., 2008) encourages "use of cognates to promote comprehension" (p. 81).

If everyone in your class shares their first language, you might consider having a working list of cognates in the room or on the board, or you might have the students create cognate dictionaries, which they can add to as the year progresses (J. Williams, 2001).

Identifying Cognates with Underlining. When teaching individual lessons that involve text, you can have students identify cognates with the help of photocopies and an overhead transparency (J. Williams, 2001). For example, if you are teaching precalculus at the beginning of the year and reviewing number lines, you might be reading the following passage from *Precalculus: A Graphing Approach* published by Holt, Rinehart, and Winston (Hungerford, Jovell, & Mayberry, 2002):

> Mathematics is the study of quantity, order, and relationships. This chapter defines the real numbers and the coordinate plane, and it uses the vocabulary of relations and functions to begin the study of mathematical relationships. The number patterns in recursive, arithmetic, and geometric sequences are examined numerically, graphically, and algebraically. Lines and linear models are reviewed. (p. 3)

As you read this passage together as a class, you could put the text on an overhead. After reading it, you could help the students scan the passage and identify cognates in Spanish, for example, "Do you see any words that look like words you know in Spanish?". Together you could underline the cognates until the paragraph had many of these words shown underlined:

> Mathematics is the study of quantity, order, and relationships. This chapter defines the real numbers and the coordinate plane, and it uses the vocabulary of relations and functions to begin the study of mathematical relationships. The number patterns in recursive, arithmetic, and geometric sequences are examined numerically, graphically, and algebraically. Lines and linear models are reviewed. (p. 3)

The following are examples of the cognates for some of the words we have underlined:

English	Spanish
mathematics	matemática
study	estudio
number	número

As students look at their underlined text, they should see a very different text. In total this passage has fifty-six words. Twenty-seven, or roughly 50%, of the words are cognates. This fact decreases the vocabulary load substantially for ELL students.

At first look, this text may seem difficult for ELLs, but after the proper native language scaffolding is provided it can become much more accessible for them, particularly those who both are literate in their native language and have had prior exposure to math terminology. However, ELLs will still need extra time to read the passage and make these connections—to work to understand their meanings within the English sentences in which they are presented. So they will have the word knowledge to help them, but still need time and support to capture the full message as presented in English.

Modeling the process of identifying cognates provides your students with a real tool they can use every time they encounter a text that looks difficult. Although cognates will vary from language to language, text to text, and subject to subject, identifying them is always an important step that provides students support in understanding difficult texts.

Providing Cognate Tables and Word Charts

If you have multiple languages in front of you, as most of us do, the situation becomes more complicated, though not impossible. First, you can still teach the concept of a cognate. Second, you can provide students with a chart or list where they can keep track of cognates in their primary language. Third, you can provide them with already completed cognate lists related to the specific content being covered. The following is an example of the third option in a physics class using the theme of thermodynamics. Before starting this unit you could create a list of cognates so that the students would have it as a reference during the unit, for either class discussions or text readings. Table 3.2 presents a list of important cognates in French for the thermodynamics unit. This list could be used for Haitian students, French students, or French-speaking African students.

You do not need to speak French to compile the list in Table 3.2; all you need

TABLE 3.2   French Cognates in Thermodynamics

Important Terms in Thermodynamics	French Cognates
internal energy	énergie interne
conservation of energy	conservation de l'énergie
system	système
transfer (verb)	transférer
pressure	pression
volume	volume
matter	matière
process	processus
constant	constant
action	action

is a French-English dictionary. This simple two-column chart will help students better understand thermodynamics by helping them feel more comfortable with the necessary terminology. Literate students will do many things with this list, such as access native language materials on the Internet that explain the same concepts they are learning in English. Teachers can make it their responsibility to check that students have this sheet available at all times for reference, and they can encourage students to use it to branch out and locate other learning resources that may give them more information about the topic.

If you like cognates as a way to both utilize the native language in the classroom and make material more comprehensible for your students, you can find many important cognate lists available online (Table 3.3).

In addition to the Internet, cognate dictionaries are available, such as *NTC's Dictionary of Spanish Cognates* (Nash, 1993), which is thematically organized. It can easily be bought online (cognate dictionaries in a few other languages are available as well).

Although cognates are definitely a wonderful way to purposefully use the native language, there are two potential problems with helping students access and use cognates to improve their English proficiency. First, the ability to benefit from the use of cognates is reliant on students having been exposed to these words in their primary language. So this strategy may not work if the students have low levels of proficiency or have not been educated in their native language. Second, although some languages are high in cognates because they share the same alphabet, other languages have few, if any, English cognates. As always, you use the cognate strategy when, where, and with whom it applies.

TABLE 3.3   Useful Web Sites for Cognates

Language	Web Site for Cognates
Portuguese	http://www.learn-portuguese-now.com/cognates.html
German	http://german.about.com/library/blcognates_A.htm
Russian	http://languagedaily.com/home/index.php?title=Russian_cognates
Spanish	http://www.spanishstudies.com/spanish_cognates.htm http://www.latinamericalinks.com/spanish_cognates__letter_a.htm
French	http://french.about.com/library/vocab/bl-vraisamis.htm

Strategy 3: Providing Instructions and Clarifications in the Primary Language

It is often the case that secondary ELLs do not understand the task that is being assigned to them. They might very well be able to complete the task if they understand the instructions. This problem is especially likely to occur with beginner and intermediate students, although it may happen on occasion with advanced students. Teachers often work very hard to make their assignments accessible to ELLs by providing important visuals and accessible text, but the instructions for these tasks may require both more language and less accessible language. Teachers should feel comfortable translating instructions if all attempts in English have been exhausted and the student seems stuck. It is just a way to give students a fighting chance to perform the task at hand. So translating directions is a real boost to secondary ELLs, because translating instructions helps them complete their work and gain the desired knowledge (Cook, 2001). This same philosophy holds true when students are already engaged in a task and may get tripped up by a certain phrase or term, needing a quick interpretation into the primary language to complete their assignment. Most often secondary students will be quite honest with you and say that they simply do not understand the directions. Furthermore, many students actually do understand the directions, but are simply not confident in their understanding and like to check by receiving the directions or clarifying points in their primary language as well. If the student was correct, this will build up her confidence because she will realize she understood, and if she was not correct, it will save her the hassle of completing an assignment incorrectly and having to go back, or sitting silently in frustration.

What if you would like to do this for your students, but do not speak the language(s) of your students? By accessing some resources, you may be able to provide written instructions in your students' primary language using several different means. First, you could try to use online translators, which will be your quickest, but least trustworthy, source. Two such available translators are www.babelfish.altavista.com and www.freetranslation.com. However, always be aware that mechanical translators can never match the translations we get from highly literate bilingual individuals, and in fact very frequently they do not yield intelligible translations for the ideas we wish to convey. Therefore, they are best used when you are searching for a particular word or trying to give students one or two words that might help them understand the concept you are trying to convey. You might also use electronic bilingual dictionaries like the Franklin translator mentioned earlier (http://www.franklin.com/handhelds/translators/)

If you find yourself often wanting translations of instructions or directions that are used again and again, a second option would be to go to neighborhood resources or to resource books created for this purpose. For example, you can seek out community translators at social service centers or educational agencies. Visit publishers like Ammie Enterprises (http://www.ammieenterprises.com/) that have published titles like *Spanish for the School Nurse's Office, School Office Spanish, School Letters in English and Spanish, Reporting to Parents in English and Spanish,* and so on. Or try this book from Scholastic Publishing: *The Multilingual Translator: Words and Phrases in 15 Languages to Help You Communicate with Students of Diverse Backgrounds* (Moore, 1994). Even if these translations are not perfect, they will help your students understand the gist of what they are supposed to do, and therefore serve their purpose. The idea would be to create a bank of these directions that you can use again and again when presenting assignments to ELL students, so it is worth the effort.

Supporting the Content

Strategy 4: Preview/View/Review

In cases where all students speak the same language and the teacher is proficient in that language or some students are proficient bilinguals, it is useful to try to support the learning of content by actively using the students' primary language for previewing or reviewing a lesson, or clarifying concepts during a lesson. This approach is particularly helpful in content classes where the focus is on learning concepts in history, science, music, and such, and the learning of English is secondary. It is also useful for beginning students, who struggle to access content through English because their vocabularies are so limited. It is precisely for situations like this that the SIOP model (Echevarría et al., 2008) encourages "ample opportunities for students to clarify key concepts in the native language, as needed with a paraprofessional, peer or native language text" (p. 128).

As alluded to previously, one of the most successful strategies you can employ to use the native language to support the building of content knowledge is "preview/view/review" (Y. Freeman & Freeman, 1998, 2002). Essentially, the idea is to preview the content in the primary language. For example, if, in music class, the students were studying Beethoven, they would first preview the topic in their primary language. Obviously, this step is most easily carried out by a teacher who speaks that language, although it can also be facilitated through recorded or written summaries, short readings, films, or inviting parents or students to run this part of the lesson (D. Freeman & Freeman, 2007). If none of these options are available or if you face a class with multiple languages, you can also have students simply brainstorm the topic in same-language groups or provide readings and summaries in multiple languages (D. Freeman & Freeman, 2007). You could also simply instruct higher proficiency students, or paraprofessionals, to translate a preview of what you are about to study for a lower proficiency student.

After previewing the material in students' primary languages, you would conduct the lesson in English, reviewing and expanding upon the same topics, but now in English. As a result of previous exposure to the material in their own language, students will have an easier time understanding the academic content, and this procedure will allow them to pay more attention to the English being used (D. Freeman & Freeman, 2007).

The last step occurs at the end of a lesson or unit presented in English. Here you would review all the material presented with short summaries in their native language. Once again, this can take place in multiple forms ranging from whole-class discussion, to same-language groups led by higher proficiency students or paraprofessionals, to having students write summaries, key findings, or questions in their primary language. The idea behind this method is to allow students access to important concepts in their own language while teaching them predominantly through English. As David and Yvonne Freeman point out, "Simply translating everything into a student's first language is not productive because the student will tune out English, the language that is harder to understand" (2007, p. 93). Preview/view/review, however, allows students to access their first language to provide background knowledge or to clarify without resorting to simultaneous translation.

Strategy 5: Using Peers, Paraprofessionals, and Mentors

Accessing the primary language through peers, paraprofessionals, and mentors is an extremely useful way to bring the primary language into the classroom. The most common use of peers in ELL classrooms is pairing lower proficiency students with higher proficiency students who speak the same native language in order to create a mutually beneficial relationship. Higher proficiency students can often help acclimate lower proficiency students to the school environment—providing school tours and helping them understand classroom rules using the native language as needed (D. Freeman & Freeman, 2007). In addition, they will be able to help with assignments.

For the higher proficiency students there are multiple benefits as well. First, they get to show their knowledge of the primary language and be proud of being proficiently bilingual. Second, the higher proficiency students may learn new things about the primary language from the lower proficiency students (D. Freeman & Freeman, 2007). Additionally, because the higher proficiency students know that they are being chosen because of their English proficiency, they will gain confidence in their English skills and be forced to engage in metacognitive thinking—they now no longer can simply conjugate a verb or choose a tense, they have to be able to explain why they made that decision so that the lower proficiency student can learn. So the idea is for them to use a combination of the native language and English wherever possible to help the lower proficiency students understand and participate.

Although teachers should create and foster these types of relationships among peers, it is important to make the roles of each student clear. Higher proficiency students need to understand that it is their job to serve as tutor and helpers, not doers. Lower proficiency students needs to understand that they are still responsible for their own work and that the partner is there to help them. Too often high school students will simply allow others to do their work for them, and teachers need to be vigilant in making sure that they do not. Teachers can encourage pairs of students to use the native language only when necessary, and not simply translate everything regardless of whether the translation is needed or not.

In addition to peers, teacher can also consider using bilingual paraprofessionals or, if those are not provided at the school, bringing bilingual mentors into the classroom. If there are ESL students in your classroom, then there are clearly bilingual people in your community, and you as a teacher can seek them out. Ask them to come into your classroom or help out after school by tutoring your students. In addition to providing reinforcement of content through the primary language, their presence will provide students with models of people who have already accomplished what they themselves are struggling with. They will see that there is a light at the end of the tunnel. Once again, though, you will want to be explicit with the paraprofessionals, mentors, or tutors as to what you want them to cover and how much of the native language you would like them to use.

Supporting the Student Socially

Strategy 6: Talking with and Relating to Your Students

This strategy is uniquely available to teachers who have at least a working knowledge of, or some conversational ability in, the primary language of their students. For many secondary students, as discussed earlier, feeling comfortable is an important part of staying in school. For most students, they feel outside their comfort zone when communicating in English, so it is good to let the students relax at some point during the day. Although during sheltered content or ESL classes the primary language of instruction is and should be English, it is always a good idea to speak to your students in their language before and after class. This allows you to find out about their past and learn about who they are. This practice is very important for students who spend a majority of their day confused and disconnected from what is going in. Conversing in their primary language allows them to be themselves in a language in which they feel comfortable. Forging this connection and creating a space where students feel comfortable being themselves may very well be the reason that students stay in school. A few minutes of conversation can go a long way toward forging a meaningful relationship with kids. That relationship can also enhance a student's motivational level in your class. Some students, especially those who are at the beginning or intermediate level, do not feel they have an identity in English and therefore do not feel as though a teacher can know them if they only speak to them in English. As a student named Chisel put it,

> Durante mi primer año acá, no había un Chisel en inglés, y por eso solo me sentía como dos maestros me conocían—los únicos dos que me podían hablar en español. El resto me parecían amables, pero no podían conocerme porque todavía no podía existir en su idioma.

> During my first year here, there was no Chisel in English, and because of that I only felt as though two teachers really knew who I was, the only two teachers who could speak to me in Spanish. The other teachers seemed nice, but they couldn't truly know me because I did not yet exist in their language.

This idea of existing in and through a language is profoundly important. Many students simply do not yet have an identity in English, and therefore at the beginning of their schooling experience do not feel as strong a connection to people who only speak English as they do to those who use some of their native language. For this reason, when you actively try to engage them outside the classroom through their home language, it shows your desire to really know them and form a relationship with them, your deep respect for their primary language, and the value you place on the bilingualism they are in the process of developing.

When Not to Use the Native Language

It should be clear by all that has been recommended in this chapter that we believe in and endorse the use of the primary language. Yet we also believe that there are times when students should not use their native languages. Teachers must not let their desire to respect students' native language, or understanding that the native language can be a resource, to get in the way of the fact that a major goal of our work with ELLs is to teach them academic English and content through English. So, as teachers, we will also want to encourage and support students toward the use of English and understand when students actually need support in their native language and when they may use it instead of doing the hard work of trying to communicate in English. This decision is dependent upon the needs of each individual learner, but teachers need to be willing to say, "No—this *must* be done in English." Otherwise, some students may overrely on the native language instead of jumping in and accepting the challenge of English. As pointed out by Linda Ventriglia (1982) in *Conversations of Miguel and Maria,* many students pass through a crystallizing phase in which they choose to "maintain their identity with native language culture and to initially reject the second language" (p. ix). Teachers need to guide students and decide when they are willing to permit the use of the native language and when it is not necessary or desirable. At these times, teachers can gently push their students out of the crystallizing phase, so students learn enough English to succeed, all the while showing that they value the native language and bilingualism. It is helpful if decisions governing native language use are made as a team, but if not, at the very least a teacher needs to let the students know the rules for his or her class. It's helpful to post or review these rules at the beginning of the year so everyone understands them. So by all means, give students access to their native language, but remember to make it clear to students when they must work only in English.

Conclusion

There is little doubt of the importance of people's native tongue to their development both academically and socially. Research has clearly shown that the native language is important and useful when learning a second language. Furthermore, America's role within the global economy is changing so rapidly in the global economy that it is shortsighted to not see the economic, social, and academic advantages of multilingualism. Therefore, as teachers, in order to provide our students with a truly equitable education and a bright future in a new global reality, we have to support and preserve their native language competencies. In working toward better serving your students' needs you should consider using the following checklist to monitor how well you feel you are supporting your students through the use of the native language. This method will help you discover how many strategies you are actively using and how many you may still want to adopt.

Checklist

Strategies for Supporting the Native Language

- [ ] I actively promote an additive schoolwide position toward the use of native languages.
- [ ] Whenever possible, I assess my students in their native languages.
- [ ] I differentiate the need for native language support based on students' proficiency levels.
- [ ] I utilize community resources to bring in native language materials.
- [ ] I utilize the native language to clarify instructions and directions.
- [ ] I encourage students to use cognates as an aid to comprehension.
- [ ] I promote the use of bilingual dictionaries and translators.
- [ ] I talk with and engage my students as people through their primary language.
- [ ] I support my content with native language material in various media forms.
- [ ] I foster the instructional use of native language peers and mentors.
- [ ] I create visible signage in students' primary languages and reflect their cultural beliefs.
- [ ] I provide after-school opportunities for my students to develop and use their primary language through, for example, heritage language classes.
- [ ] I insist on times when the native language is not permissible.
- [ ] I use the native language as a medium through which to contact and communicate with families.

CHAPTER 4

Language and Literacy Frameworks to Guide Teachers' Work with Secondary English Language Learners

Qian, China

> If you don't know where you're going, how will you know when you get there?
>
> Anonymous

Guiding Questions

- What principles should guide literacy instruction with adolescent English language learners?
- What literacy frameworks and standards should be honored in our work with students?
- What should a strong schoolwide literacy program look like? What program characteristics are recommended by leading literacy associations and adolescent literacy experts?
- What types of literacy do ELL students need in the 21st century?

A number of national literacy initiatives have been launched in recent years to address the current literacy crisis in secondary schools—for native speakers of English as well as for English language learners (ELLs). Professional associations including the National Council of Teachers of English (NCTE, ELL Task Force, 2006, 2007b) and the International Reading Association (Moore, Bean, Birdyshaw, & Rycik, 1999) have published exploratory reports, and the U.S. Department of Education's National Literacy Panel on Language-Minority Children and Youth has commissioned research reviews (August & Shanahan, 2006a). As noted in Chapter 1, the achievement of academic literacy—or the lack of such achievement—is one of the major challenges facing ELLs entering U.S. secondary schools. It is the pervasiveness of the literacy crisis—among native speakers as well as ELLs—that provides us with an opportunity to change secondary instruction in ways that will engage ELLs and native speakers alike, ultimately promoting higher levels of literacy for all.

In this chapter, we outline key principles in adolescent literacy instruction, drawing from the leading streams of research and practice, to frame our work with adolescent ELLs. Later, we talk about the frameworks and standards that should guide our practices and the characteristics of literacy programs that have been recommended by leading literacy associations and adolescent literacy specialists. We also identify the various types of literacy that are needed by ELLs. The overarching purpose of this chapter is to provide the foundation upon which the subsequent, practical chapters will build.

Our Philosophy Regarding Literacy Instruction for Adolescent ELLs

Our philosophy for bringing about the changes needed in secondary literacy education, particularly as it relates to ELLs, is built on the following eight principles:

1. Effective instruction is learner centered.

2. Students succeed when classrooms become communities of learners.

3. Effective teachers view diversity as a resource, not a deficit.

4. Assessment should be more a formative than a summative process.

5. Listening, speaking, reading, and writing are best developed in an integrated manner, as needed in specific contexts and driven by content learning.

6. Students should engage in wide reading of age-appropriate, reading-level-appropriate, high-interest literature.

7. Students should engage in producing language—both written and oral—in every classroom every day.

8. Literacy instruction is the responsibility of all teachers, across all disciplines, not just English and ESL teachers.

Each of these principles will be discussed in more detail in the following subsections.

Effective Instruction Is Learner Centered

One unquestioned tenet of education is to start where the learner is and to build from there. Our mission in creating literacy programs, then, should be to offer developmentally appropriate language and literacy instruction, while keeping our eye on the schoolwide and districtwide goals we are trying to achieve, so that the gap between where students *are* and where they *should be* does not become an unbridgeable abyss.

For ELLs, the need for learner centeredness is especially critical. English language learners are going through predictable developmental stages of second-language development in listening, speaking, reading, and writing. Under various classification systems, these stages are given different labels, such as the following:

• Beginning, intermediate, advanced

• Preproduction, early production, speech emergence, intermediate proficiency, proficiency (Krashen & Terrell, 1983)

• Entering, beginning, developing, expanding, bridging, reaching (WIDA Consortium, 2004, 2007; TESOL, 2006)

Regardless of how language proficiency is classified, teachers must know how to frame instruction around what learners can *do*. Figure 4.1 provides a picture of what ELLs are capable of doing at three general proficiency levels: beginning, intermediate, and advanced. Different states and provinces may categorize proficiency levels using a variety of English language proficiency (ELP) categories; for the purposes of this book, however, and for the sake of simplicity, we will be referring to these three general proficiency levels. They provide useful information for lesson planning and for working with ELLs.

Whichever language proficiency classification system is used, it is clear that instruction for ELLs must be developmentally appropriate to support second-language growth and development.

Instruction of ELLs must also be sufficiently rigorous. Certainly we know that the current stage of language proficiency of our ELLs is not a reflection of their capacity for high-level academic work. So we need to create learner-centered environments where they are able to demonstrate understanding of rigorous academic content in formats that are not limited to essays, language-heavy tests, or other language-dense assessments. In other words, the academic challenge should be kept high, yet at the same time respectful of the level of their developing second-language proficiency in English. At the same time, instruction must advance ELLs' language and literacy skills so that they attain full proficiency and high levels of literacy in their second language. With ELLs, it is essential to scaffold instruction to match our learners' second-language characteristics while at the same time allowing them to demonstrate understanding of advanced concepts and critical thinking abilities.

Instruction must also be culturally responsive (Gay, 2000; Irvine & Armento, 2001; Ladson-Billings, 1992). English language learners bring differing cultural frames of reference to schools and rich life experiences that vary in important ways from students born in the United States. Because a good proportion of ELLs at the secondary level are new arrivals or late entrants to the United States, we need to understand their cultural frames of reference and the nature of their background knowledge to provide effective instruction that connects with what they know and value. Yet predefined curricula, especially at the secondary level, often assume prior knowledge that adolescent ELLs may not have, regardless of the quality or extent of their previous education. For example, the curriculum may assume knowledge of U.S. history or geography (e.g., the states that comprise the New England states, the Civil War) or presume knowledge of literary figures (e.g., Paul Bunyan, Johnny Appleseed) commonly known by students born and raised in the United States and educated in American schools. While ELLs may not have that particular "cultural capital," they do have knowledge—just not the knowledge upon which American curricula are built. So we need both to give them the new cultural capital and also to use the capital they bring with them to school.

According to Weinstein (2004), learner-centered approaches for ELLs assume an inquiring stance where teachers strive to get to know their learners and their context, build on what learners know, balance the teaching of skills with meaning making and knowledge creation, strive for authenticity (authentic texts, tasks), promote a shared responsibility for learning among students and their teachers, and build communities of learners. In this approach, the texts that students are provided—and that they create—acknowledge and reflect these principles. Literacy is viewed as a sociocultural endeavor.

In short, experts agree that secondary students engage in reading or discussion when they can see how these tasks, as well as the subject matter, relate to their lives (NCTE, 2007a). In this book we will look at ways in which teachers can engage ELLs in literacy activities that have relevance to their lives.

Learner-centered instruction for ELLs incorporates all these notions—culturally, linguistically, and academically responsive instruction that challenges learn-

FIGURE 4.1 Beginner, intermediate, and advanced proficiency levels for ELLs

LANGUAGE DOMAIN	BEGINNER	INTERMEDIATE	ADVANCED
Listening	*Recognizes* • One-step commands • Yes/no questions *Understands* • General language of content areas • Basic family, school, and personal preferences *Benefits from* • Sensory, graphic, or interactive support • Slowed, enunciated speech • Frequent repetition • Body language and gestures *Responses may include* • Nonverbal action • Native-language or target-language utterances	*Recognizes* • Multistep commands • Simple questions • Expanded sentences *Understands* • Most general and some specific content area language • More complex interpersonal and school-related discussion *Benefits from* • Sensory, graphic, or interactive support • Slower speech • Frequent clarification • Body language and gestures	*Recognizes* • Multistep commands • Complex questions • Expanded sentences and varied sentence structures *Understands* • Specific and specialized content area language • Complex interpersonal, abstract, and academic discussions *Continues to benefit from* • Sensory, graphic, or interactive support • Clarification • Body language
Speaking	*Vocabulary* • Limited command of words for common objects • Basic interpersonal and content area vocabulary *Fluency* • Memorized or fixed phrases • Some short, simple sentences • Long silences and hesitation common *Grammar and syntax* • Single words • Memorized chunks or phrases • Basic language patterns • Simple sentence structures *Comprehensibility* • Meaning often impeded by grammatical and pronunciation errors • Pronunciation heavily influenced by primary language	*Vocabulary* • Expanded knowledge of common words and expressions • Adequate interpersonal and content area vocabulary *Fluency* • More novel sentences • More complex sentences • Frequent pauses when searching for a word *Grammar and syntax* • Basic sentences • Familiar phrases • More complex language patterns *Comprehensibility* • Most meaning is retained, despite errors • Some nonnative intonation patterns exist	*Vocabulary* • Descriptive words and expressions • Specific and technical content area terminology • Some idiom usage *Fluency* • Novel, original speech • Ability to rephrase, elaborate • Occasional pauses when searching for a specialized word or expression *Grammar and syntax* • A variety of sentence structures • Familiar phrases • Complex, subjunctive, conditional language patterns *Comprehensibility* • Minimal phonological, semantic and syntactic errors do not impede overall communication • May commit errors typical of native speakers

Reading	*Vocabulary* • Recognizes some sight words • Frequent use of bilingual or ESL dictionary to look up unknown words *Decoding and Fluency* • Knows some letter sounds • Attempts to sound out words • Reads familiar words or phrases aloud • May not recognize some punctuation cues • Can follow along as text is read aloud *Comprehension* • Uses illustrations and nonprint features to construct meaning • Demonstrates basic comprehension of main idea, sequencing	*Vocabulary* • Recognizes names, words by sight • Uses a dictionary and thesaurus to expand vocabulary *Decoding and fluency* • Uses phonetic clues • Attempts to sound out words • Uses sentence structure clues • Reads and finishes a variety of texts with guidance • Reads silently for short periods of time *Comprehension* • Decreasing dependence on illustrations; increasing reliance on print • Recognizes features of different text structures, genres • Responds to texts in various modes (drawing, mapping, diagramming) • Constructs meaning from texts that contain background knowledge relevant to student's experience	*Vocabulary* • Reads and understands most new words • Uses knowledge of word parts to make associations and connections between words and word groups *Decoding and fluency* • Reads with considerable fluency • Reads independently • Reads silently for extended periods *Comprehension* • Reads and comprehends at or near grade-level texts • Uses a variety of reading strategies to comprehend and extend the meaning of complex and/or abstract texts • Interacts with texts in various modes (predicting, reacting, inferring, evaluating, analyzing)
Writing	*Vocabulary range* • Uses high-frequency words from school setting and content areas • Lacks key vocabulary • Uses familiar words *Sentence fluency* • Can write single words or short phrases independently *Language use* • Simple sentences • Chunks of language—phrases, short sentences *Mechanics and conventions* • Uses inventive spelling • Frequent errors in conventions (punctuation, spacing, capitalization) *Clarity* • Struggles to express ideas clearly • Communicates meaning through pictures, illustrations • Begins to convey meaning through words	*Vocabulary range* • Uses general, specific, and some technical language related to content areas • Occasionally lacks needed vocabulary *Sentence Fluency* • Can write short answers to questions • Can create original paragraphs *Language use* • Experiments with a variety of sentence structures • Uses a limited amount of transitions *Mechanics and Conventions* • Errors in conventions (punctuation, spacing, capitalization) occasionally impede comprehension *Clarity* • Expresses ideas coherently most of the time • Begins to write a paragraph by organizing ideas	*Vocabulary range* • Uses technical language related to content areas • Facility with, and variety of, needed vocabulary • Incorporates idioms and expressions • Uses descriptive, expressive language *Sentence fluency* • Can write extensive answers to questions • Can create original, multiparagraph texts *Language use* • Skillfully uses varied sentence structures and lengths • Consistently uses a variety of appropriate transitions *Mechanics and conventions* • Writes with few grammatical and mechanical errors *Clarity* • Conveys meaning clearly • Presents multiparagraph organization • Shows a clear development of ideas

ers while at the same time matching their stage of proficiency and level of acculturation (Cloud, 2002; Echevarría, Vogt, & Short, 2008). There are other reasons, however, to offer learner-centered instruction; the greatest among them that all high school reform initiatives call for personalization of high school learning environments (outlined in Chapter 1). Certainly we want to personalize instruction for this group of adolescents as much as, if not more than, we seek to do for all adolescents in our classrooms. Personalization is a centerpiece of the reform initiatives going on in secondary schools for a very important reason: It is a major strategy in creating a sense of community and belonging for all learners (Committee on Increasing, 2003; Stipek, 2006). We want to keep learners engaged in school, especially ELLs who are at high risk of dropping out, by creating meaningful relationships with teachers and other school-based personnel—adults who understand how to shape instruction to build the skills ELLs need to attain their postsecondary goals.

Students Succeed When Classrooms Become Communities of Learners

Secondary teachers are well aware that learning happens in sociocultural contexts—schools, classrooms, communities. We know that many adolescents choose to learn from teachers they trust, and choose whether or not to learn based on their comfort level in a classroom. Adolescent ELLs are particularly vulnerable in secondary school because their motivation to learn depends in great part on how safe they feel—socially, culturally, emotionally—in the school and in the classroom. As pointed out in Chapter 1, there are many unique challenges faced by students new to English and to the dominant culture. One of these is that ESL students often have had little or no contact with native-speaking students in the same school and sometimes limited contact even with ESL students of other cultural or linguistic backgrounds.

It is essential that teachers create a safe learning environment for all students. In addition to teachers knowing their students, teachers must continually build community within the classroom so that students know each other and work together. For this reason, cooperative learning is a powerful instructional method because it provides ELLs with access to peers as well as input and interaction (Kagan, 1995)—two key conditions for language learning (Lightbown & Spada, 2006; Brown, 2006). Another known benefit of cooperative classrooms is that they help students to come to know and appreciate one another and thus to lessen stereotypes and biases that create cultural conflict in schools and communities (Kagan, 1994: Johnson, Johnson, & Holubec, 1994). Chapters 5, 6, 7, and 8 offer instructional methods to use with adolescent ELLs—such as cooperative learning—that help us develop language while creating a sense of community. This principle is no less important to ELLs in general education classrooms, where they continue to build academic literacy side by side with native speakers, as will be shown in Chapter 9.

Creating a sense of community is a primary support for ELLs (Weinstein, 2004). Connecting language and literacy learning with students' lives and experiences generates both the desire to speak and write in order to share important information with others and the desire to read and listen in order to hear about the experiences of others to whom they can relate.

Effective Teachers View Diversity as a Resource, Not a Deficit

In order to capitalize on the linguistically and culturally diverse classroom, all students must feel valued, and diversity itself must be valued—not implicitly, but explicitly. When learners feel valued, they contribute. When learners feel they belong, all forms of learning are enhanced: content, language, literacy, and intercultural understanding. Multiple language and cultural backgrounds in the classroom provide multiple ways of understanding any given task, as well as multiple ways of acquiring, interpreting, and storing new knowledge (Hollins, 1996). As you saw in Chapter 3, we want to make use of students' native language resources rather than ignore or restrict access to this important learning tool. Certainly in the acquisition of literacy skills in English, we know that the native language has important contributions to make, and we need to communicate to learners that their native language is important and desirable and that we welcome connections they make between their language and English in our classrooms.

Teachers who explore their own cultural characteristics and who seek to understand and appreciate the cultures of others model a positive cross-cultural stance needed by all individuals in a highly culturally diverse society. Further, teachers who welcome alternative perspectives in their classrooms also welcome the type of critical thinking involved in deliberative discourse that emphasizes "the forms and norms of discourse that support and promote equity and access to rigorous academic learning" (Michaels et al., 2008, 283). Diversity in experience, values, norms, and perspectives enriches the classroom and all human experience, and it is something we want our learners to appreciate for their futures as citizens living in a global society. In short, by viewing linguistic and cultural diversity as a resource, we tap its potential to promote learning, critical inquiry, and cross-cultural understanding.

Assessment Should Be More a Formative Than a Summative Process

Because our ELLs are going through a known developmental process, monitoring their progress as they acquire English is key to seeing the results of our teaching efforts. We want to use assessment approaches that are more formative for this reason (Echevarría et al., 2008; Gottlieb & Nguyen, 2007). Formative assessment is viewed by Gottlieb and Nguyen (2007) as "assessment for learning," which involves the collection, analysis, and use of data on a regular basis to directly inform and shape teaching and learning in classrooms (p. 45). We want to expect, measure, and report growth of our learners and to use growth models of assessment rather than comparative models of assessment that set fixed benchmarks and then view all learners below the benchmark as "below standard," when in fact meaningful growth is going on.

Process-oriented assessment in secondary educational environments is important for an even more fundamental reason. Keeping class work focused on processes, rather than solely on an end product, is essential for engaging all students in learning. With the current national focus on high-stakes testing, many teachers feel pressured to emphasize exams and final projects over process learning. The problem with summative (end-of-task) assessment is that students need to witness their progress day by day and week by week, not just once a quarter or once a year. The greatest opportunity for learning is through revisiting and revising, not through a single, monolithic end product. We know that learning is a recursive process. Therefore, students need to see how they are doing *as they go*, not just after they have "arrived." For this reason, it is essential that teachers focus on how students are doing along the way.

Moreover, measurement experts caution against use of summative standardized testing in English with ELLs, since the validity and reliability of such measures are questionable at best given that they are being administered in a language that students are still in the process of learning (Solórzano, 2008). Formative assessment is essential for learning, and it must be especially explicit with respect to language proficiencies in listening, speaking, reading, and writing. You will see evidence of this philosophy in the next five chapters as we focus on growth models of assessment, not end-of-program, end-of-course, or high-stakes annual assessments of learner abilities.

Listening, Speaking, Reading, and Writing Are Best Developed in an Integrated Manner, as Needed in Specific Contexts, and Driven by Content Learning

Language instruction at the secondary level tends to focus more on text comprehension, concept, and vocabulary development, and, as noted in Chapter 1, especially on the development of academic language.

> The vocabulary of academic language goes well beyond that used in most social conversations. It is only through structured talk about academically relevant content that students will learn the words needed to engage in class discussions and to comprehend what they read in various subjects. Memorizing word lists rarely works. Words must be learned and used in context. (American Educational Research Association [AERA], 2004)

According to Short and Fitzsimmons (2007), teachers need to consciously develop this type of language and literacy so that ELLs can succeed in academic settings. Whether you are a language or literacy specialist or a content teacher, their book was designed to offer ideas for helping ELL students to build the academic language and literacy needed to be successful in the classroom.

Since reading, writing, listening, and speaking are not discrete tasks, but interdependent and interactive (Genesee, 2006), they are best developed in an integrated manner. At the secondary level especially, students are required to talk as well as listen, write as well as read, and they must be able to do these things "in structured and supported ways" (AERA, 2004). The best way to do so in a secondary setting is to learn these language skills *through* discipline-specific content, rather than *in addition to* it; that is, language learning should be driven by content learning, such that language development is specific to the structured and supportive contexts that each discipline provides (e.g., the language needed to work with a lab partner and write a lab report in a chemistry class). Language is best learned, after all, when it is a by-product of learning interesting, relevant content. Just as, "extensive oral English development must be incorporated into successful literacy instruction" (Cloud, Genesee, & Hamayan, 2009; Mota-Altman, 2006; August & Shanahan, 2006a), all four skill areas must receive ongoing language and content attention during instruction.

Students Should Engage in Wide Reading of Age-Appropriate, Reading-Level-Appropriate, High-Interest Literature

Reading is a complex activity, requiring students "to master two separate skills: recognizing or decoding the words and understanding what the text says" (AERA, 2004; August & Shanahan, 2006a). To assist adolescent ELLs in developing their skills as readers, we must both engage and support them. Studies document that encouraging students to read a wide range of proficiency-level-appropriate books helps to build students' reading skills (Slavin & Cheung, 2003), so one key strategy is to have plentiful materials in the classroom and in the school library that are appropriate for the levels at which students read.

It is not enough that the books be appropriate for proficiency level, though. Since intrinsic motivation is very important to all learning, especially to language learning, ELLs will be more motivated to engage in reading and writing and will advance more rapidly when reading high-interest literature (Krashen, 2004). This statement is also true of content classrooms—students must engage in personally meaningful reading and writing, writing that is motivated by learner need and curiosity. If ELLs are motivated to engage in reading and writing, they will advance more rapidly than when reading and writing feel like an exercise to be completed for a grade.

Closely tied to this type of instruction is the use of relevant adolescent literature—in which themes of being the new kid, fitting in, being your own person versus being part of the crowd—create the high interest needed to motivate students to read. While most educators still concede that a knowledge of literary classics provides a useful kind of cultural capital that facilitates class mobility—and hence fulfills a social function—we cannot afford to teach the classics exclusively if doing so means that we spend more class time on Shakespearean or Dickensian English than on 21st-century standard American English. To build student comprehension of English within what Vygotsky called the "zone of proximal development," (Vygotsky, 1978), ESL and English language arts classes must make regular use of high-quality, high-interest adolescent literature. Our goal is to make habitual readers of students, through use of engaging, well-written texts that reflect the reality of being a language minority in the United States, while at the same time promoting close reading, an essential skill for developing critical thinking. Helping students to become habitual readers also requires encouraging ELLs to continue to read in their primary languages if they possess literacy in those languages.

Students Should Engage in Producing Language—Both Written and Oral—in Every Classroom Every Day

In one classroom, students noticed that "we need to practice our English, but teachers don't ask us to speak" (Mota-Altman, 2006). Many ELLs lack sufficient opportunities to practice their new language, yet practice is precisely what is needed in order for students to develop proficiency, because receiving comprehensible input, negotiating language through interaction with others, and producing language are keys to language development. If we choose themes that engage our learners, they will want to speak and share their thoughts with us. If we motivate learners with engaging reading material, they will want to talk and write about it. We need to engage our learners fully so that they cannot wait to speak and they want to write. This means selecting topics that promote real dialogue and sharing—high-interest topics that draw even the most reluctant learner into speaking and writing activities. Powerful stories generate lots of talk and lead to the desire to write and share, when adequate scaffolding is provided to ELLs. This is the kind of curricula we urge—not dull and lifeless exercises designed to give rote practice at a skills level, but rather the building of skills through authentic, purposeful communication.

When we identify learners' interests and needs and learn about the issues and challenges they face, we fully engage them. When we create opportunities for relating perspectives and experiences and for analyzing problematic situations they face and collectively develop strategies for action, we motivate learners, and this activity generates language, both oral and written. In the chapters that follow we describe how to support motivated students to speak and write in English.

All teachers need to provide this practice, and how we organize our classes has an impact. It is not okay for ELLs not to participate—to sit silently while others do all the talking. According to their level of proficiency, they need to respond to language (nonverbally initially) and produce it (in stage-appropriate ways, according to their levels of literacy). All secondary teachers can learn how to engage ELLs to create maximum practice opportunities. Teacher-fronted classes generally do not promote maximum opportunities for language use. So, learner-centered classes, with students in well-formulated group activities, generally support more language use and hence more opportunity for language development. We will give suggestions in the chapters that follow as to how best to engage ELLs and give them the practice they need—and in many cases that they actively seek.

Literacy Instruction Is the Responsibility of All Teachers, across All Disciplines, Not Just English and ESL Teachers

At the secondary school level, where classroom teachers "impart knowledge about subjects such as science and history in which they are expert," literacy and language development are most often left completely to ESL and English language arts (ELA) teachers who "often have sole responsibility for guiding students' reading growth while still being held accountable for covering a literature program, teaching grammar, offering personal advisory programs, and so on" (Moore et al., 1999). If ESL and ELA teachers are solely responsible for literacy instruction, though, then the most that can be expected of ELLs' literacy development is basic or functional literacy and a focus on classic and contemporary adolescent literature—not an acceptable end goal for a comprehensive literacy program. The real goal of a schoolwide literacy program, rather, must be *academic literacy*—reading, writing, and speaking across the disciplines (Fang & Schleppegrell, 2008; Schleppegrell, 2004, 2001; Schleppegrell & Colombi, 2002)—and this type of high-level, content-specific literacy cannot be achieved solely in the English classrooms; it is the responsibility of everyone in school. Indeed, academic literacy in each content area has its own demands, as noted by literacy experts:

> In academic contexts, there are clearly recognized text types that are characteristic, and these text types are instantiated through grammatical features that are common to school-based uses of language and that reflect the purposes for which language is typically used in schooling. (Schleppegrell, 2001, p. 432)

Researchers agree that "the best way to help students learn both English and the knowledge of school subjects is to *teach language through content*" (NCTE ELL Task Force, 2006, italics added). Secondary ELL specialists concur (Echevarría et al., 2008; Ivey & Fisher, 2006; Short & Fitzsimmons, 2007).

Now that we have stated our philosophy of teaching ELLs, the next section lays out existing frameworks and standards for literacy development and shows how these can shape literacy programs.

Literacy Frameworks and Standards

This book is designed to help language and content teachers to meet the literacy needs of adolescents that have been established through numerous national initiatives and reports on literacy, focusing on the specific needs of ELLs. To reach this goal, we will present the frameworks and standards that should guide teachers' work with adolescent ELLs.

Literacy Frameworks

In 1999 the Commission on Adolescent Literacy of the International Reading Association found that our national focus on literacy in the elementary grades needed to be expanded to secondary students:

> Adolescents entering the adult world in the 21st century will read and write more than at any other time in human history. They will need advanced levels of literacy to perform their jobs, run their households, act as citizens, and conduct their personal lives. . . . In a complex and sometimes even dangerous world, their ability to read will be crucial. Continual instruction beyond the early grades is needed. (Moore et al., 1999, p3)

Moreover,

> Today's adolescents enter school speaking many different languages and coming from many different backgrounds and experiences, so their academic progress differs substantially. Some teens need special instruction to comprehend basic ideas in print. (ibid, p.4)

No one has to tell secondary school teachers that literacy is of critical importance in secondary schools and for their students' future success—we are very aware of our students' needs. The question is, though, what do we do about it? What would a good schoolwide literacy program look like that encompasses the diversity of students present in our classrooms?

The following list describes 10 program characteristics recommended by leading literacy associations and adolescent literacy experts. These are useful recommendations for what a strong, schoolwide literacy program should look like, particularly in schools with ELLs.

Recommended Program Characteristics

1. *Literacy and oral proficiency in language-minority students' first language is used to facilitate literacy development in English.* The recognition of cognates, literary genres, and active use of reading strategies are often transferable to the second language (August & Shanahan, 2006a; Cloud et al., 2009) and therefore are to be encouraged.

2. *Age-appropriate and reading-level appropriate reading materials are used* (Biancarosa & Snow, 2004; Ivey & Fisher, 2006), particularly literature that students *want* to read (Moore et al., 1999); along with *intensive, individual support for low-level readers* (Heller & Greenleaf, 2007; Ivey & Fisher, 2006) delivered by well-prepared reading specialists (Moore et al., 1999).

3. *Teachers of ELLs understand that cultural attitudes toward and uses of literacy may differ from one culture to the next* (Jiménez, 2005) *are employed*—teachers who

recognize and understand the complexity of reading and are respectful of the differences among individual adolescent readers (Biancarosa & Snow, 2004).

4. *Reading instruction builds both reading skills and the desire for and interest in reading increasingly complex materials* (Ivey & Fisher, 2006; Moore et al., 1999). Furthermore, *oral language development is taught alongside reading and writing*, as "literacy programs that provide instructional support of oral language development in English, aligned with high-quality literacy instruction, are the most successful" (August & Shanahan, 2006a).

5. *Vocabulary building and word study are a routine and active part of every class, as are the identification and interpretation of idiomatic expressions* (Graves 2006; Jiménez, 2005). Vocabulary instruction includes helping students to develop strategies for identifying and learning new words, such as recognizing context clues for new words they encounter. Vocabulary instruction also includes deliberately frequent contact with the same words (repetition), frequent verbal and written use of new words (active engagement), and direct instruction on new vocabulary (Alliance for Excellent Education [AEE], 2004; Graves, 2006).

6. *Teachers provide explicit literary instruction in the curriculum and model reading comprehension and study strategies across the curriculum.* In doing so, teachers help students develop a metacognitive approach to reading, including questioning themselves about what they have read, synthesizing information from various sources, organizing information in notes, interpreting symbol systems in science and math classes, and developing new vocabulary (Moore et al., 1999; AEE, 2004). Among students reading below grade level, most are able to sound out words; decoding is not the challenge; helping students to comprehend what they read is (Biancarosa & Snow, 2004; August & Shanahan, 2006a).

7. *Reading and writing tasks are made relevant to students' lives to increase student motivation to read and write.* This motivation must be nurtured through high-interest literature, especially literature featuring writers and characters from diverse backgrounds, and by engaging students in writing that taps into their individual interests (Heller & Greenleaf, 2007; Jiménez, 2005; Weinstein, 2004). Literacy programs should also consciously address and discuss with students the question "Why read?" (Jiménez, 2005), focus on reading as a strategy for learning, and include a cooperative learning environment designed for students to discuss what they read (AEE, 2004).

8. *Writing instruction takes place in an environment in which students' writing has an authentic purpose and audience, in which writing is relevant to students' lives, in which content is at the center of the writing process, and in which critical thinking skills are engaged—not just regurgitation of delivered material* (AEE, 2004; Samway, 2006). In these environments writing is viewed as a recursive, five-stage process with meaning at the center: prewriting (brainstorming, outlining), drafting, revising, rewriting, and publishing.

9. *Students' reading levels* (for all languages in which they have literacy) are routinely assessed upon entry to middle school and high school (Heller & Greenleaf, 2007) *and ongoing assessment to gauge progress and modify instruction* (AERA, 2004) *is also common.* Not only are assessment results used to shape

instruction so as to help students develop as readers (Moore et al., 1999), but also teachers give learners usable feedback based on clear, attainable, and worthwhile standards (AEE, 2004).

10. *Teachers receive ongoing professional development in language development and secondary literacy instruction* (Heller & Greenleaf, 2007; Ivey & Fisher, 2006; Short & Fitzsimmons, 2007). When it comes to ELLs, of course, this professional development must be made specific to the development of literacy in a second language.

These program characteristics are the hallmark of responsive adolescent literacy programs—indicators of what a strong, school-wide literacy program should look like. The goal of this book is to offer you practical strategies to work toward these program characteristics while at the same time acknowledging the language standards and definitions of literacy that also guide our work.

Standards, Literacy Definitions, and Their Impact on Teachers' Work

When we talk about literacy standards, we refer not only to national and state content-area standards for academic literacy (English language arts, mathematics, science, social studies, health, etc.), but also to standards developed particularly to measure the growth and development of proficiency in English as a second language. When crafting literacy instruction for ELLs, we must also pay attention to state and national language proficiency standards such as the *PreK–12 English Language Proficiency (ELP) Standards* from Teachers of English to Speakers of Other Languages (TESOL, 2006). These were developed from the *World-Class Instructional Design and Assessment English Language Proficiency Standards* (WIDA Consortium, 2007); and WIDA standards had been adopted by 17 states and the District of Columbia at time of publication (http://www.wida.us). These standards provide a useful tool for instructional design and to direct our literacy work with ELLs.

The WIDA/TESOL ELP standards, like many state-adopted English language proficiency (ELP) standards, include the notions of social and academic literacy and directly address the development of academic literacy across all academic areas. They state that ELLs must

- Communicate for social, intercultural, and instructional purposes within the school setting (Standard 1)
- Communicate information, ideas, and concepts necessary for academic success in the area of language arts (Standard 2)
- Communicate information, ideas, and concepts necessary for academic success in the area of mathematics (Standard 3)
- Communicate information, ideas, and concepts necessary for academic success in the area of science (Standard 4)
- Communicate information, ideas, and concepts necessary for academic success in the area of social studies (Standard 5)

In order to design standards-based instruction for ELLs, we need to know not only the standards specific to the content subjects we teach but also the *language* standards we must reach. Thus all teachers, irrespective of discipline, need to become familiar with state and national standards for English language arts and English language proficiency), as we are all charged with promoting language and literacy development while advancing learner knowledge and skills that correspond to the courses we teach.

At the same time, it is important to put all standards in their proper place so that we do not lose sight of the need to offer culturally responsive pedagogy—instruction and assessment that respond to the backgrounds, needs, and interests of our students. Ramírez (2008) proposes the adoption of a general pedagogical framework he labels *strategic alignment*, a pedagogic-ideological position that expands the frame of accountability to all stakeholders of the educational process, most critically to the students we teach. Practitioners using this framework would align to standards and mandates represented by the current educational policy, including ELP standards, but more importantly, they would also align to best practices in teaching ELLs and to the specific needs and backgrounds of their learners. Using culturally and linguistically responsive pedagogy, teachers would insure that they use the cultural and linguistic resources students bring to the classroom as well as the latest research on promoting language and literacy development for ELLs. So standards are best incorporated in an integrative manner, where teachers do not lose track of the backgrounds, needs, and rights of students to whom the standards are being applied. Teachers can accomplish this goal through the type of "strategic alignment" process Ramírez advocates when they plan instruction.

There Is More Than One Kind of Literacy

For the purposes of the chapters that follow, we adopt the following definition of *literacy*:

> As spelled out in many state and national standards, literacy is multifaceted. To be considered literate today, individuals must read and write; speak, listen, and view; think critically; analyze and synthesize multiple streams of information; and produce new information in all these modes.

There are many ways in which we are literate, in which we use not just language but also images, layouts, symbols, forms, and formats, to understand, analyze, synthesize, and create new information. We are computer literate, financially literate, visually literate, scientifically literate, academically literate, media literate, and on and on. Literacy is not, then, just about English class. It is about survival in a data-rich world, survival in the global realities of the 21st century. So there are many types of literacy that we must develop in all learners, including ELLs, in a 21st-century secondary school literacy program. Here are some of the most essential:

- *Computer and technology literacy:* Students already access the internet for socializing (MySpace, Facebook), entertainment (YouTube), and reading and writing blogs; they use cell phones and PSPs for text messaging, playing video games, and taking and storing photographs; they also use iPods and other MP3 players to record and store music, photographs, and the "411" on their friends and family. In academic settings, students also access the internet for research and use search engines such as Google, and they are increasingly being required to compose at the keyboard and to record and store their work in electronic portfolios. Digital portfolios are not only a more efficient way of storing information; among college students, maintaining an electronic portfolio has been linked to higher academic performance, higher retention rates, higher levels of metacognition, reflection, and audience awareness in writing (Goldberg et al., 2003; NCTE, 2007b). As virtual universities—the digital version of "distance learning"—become a greater option for more students, so will virtual components of secondary schools, such as online syllabi, assignments, and tests.

- *Workforce literacy:* In order to be ready for the workplace, students must have high-level written and oral communication skills and academic knowledge, but they must also be able to collaborate, think critically, lead effectively, and use moral judgment. They must have organizational, critical-thinking, and problem-solving skills, must be creative and socially responsible, and must above all have a work ethic (Partnership for 21st Century Skills, 2007).

- *Financial literacy:* Do students understand how to open a checking or savings account, write a check, save for college and retirement, create and keep to a budget, and apply for a credit card, car loan, or mortgage? Do they understand interest rates and compound interest? As recent history has shown, students need financial literacy (National Endowment for Financial Education [NEFE], 2007).

- *Visual literacy:* Many students are visual learners, but how visually literate are they? How acute are their skills of observation when they are looking at something other than a video game or a favorite web page? Can they read and understand political cartoons, bar graphs, and pie charts? Can they watch a complex film or documentary and follow the narrative, even when the dialogue and voiceovers contradict the images? Do they understand how textbooks and web sites are organized, strategically using text boxes, sidebars, and menus? When looking at the results page of an internet search, can they tell the difference between an information link and an advertising link?

- *Life skills literacy:* Do students understand how to read a lease or other contract, how to fill out a job or college application, how to write and maintain a résumé? Can they effectively communicate and resolve errors in their bills or paychecks? Can they persuade their local representative to take actions on behalf of their community? Can they read nutritional labels? Do they know how to fill out loan applications, read a ballot, research candidates in an election? Do students know how to adapt the register of their language to specific social or professional contexts? All these types of skills are needed to function as an informed adult in American society.

- *Academic literacy* (Fang & Schleppegrell, 2008, Schleppegrell, 2004, 2001):
  - *Scientific:* Do students understand the scientific method and how new knowledge and theories are vetted for scientific integrity? Do they understand the basic principles of anatomy, geology, biology, physics, and chemistry? Can they write a lab report that outlines materials and methods but that also answers the question "So what?"
  - *Mathematical:* Do students have functional knowledge of numbers and problem solving? Can they determine, from reading a problem, which formulas they must use to solve it? Can they explain how they got their answers? Do students fully understand how their grades are calculated in each of their classes?
  - *Historical and sociological:* Do students understand how to think like a historian or a social scientist, to compare multiple historical perspectives on an

event, and to conduct research using observation and primary and secondary sources? Do they understand how anthropologists, sociologists, psychologists, and historians use such research to reach their conclusions and how to convey their conclusions to others?

- ○ *English language arts:*
  - —*Writing:* Can students write in multiple formats, showing awareness of audience, clarity of purpose, and purpose-appropriate tone? Can students proficiently produce personal, factual, and analytical writing?
  - —*Speaking:* Do students understand what it takes to communicate effectively with others, using eye contact, body language, and inflection? Do students understand rhetorical strategies and how they can be used to persuade an audience?
  - —*Literary and poetic:* Can students do close analytical readings of literary texts? Can they discern the differences between style and content? Can they distinguish an author's point of view from that of a story's narrator? Can they recognize and use figures of speech and literary allusions?
  - —*Language development, knowledge, and skills:* Do students understand components of language? Are they able to use the correct verb tense and subject-verb agreement? Do they know how to use social or written context to gauge meaning? Can students hold conversations or read in more than one language? Do they understand how dictionaries and thesauri work?
- *Media literacy:* The current generation of secondary students has grown up with television and the Internet, but how media savvy are they? When surfing the net, to what extent can they distinguish between trustworthy data and a sales pitch? Do they understand plagiarism and intellectual property? When using sparknotes.com and pinkmonkey.com (the modern equivalent of Cliff Notes), do they see these as supports for understanding class work, or substitutes for understanding class work?

Preparing secondary students to be literate today means more than just instruction in reading comprehension and composition, just as preparing secondary ELLs to be literate means more than just helping them to achieve basic comprehension and basic production of English. Literacy is context specific, and because students encounter language across a full spectrum of contexts, literacy programs must teach literacy skills across that spectrum.

Who is responsible for teaching these different literacies? Clearly, not just ESL and ELA teachers. The primary responsibility of ESL teachers is to promote English language development. Teachers of English language arts are responsible for literature, creative writing, and personal and reflective writing—as much content and skill building as any other content-area teacher. So instruction in literacy must lead the *schoolwide* agenda in secondary schools. Teachers across all disciplines must be philosophically and practically and pedagogically aligned around literacy instruction, each taking on a different, but integral, component of academic literacy. How might we distribute this work? Who is best equipped to take on each part? Figure 4.2 outlines one way to distribute these responsibilities, but each school should discuss this topic and come to its own satisfying resolution.

Figure 4.2 shows ways in which the literacy skills of listening, reading, writing, and speaking must span a spectrum of academic and social contexts. While

	ACADEMIC REGISTER Vocabulary, Structures, Discourse					SOCIAL REGISTER Vocabulary, Structures, Discourse	
	Mathematics	Science	Social Studies	English Language Arts	Art, Music, Dance, PE, etc.	Life Skills Literacy	Personal Literacy
	Financial Mathematical	Scientific	Academic Literacies Historical Sociological	Literary	Artistic Sports/Health	Life Literacies Work/Career/Family	Expression/Communication
Listening							◇
Speaking							◇
Reading							◇
Writing							◇
Visual							◇
Multimedia							◇
Computers and technology							◇

FIGURE 4.2   Assigning literacy instruction responsibilities across secondary schools: Where does each of us fit?

some literacies may be more specific to either academic or social registers (such as financial literacy to mathematics), others, such as media and computer literacies, can span all domains.

Conclusion

The purpose of this chapter was, first, to articulate important understandings about literacy that underlie the remaining action-oriented chapters of the book and, second, to provide the foundation upon which you can build your own teaching practice.

As you consider which parts of each chapter pertain to your teaching, keep in mind that in different states and districts placement practices for ELLs vary significantly. It is useful to be aware of these so that you can plan for your ELLs' specific needs and situations. English language learners may be placed in classes in one or more of the following ways:

- *Sequential ESL to mainstream*: ELLs may be placed in mainstream ELA only after they have transitioned out of ESL classes (but note that this transition may have taken place as little as one month or as many as eleven years before a student joined your classroom).

- *Exited or waived from ESL classes:* ELLs may have been exited or never enrolled in ESL classes in secondary schools for a number of reasons, including the following: they reached proficiency in their previous school; they reached proficiency in your school (note, though, that proficient ELLs continue to be monitored after they exit ESL classes); their parents do not want them in sheltered ESL classes.

- *Concurrent ESL and mainstream:* ELLs may be participating in ESL and ELA classes concurrently rather than sequentially.

- *Pull-out/push-in programs:* ELLs may be in "pull-out" or "push-in" programs that provide language support for students placed in mainstream classes.

The next four chapters, then, are not solely for use in ESL classrooms, especially if you work in a school where ELLs are placed in ESL and mainstream classes concurrently. Rather, they present a range of strategies for developing ELLs' oral language, reading skills, writing skills, and listening skills in any classroom where there are ELLs. The strategies presented in Chapters 5 through 8 can and should be used in all classrooms to build literacy across the curriculum. Chapter 9 addresses the special concerns that ELA teachers have when ELLs are enrolled in their mainstream English classes.

Checklist

Eleven Ways to Structure Literacy Programs for ELLs

☐ My literacy program is structured to meet the English language proficiency (ELP) standards for my state.

☐ My literacy program creates a learning environment that is socially, culturally, and emotionally safe for ELLs.

☐ My literacy program is built around the specific proficiency levels of my ELLs.

☐ My literacy program incorporates a wide variety of high-interest, age-appropriate literature.

☐ My literacy program celebrates diversity of culture and language in explicit and implicit ways.

☐ My literacy program focuses and builds on what students *can* do rather than on what they *cannot* do.

☐ Most of the assessment that takes place in my literacy program is formative, rather than summative, allowing students to revise and learn from their mistakes. Assessment is used as a tool for learning.

☐ My literacy program incorporates cooperative learning.

☐ My literacy program integrates listening, speaking, reading, and writing in meaningful learning contexts.

☐ My literacy program extends across the entire secondary curriculum, not just ELA and ESL classes.

☐ My literacy program considers multiple literacies.

CHAPTER 5

Oral Language

Johnny and Erilenny, Dominican Republic

> Studies indicate that, in most classrooms, teachers dominate the linguistic aspect of the lesson, leaving students severely limited in terms of opportunities to use language in a variety of ways (Goodlad, 1984; Marshall, 2000). When students were given an opportunity to respond, it usually involved only simple information-recall statements, restricting students' chance to produce language and develop complex language and thinking skills. (Echevarría, Vogt, & Short, 2008, pp. 115–116)

Guiding Questions

- Why is it so difficult for English language learners to speak in class?
- What aspects of English are important to understand in order to help English language learners develop their oral language skills?
- How can we determine what academic oral language skills students need in our classrooms?
- What oral language abilities do students have at the different levels of language proficiency, and what skills should they be working toward?
- How can we shape verbal interactions for the various proficiency levels of our students?
- What strategies are most effective in promoting oral language development in the classroom?
- What are the best practices for correcting students' oral language errors?

The ease and efficiency of language for the communication of our thoughts is something we often take for granted, especially if everyone around us speaks a common language. In general, secondary teachers are primarily concerned with the subject they teach, and many do not see the "hidden" language demands or language-learning opportunities in content-area learning. However, oral language is fundamental to all communication. We draw on our oral language to communicate with others, from basic everyday needs to complex academic content. Students learn content primarily through language, and they demonstrate their understanding of that content primarily through language. Unfortunately, many secondary classrooms offer few opportunities for students, particularly English language learners (ELLs), to use and develop English while learning content.

This chapter helps you see the integral role of oral language in secondary classrooms so that you can better engage all your students, particularly your

ELLs. First we describe challenges that ELLs face with respect to developing oral language in secondary school and the essential role oral language plays academically and socially. Next we identify aspects of oral language that matter in secondary classrooms and the kinds of verbal interactions students of different proficiency levels can handle. Then we provide a how-to guide that teachers can use to look closely and critically at oral language use in their own classrooms. The majority of the chapter shares teaching tips and instructional strategies that teachers can use to promote oral language use and development in their classrooms, as well as data that can help guide instruction. These strategies enrich the quality of classroom interaction not only for ELLs, but for all students—including English speakers who struggle with reading and writing grade-level content-area material.

The Challenges of Getting ELLs to Talk in the Secondary Classroom

There are many challenges teachers face in getting adolescents to express their ideas in the classroom or participate in a text-based discussion. First and foremost, teachers have to make sure students understand what is being said to and asked of them, both by the teacher and by classmates—referred to as giving students "comprehensible input" (Krashen & Terrell, 1983). Other in-class challenges include

- Culturally diverse learners' lack of background knowledge of U.S.-based topics (government, geography, authors, health care practices, etc.) and experiences

- Students' insecurity about speaking (e.g., fear of not being understood because of an accent)

- Students' anxiety about being judged as a competent thinker when speaking in a second language

- Students' lack of vocabulary and phrasing to express a specific idea

- New students' feeling shy as a result of being in a new environment

- Something as basic as not understanding the underlying classroom routines or expectations when participating in class discussions

Students' willingness to speak may also vary greatly from teacher to teacher and class to class depending on students' self-confidence and comfort levels. It can also be common to find that the same student is very quiet in a teacher-fronted, lecture-format classroom, yet orally engaged in a more student-centered, cooperative learning environment (Hertz-Lazarowitz & Shachar, 1990).

There are also influences from outside of the classroom. Some middle and high school students are resistant speakers who refuse to speak entirely, no matter the context. Other students only have the time they spend at school to practice speaking English; they do not have any friends or relatives outside the classroom with whom they can interact and practice in English. Students' level of English language proficiency and strength in literacy in their first language also matters in terms of giving students a jump start in the secondary classroom, as we saw in Chapter 3.

A frequently discussed challenge for secondary second-language learners is learning the language of school (Schleppegrell, 2004). It is important for teachers to understand that there are two types of proficiency that secondary students need to develop. Some students may have a high level of what Jim Cummins has called *conversational fluency,* or *basic interpersonal communication skills* (BICS), but face significant challenges in developing *cognitive academic language proficiency* (CALP), or *academic language* (Cummins, 1981, 2006). Many current and some former ELLs sound like they speak English fluently, especially when they are talking about concrete topics they know well or using everyday language they have practiced a lot. However, these same students often really struggle with the oral academic English they need to communicate effectively about the abstract, complex content-area topics that they are learning about at school.

Helping ELLs develop social and academic oral English can go a long way in helping students overcome the challenges they face as new arrivals in the complex social environment of secondary school, a challenge noted in Chapter 1. As students begin to use their developing oral English to communicate socially and academically, they will be better able to connect with peers and adults both in and outside the classroom, and to develop a positive identity within the new school and community culture. This communication could focus on academic issues such as homework or career planning, or social rules and norms such as scheduling classes or navigating the lunch line. Oral language can also play a major role in helping ELLs get involved in extracurricular activities, which provide opportunities to use English with a different social group with whom they can experiment and refine their developing oral language skills.

The ability of students to stay motivated and achieve success in secondary school depends on their ability to engage in their learning and feel connected to and supported by those in their learning environment. Students must be able to understand and process the predominant language of instruction to succeed. Likewise, students need oral language to engage in the collaborative learning process and to express themselves so they can seek assistance and support when needed. Acquiring oral English can boost motivation, which in turn can foster regular school attendance—a sure contributor to secondary students' success.

Oral language skills are invaluable not only for the students in their communication with teachers and guidance counselors, but also to aid their family members who would like to be involved in their education. English language learners, even in the earliest development stages, often act as linguistic brokers for family members who wish to become involved in the school or meet with teachers, guidance counselors, or administrators about a student's academics. As we expand students' abilities in oral English, we are helping them do more than participate in class; we are helping them participate more effectively in all aspects of school life and aid their parents to do so also.

All this said, remember that learning English does not have to mean losing the first language. In fact, as shown in Chapter 3, learning English may help students develop a positive identity within the new culture by allowing them to express aspects of their personality and culture to the new people they meet at school. This outcome is most likely to be achieved when they know their home language and culture are valued at school. For this reason, we recommend promoting the second language, while honoring and including the home language in the ways we have already outlined in Chapter 3.

Aspects of Oral Language
That Matter in the Secondary Classroom

In this section we define a few key linguistic concepts that can help secondary teachers see the fundamental role of oral language in their classrooms. Teachers can draw on this foundation to inform their selection of strategies that increase the quantity and improve the quality of oral language used by all students, particularly ELLs, in their classes.

Linguistics is the scientific study of human language structure and use. When linguists study language structure, they traditionally focus on the following areas:

- *Phonetics and phonology:* The sound system
- *Morphology:* Word formation
- *Syntax:* Grammar or sentence structure
- *Semantics:* Word meaning
- *Pragmatics:* Language use in context

Teachers who want to learn more about these areas might turn to turn to one of the following resources:

- D. E. Freeman & Y. S. Freeman, *Essential Linguistics: What You Need to Know to Teach Reading, ESL Spelling, Phonics, and Grammar.* Portsmouth, NH: Heinemann, 2004.
- M. Swan & B. Smith, *Learner English: A Teacher's Guide to Interference and Other Problems* (2nd ed.). New York: Cambridge University Press, 2001.

A basic understanding of these aspects of language structure can help teachers appreciate some of the specific challenges their ELLs face, for example, in vocabulary development, pronunciation, or grammar, as they work to acquire conversational and academic English.

While an awareness of these aspects of language structure is certainly beneficial for all teachers (and essential for the ESL teacher), a broader understanding of language use within specific communicative contexts like the content-area classroom is essential. Dell Hymes' (1971, 1996) notion of communicative competence can help us understand different aspects of oral language use that matter in secondary classrooms, and it is the basis for most contemporary approaches to language teaching and learning. Communicative competence can be broadly defined as what a speaker needs to be able to do to communicate correctly and appropriately within a particular speech community. Canale and Swain (1980) identify the following four aspects of communicative competence:

1. *Linguistic competence:* The forms, inflections, and sequences used to express the message are grammatically correct.

2. *Sociolinguistic competence:* The expression of the message is appropriate in terms of the person being addressed and the overall circumstances and purpose of communication.

3. *Discourse competence:* The selection, sequence, and arrangement of words and structures are clear and effective means of expressing the intended message.

4. *Strategic competence:* The strategies used to compensate for any weaknesses in the preceding areas are effective and unobtrusive.

The first component of this framework, linguistic competence, parallels the traditional language education concern with grammar and correctness. However, communicative language teaching and learning, with its additional focus on sociolinguistic, discourse, and strategic competence, draws our attention to the fact that language is used differently in different contexts. This is highlighted in *PreK–12 English Language Proficiency Standards* (TESOL, 2006), which distinguishes social and instructional language at school (Standard 1) from the language of English language arts (Standard 2), the language of mathematics (Standard 3), the language of science (Standard 4), and the language of social studies (Standard 5).

Secondary teachers need to pay explicit attention to the kinds of oral academic language that their students need to participate appropriately in the content area that they teach so that ELLs have opportunities to listen and speak in their content areas. Equipped with this understanding of the social-interactional language and academic language (vocabulary, ways of speaking about content concepts) associated with the content area that secondary teachers teach, they can find creative ways to support the language development of all students, particularly the ELLs, in their classes.

Assessing Oral Language to Guide Instruction

Although assessment has been traditionally thought of as a way to evaluate what students have learned from instruction at the end of instruction, the ideal and most effective way to use assessment to promote instruction is to gauge where learners are and assess them in ways that respect their level of proficiency. This section will talk about how to incorporate assessment into academic instruction.

In order to effectively help students build their oral language proficiency, we must first learn as much about their prior educational and personal experiences with English as we can. You should be able to get some basic proficiency-level information about each student from the entrance assessments that most districts give to incoming students. However, what these preliminary academic assessments do not address are the affective aspects of a students' oral language, such as their self-confidence and general feeling about themselves as speakers of English. These social-emotional language factors are as important as a student's current proficiency level. For example, a student who has some basic knowledge of English but who is anxious about speaking may progress at a much slower rate than a student who comes to you with almost no knowledge of English but who is confident and energized about learning and improving his or her English language skills.

In addition to gathering information about students' social and emotional experiences and associations with English prior to instruction, it is important to gather information about their educational experiences and current English language skills level as well. You will want to inquire about students' prior exposure to and experience with oral English; their current oral language proficiency level; their proficiencies in other languages, as this directly contributes to the acquisition of English; and any opportunities they have for practicing oral language outside of school. Consider students' oral language needs outside of the school setting so you can be thinking about all the places they need to speak English.

One way of gathering this type of information is by conducting an informal survey or questionnaire at the beginning of the school year or whenever you get a

- How many years have you studied English?   1   2   3   4   5

- Do you practice English with anyone outside of school?   ☐ yes   ☐ no

- If so, who, and how often?   ☐ mother   ☐ father   ☐ friends   ☐ other
  ☐ every day   ☐ 1–2 times a week   ☐ 1–2 times a month   ☐ other

- Do you like learning English?   ☐ yes   ☐ no

- Do you like talking to people?   ☐ yes   ☐ no

- Do you like speaking English?   ☐ yes   ☐ no

- Where do you use English outside of school?   ☐ at work   ☐ shopping   ☐ at home
  ☐ on the phone   ☐ other

- What other languages do you speak?   ☐ Spanish   ☐ Creole   ☐ other

- What other languages do you understand?   ☐ Spanish   ☐ Creole   ☐ other

- What language do you speak at home?   ☐ Spanish   ☐ Creole   ☐ other

FIGURE 5.1   Sample student survey showing some examples of questions you could use.

new student. Surveys can be given to students only, or to both students and their parent(s) in order to get a more comprehensive view of students' current level of skill and needs. Be sure to take into consideration the language proficiency level of your students and their families when creating both the questions and the type of response you employ on your survey. You will want to ensure that the questions are straightforward and nonthreatening. This way you will be sure to collect clear, accurate information about each student's language experiences. While you may chose to use more open-ended and abstract questions with your high intermediate and advanced level students, use of yes/no, multiple choice, and matching questions with your beginner level students is advisable in order to make the survey as comprehensible as possible.

Students and their families are one resource for obtaining information about students' experience with English and their feelings about English, but another helpful resource is a student's prior school records, including transcripts, report cards, or personal references from prior teachers and guidance counselors. Often, students will have official school documents from the native country, but they may not realize they should bring them to school as soon as possible. The issue of awarding students credit for classes taken in their native country is addressed in Chapter 2, but it is important to mention that transcripts are also very useful in providing classroom teachers information about students' prior learning experiences and general academic history. Some students may have also studied English in their home country, a fact that would be very helpful to know. For this reason, it is wise to obtain copies of all your students' transcripts as soon as possible.

Once you have acquired a body of information about your students with regard to language and education, you can skillfully plan and carry out appropriate lessons while monitoring student progress.

Documenting Oral Language Learning Opportunities in the Classroom

The best way to go about planning compatible oral language instruction for students is by first figuring out which language forms (word forms, sentence structures, verb tenses) and functions (ways of using language to communicate, such as describing phenomena, explaining understandings of new concepts, giving examples) they will need to participate in your class. If you are aware of which language students need to understand and use within the environment of your classroom, you can focus on teaching specific oral language skills, both forms (e.g., using regular and irregular past-tense verbs) and functions (e.g., telling a sequence of events that occurred in the past). This way, students will learn how to be orally successful in class. Most likely what you teach them will apply to other classes as well, as naturally there are many communicative tasks that overlap across secondary classrooms. Furthermore, when you give students the skills to participate in your class successfully, they will be more likely to speak up, and doing so will help build their oral language confidence in other academic settings.

The following list presents some tips to consider as you begin documenting language use in your classroom. Table 5.1 shows one way to keep track of your documentation.

- *Take notes:* Keep a written record, in a notebook or notepad, of what you expect students to be able to say—the kinds of things they say when they participate. The simplest way to keep this record is, every time you request any response from a student, group, or class, just write it down. Examples may range from basic necessities such as students asking to go to their locker or to the restroom, to more complex communication such as voicing agreement or disagreement with an idea or viewpoint. Be sure to notice language forms (verb tense, use of pronouns, prepositions, adjectives/adverbs, plurals) as much as what kinds of communication is required in the classroom using English.

- *Observe over time:* We do not always do the same thing every day, so it is important to take notes on your classroom routines throughout the course of a week, a month, a unit, or whatever different cycles go on in your class, so that you do not forget or overlook any key routines students need to orally participate in your class.

- *Organize and prioritize:* Once you have documented the various oral language routines in your classroom, organize and prioritize them in the way that makes the most sense to you. You may choose to organize your instruction beginning with the least demanding verbal response required or the easiest language form to learn about, or by frequency, beginning with the language forms and functions that occur most often in your classroom. The most important thing is that the organization makes sense to you and works within your existing curriculum. As long as you focus in on what students need to successfully engage in oral language interactions in your classroom, you are providing a tremendous boost to your students.

- *Don't forget!*
  - *Student/student communication:* Students also need to be prepared to talk with their classmates, so don't forget about the language routines where the

teacher is not a participant, such as student/student interactions like pair/share, collaborative learning, and other group activities.

- ○ *Non-academic routines:*These include homework collection, asking to go to the restroom or nurse, and so on.

You can use your documentation of oral language use in your classroom in two very important ways. First, you can look critically at the quantity and quality of teacher and student talk in the classroom, with particular attention to the quantity and quality of oral language contributions by your ELLs. Then you can decide what kinds of oral language instruction is needed in your classroom.

As noted in this chapter's opening quote, most analyses of classroom interaction find that the teacher talks the overwhelming majority of time in the classroom (Echevarría et al., 2008; Rothenberg & Fisher, 2007), and this trend can be even more pervasive at the secondary level given the amount of material teachers are expected to cover in a year. Cooperatively structured classrooms yield more student talk than do teacher-fronted classrooms, and the type of participation also varies (Hertz-Lazarowitz & Shachar, 1990). Not only is the amount of student talk increased in cooperative classrooms, thus providing students with more opportunities to use their new language, but the aforesaid researchers also found that, unlike teacher-dominated classrooms where teachers give information and directions, ask narrow questions, and judge student responses as accurate or not, in cooperative classrooms the teacher asks broad questions that invite discussion and also is more responsive to student input, thus encouraging students to speak more (reported in Baloche, 1998, pp. 21–22). This is helpful because it is commonplace for ELLs to speak less than their native English-speaking counterparts in mainstream classes.

What is happening in your class? Who is speaking to whom and for how long? Look both at the number of contributions that each student makes relative to other students (paying special attention to the student's proficiency level) and relative to the teacher. Also look at the length of each contribution. Document who is asking questions, and what kinds of questions, in your classroom. Is the teacher asking most of the questions? Or are students also asking questions of the teacher, of each other, of the texts they read, and of the world they live in? What kinds of questions are being asked and by whom—simple information questions, or higher order, critical thinking questions? Answering these questions will tell you how much change is needed to get ELLs talking in your classroom.

TABLE 5.1 Table for Documenting Oral Language Demands in the Classroom

Description of Activity	Listening or Speaking?	Frequency (daily, weekly, quarterly)	Forms (key words, phrases; verb tenses; other grammar features)	Functions (students must . . .)
Pair/share	Both	About weekly	"My partner wrote/talked about . . ." (past tense, possessive pronouns)	Summarize what happened
			"I think the author is trying to say . . ." (present and present progressive tenses, definite articles)	Express an opinion
			"An example from the text is . . ." (indefinite article, prepositions, present tense of the verb "to be")	Give examples

Helping ELLs Participate in the Classroom

Once you understand the oral language used in your classroom, next you will want to understand the proficiency levels of your students, since we know that the ways learners can participate in English varies by their proficiency level (see Chapter 4). All ELLs want to communicate their understanding of what they are learning, but the amount and sophistication of the oral language a learner uses will vary depending on the language proficiency of the learner. Table 5.2 shows the kinds of language functions students can be expected to perform to demonstrate their knowledge and understanding at each proficiency level.

To use communicative functions in a language or content classroom, first decide on a focus topic, such as mythology or cell structure and function. Once you have a focus, use the communicative functions given in Table 5.2 to build your lesson plan and assessment strategies for students at the various proficiency levels. Think about what it is you want students to know, in terms of content, and then think about how they can show their knowledge, respecting their proficiency levels. This approach may mean changing some of the ways you have been inviting participation in your classroom, if you recognize that those ways have excluded beginning and intermediate ELLs because the demands exceeded their proficiency levels.

When working on oral language development, you can choose to teach (1) language forms (vocabulary, grammar), (2) language functions (naming, describing, explaining), or (3) language scripts ("I agree"; "I think that . . ."; "The author's message is . . .") within the context of your curriculum. More will be said about teaching language scripts later in this chapter because teaching ELLs "scripts" is a strategy to get kids talking.

Whatever language goal you choose, always remember to allow for sufficient practice time, so students become familiar and comfortable with the expectations of each new verbal routine that can help them participate in your classroom. Here are a couple of different implementation ideas:

- *A systematic approach:* Introduce a new phrase or verbal exchange, every day or week, depending on the criteria you choose (i.e., order of appearance, complexity, frequency). Try to focus on one communicative pattern. You can also teach about how English works (how nouns are pluralized, how verbs are formed, how prepositions are used, etc.).
- *Play it by ear:* Rather than deciding all your language objectives in advance, you may also choose to wait until the opportunity presents itself unexpectedly in your classroom to introduce a new language pattern. Recognizing the "teachable moment" creates an organic, flowing atmosphere where teachers

TABLE 5.2 Communicative Functions by Overall Language Proficiency

Beginner		Intermediate		Advanced		
Sort	Point	Create	Present	Support	Draw conclusions	
List	Match	Categorize	Determine	Summarize	Make connections	
Describe	Name	Sequence	Produce	Edit	Explain	Research
Locate	Identify	Hypothesize	Compare	Revise	Debate	Apply
Classify	Label	Discuss	Contrast	Interpret	Justify	React
Select	Draw	Retell		Author	Defend	

feel comfortable addressing the needs of their students as they arise and where students can immediately apply what they learn, a result that helps to solidify learning for the long term.

For more information on the topic of language analysis in content classrooms, see Cloud, Genesee, and Hamayan (2009), Freeman and Freeman (2009), and Schleppegrell (2004).

Integrating Language Instruction into Classroom Instruction

By using the proficiency-based descriptors in the preceding section as a guide, teachers can plan for linguistically responsive instruction and assessment—what you require students at different proficiency levels to do in your classroom. Amount of support needed, or scaffolding, should also be guided by this proficiency-based understanding of what students of various proficiency levels can do.

With knowledge of the proficiency levels of your students at your fingertips, you are ready to begin planning your instruction and also how you will check whether your goals have been met. For most units, no matter the length or subject matter, you will want to have both content goals and language goals for your students. As advocated by Echevarría and colleagues (2008) in their SIOP (sheltered instruction observation protocol) lesson planning and delivery model, it is important to articulate these goals at the outset of your planning, so that you can effectively work backward to incorporate the strategies and activities that will appropriately scaffold your students toward meeting both sets of goals. You will also want to plan how to assess students of various proficiency levels. Figure 5.2 shows an example of a unit planning template that may help you stay focused as you work through the different levels of activity and assessment planning.

In order to help you effectively plan your instruction and assessment to match the proficiency levels of your students, Table 5.3 shows some examples of types of oral language (listening and speaking) output (or performance indicators) you might request of your students at each proficiency level.

Setting Appropriate Language Targets: Oral Language Capabilities and Components to Develop by Level

In Chapter 4 we introduced three levels of proficiency to guide your work with students. Table 5.4 shows the oral language characteristics of beginner-, intermediate-, and advanced-level students, and the primary language components to develop at each stage.

Helpful Classroom Strategies for Promoting Oral Language

To promote language use, it is necessary to provide sufficient scaffolds to aid students in communicating orally. When you select scaffolds, choose scaffolds students can apply to different situations and further adapt for their own use (Ver-

ELL UNIT PLANNING DOCUMENT

CENTRAL QUESTION(S)/THEMES

TEXTS(S) AND RESOURCES

CONTENT GOALS
(Content-specific knowledge and skills)

LANGUAGE GOALS
(Content-specific vocabulary words and sentence structures needed to communicate content)

STANDARDS
(School, District, State, or National Standards)

PERFORMANCE INDICATORS
(What students will do to participate in English)

FORMATIVE AND SUMMATIVE ASSESSMENT

DEPARTMENT/COURSE _____

CIRCLE ONE: FALL   WINTER   SPRING

FIGURE 5.2   ELL unit planning template. *Source:* Hope High School, Providence, RI *Unit Mapping Template*, 2007, adapted from Wiggins and Tighe, 2005.

TABLE 5.3   Oral Language Performance Indicators by Proficiency Level

Language Domain	Beginner	Intermediate	Advanced
Listening	Follow instructions from peers or teachers related to a sequence of events.	Compare and contrast using visuals in English language arts (ELA) or around content area topics (WWII propaganda, scientific or mathematic processes).	Analyze meaning and use of new vocabulary and idioms related to focus-topic texts read aloud.
Speaking	Ask and answer *wh-* or either/or questions using pictures, or label diagrams using learned vocabulary.	Verbally describe a sequence of events (using visual support)... *ELA:* ... from a narrative text using present tense. *Social studies:* ... from a history text using learned vocabulary and past tense.	Formulate and assert an opinion on a topic of choice and argue persuasively, using persuasive language and appropriate volume, tone, and word choice.

Source: Adapted from WIDA's English Language Proficiency (ELP) Standards (World-Class Instructional Design and Assessment, 2007).

plaetse & Migliacci, 2008). This section will focus on written and visual scaffolds that support oral language production and will show how to provide these in the different content areas. It will also discuss ways of helping students learn turn taking and other rules for participating in American classrooms.

Acquiring Discussion Rules

To help students have positive experiences speaking English in U.S. classrooms, instruct them about common discussion expectations. Scaffolding for discussion rules will serve as a foundation for all forms of oral language interactions the students may have, both in and out of the classroom. Forms of discussion rules include taking turns, being aware of one's register (volume, tone, etc), staying on topic, and responding intelligently.

One way to scaffold turn taking is by first introducing the term. The concept "taking turns" is an idiomatic expression that cannot be understood by simply understanding the words "taking" and "turns." Therefore, students need to be taught what "taking turns" actually means before you can use the term as an instructive tool in the classroom. The idea of taking turns can be modeled and scaffolded first through the use of nonverbal actions. For example, you could demonstrate what it looks like when students take turns walking into a classroom or ordering lunch at the lunch line. Similarly, it is important to demonstrate what taking turns does *not* look like in order for students to have a basis for comparison. In providing models and examples, it is crucial to use examples that all students will be familiar with; therefore, school routines work well for demonstrating appropriate turn taking at school.

Another important aspect of discussion rules is being aware of one's *register*, in terms of one's volume, tone, and level of formality. Again, instruct the students first as to what the word "register" means in the context of discussion. Many students may be familiar with the word "register" in terms of enrolling in a school and choosing one's classes or in the phrase "cash register." This is a good opportu-

TABLE 5.4 Beginner-, Intermediate-, and Advanced-Level Oral Language Characteristics and Components to Develop

	Oral Language Characteristics and Abilities	Oral Language Components to Develop
Beginner listening	Ability to understand simple, one-step teacher commands or instructions related to classroom routines and instruction, including • Pointing to, locating, identifying, or selecting requested information • Drawing, naming, labeling, or listing to demonstrate understanding Ability to understand peers' simple answers related to teacher prompts and questions	Ability to understand simple, two-step commands related to instruction, including • Matching, sorting, comparing/contrasting, or classifying in order to demonstrate understanding Ability to understand peers' questions and answers related to classroom discourse
Beginner speaking	Ability to give one-word or simple sentence responses to teacher questions (related to classroom routines and instruction) Ability to ask simple questions	Ability to use increasingly complex responses to teacher or peer questions (related to classroom routines and instruction) Ability to produce simple oral descriptions Ability to ask increasingly complex questions
Intermediate listening	Ability to understand simple, two-step commands related to instruction, including • Matching, sorting, comparing/contrasting, or classifying in order to demonstrate understanding Ability to understand peers' questions and answers related to teacher or peer questions	Ability to understand complex, multilevel commands related to instruction, including • Drawing conclusions, making connections, defending and justifying, and researching Ability to understand oral discourse from off-air media sources (TV, movies, radio)
Intermediate speaking	Ability to give simple, though increasingly complex, sentence responses to teacher or peer questions related to classroom routines and instruction Ability to produce simple oral descriptions Ability to give brief oral summaries of short texts Ability to give oral support to oral claims or arguments Ability to orally interpret, or rephrase instructional texts	Ability to share opinions and participate in classroom discussion Ability to orally justify and defend one's views on concrete instructional topics Ability to describe using descriptive language Ability to ask increasingly complex questions grounded in instructional focus Ability to make simple connections between instructional content and text, self, world Ability to retell and summarize simple informative and narrative texts
Advanced listening	Ability to understand complex, multilevel commands related to instruction, including: • Drawing conclusions, making connections, defending and justifying, and researching Ability to understand main ideas and concepts of oral discourse from media sources (TV, movies, radio, Internet downloads, Web-based lectures)	Continue to work on the ability to understand complex, multilevel commands related to instruction, including • Drawing conclusions, making connections, defending and justifying, and researching Ability to understand the majority of oral discourse from outside sources (TV, movies, radio, Internet downloads, Web-based lectures)

	Oral Language Characteristics and Abilities	Oral Language Components to Develop
Advanced speaking	Ability to share opinions and participate in classroom discussion	Ability to share opinions and participate in classroom discussion and debate
	Ability to orally justify and defend one's views on concrete instructional topics	Ability to orally justify and defend one's views on abstract topics and issues
	Ability to describe using a range of descriptive language	Ability to describe using rich descriptive language, imagery, and figurative language
	Ability to ask increasingly complex questions grounded in a topic of instructional focus	Ability to ask increasingly complex questions, including abstract, multilevel questions
	Ability to give oral support to oral claims or arguments	Ability to articulate connections between instructional content and text, self, world
	Ability to make simple connections between instructional content and text, self, world	Ability to orally interpret, or rephrase instructional texts
	Ability to retell and summarize informative and narrative texts	Ability to give oral summaries of short or medium-length instructional or narrative text
		Ability to strongly articulate deep connections between instructional content and text, self, world

nity to introduce or further discuss the idea of multiple-meaning words and the importance of using context to understand word meanings. Halliday and Hasan (1985) use the terms *mode* (the means of communication, i.e., written, spoken, read, listened to, or viewed), *field* (the subject matter discussed), and *tenor* (the relationship between the communicator and receiver) to talk about the different situations that influence how people use language (Rothenberg & Fisher, 2007). As students gain a sense of their new language, they most quickly become at ease using oral language to speak (mode) with their friends (tenor) about personal topics (field), but struggle more with writing (mode) for academic purposes (field) for a teacher or unknown audience (tenor). There are five language registers that have been identified, defined by when and how each is used. They are *fixed/frozen, formal, consultative, casual,* and *intimate* (Montano-Harmon, 1999). Again, students experience the most ease in acquiring intimate and casual language registers, the registers used with close family and friends, and more difficulty acquiring consultative, formal, and fixed/frozen. Teaching students the meaning of each language register, as well as the when, how, why, and with whom of using each register, will assist them in learning to distinguish between appropriate and inappropriate ways of communicating in different situations. Once you explain the meaning of register in terms of discussion, you can further demonstrate by modeling different volumes, tones, and body language in different imagined situations, and have students evaluate appropriate and inappropriate registers for each situation. Being aware of one's register is a concept that most students are aware of when it is brought to their attention, and so by teaching them the terminology, as well as teaching that this concept is important to the way in which students develop and use oral language, students become empowered to monitor and adjust their own register appropriately in various communicative situations.

Learning how to stay on topic during a discussion is another important skill for students to learn and master. It is important to clarify for the students that there is a time for making connections and reflecting on a topic, discussion, or text, but that during a discussion about a particular idea or topic, it is important to stay focused and work through the topic or idea at hand. Limiting, or focusing, student discussion is a difficult task for many teachers, especially teachers of ELLs because as teachers, we do not want to silence a student's voice and, at the same time we want our ELLs to have as many opportunities as possible to practice their emerging oral language skills. So how does one keep a discussion focused and flowing, while at the same time not silencing students' voices and allowing them to have ample opportunities to speak in class? We believe the answer lies in how a teacher sets up the class and, more importantly, the specific discussion. By communicating the different facets and goals of each unit, class period, and activity to students, students will know what to expect and how to direct their thinking. Simply explaining to students that they are to try and stay on topic and respond to the topic at hand will help them do just that, and it will also prepare them if you must interject in order to focus the discussion. You may also allow for more open discussion later on in the class period or unit to allow students the opportunity to speak more freely about a particular topic or issue.

Notions of what is "on or off topic" have cultural underpinnings (Verplaetse & Migliacci, 2008). What is considered "on topic" in one cultural group (providing contextual information, not just factual information) is considered "off topic" in another culture. It is important to tell students you will give them feedback regarding what is on or off topic in a discussion from an American perspective to

---

Vignette: Preston and Staying on Topic

During a unit on immigration, as students were discussing reasons why people immigrate to the United States, I asked students to share their personal experiences. Preston, always eager to contribute to discussions, began by telling why he and his family immigrated to the United States from Liberia, then diverged by talking about what he missed about Liberia. Though Preston's comments about what he missed were relevant in terms of the broad topic of immigration, they were off the current topic of discussion. The specific topic of what immigrants miss most about their home countries was going to be the discussion topic for a future class. Therefore, in order to focus the discussion back on reasons for immigrating, but not silence Preston's or any other student's voice, I reinforced Preston's comments about the reasons he gave for why his family came to the United States, but then reminded him and the rest of the class that discussion of one's home country would be the topic for another class. I further suggested that students should be thinking about or even making notes about such opinions so that they are prepared to share in that future discussion. In this way, I was able to make a point of refocusing the class, communicate the importance of staying on topic, and at the same time validate Preston's contribution to the discussion, and encourage reflection and future participation by all students.

Erin Leininger

help them navigate their new culture's expectations about what to include and what to leave out.

Acquiring Discussion Tools: Scripts and Idea-Linking Words

Once students understand turn taking, appropriate register, and how to stay on topic, it is crucial for teachers to provide students with the tools they need to actually participate in a discussion. Depending on the oral language ability of the student, teachers can provide sets of sentence starters or scripts and transition words for students to use at different points in the discussion to link one idea to another. For example, students may want to agree or disagree with something another student says, ask a question, share an idea, or give feedback. Tables 5.5 and 5.6 provide lists of sentence starters or scripts and transition or idea-linking words to share with students, together with the communicative function, so that students can determine when to use such scaffolds in a discussion.

Many of these sentence starters and transition words contain language that many beginner- and some intermediate-level students may not be familiar with. Therefore, it is important not only to review each sentence starter with the students, but also to go over the different functions they serve in a discussion (and also in writing). Most importantly, always model the use of such scaffolds in everyday classroom activities and lessons showing students how to use these language-building helpers. When teachers model the use of the sentence starters and transi-

TABLE 5.5 Discussion Tools: Sentence Starters and Scripts

When to Use in a Discussion	Sentence Starter or Script
To better understand	One point that was not clear to me was . . . Are you saying that . . . Can you please clarify?
To share an idea	Another idea is to . . . What if we tried . . . I have an idea, we could try . . .
To disagree	I see your point, but what about . . . I'm still not convinced that . . . Another way of looking at it is . . .
To challenge	How did you reach your conclusion? What makes you think that? How does it explain . . .
To look for feedback	What would you do to improve this? Does this make sense? How could my idea be improved?
To provide positive feedback	One strength of your argument is... Your idea is good because . . .
To provide constructive feedback	The argument would be stronger if . . . Another way to do it would be . . . What if you said it like this . . .

(Based on Kinsella, 1999)

TABLE 5.6   Discussion Tools: Transition (Idea-Linking) Words

Communicative Function	Transition Words
Illustration	Thus, for example, for instance, namely, to illustrate, in other words, in particular, specifically, such as
Contrast	On the contrary, contrarily, notwithstanding, but, however, nevertheless, in spite of, in contrast, yet, on one hand, on the other hand, rather, or, nor, conversely, at the same time, while this may be true
Addition	And, in addition to, furthermore, moreover, besides, too, also, both/and, another, equally important, first, second, etc., again, further, last, finally, not only/but also, as well as, in the second place, next, likewise, similarly, in fact, as a result, consequently, in the same way, for example, for instance, however, thus, therefore, otherwise
Time	After, afterward, before, then, once, next, last, at last, at length, first, second, etc., at first, formerly, rarely, usually, another, finally, soon, meanwhile, at the same time, for a minute, hour, day, etc., during the morning, day, week, etc., most important, later, ordinarily, to begin with, afterward, generally, in order to, subsequently, previously, in the meantime, immediately, eventually, concurrently, simultaneously
Space	At the left, at the right, in the center, on the side, along the edge, on top, below, beneath, under, around, above, over, straight ahead, at the top, at the bottom, surrounding, opposite, at the rear, at the front, in front of, beside, behind, next to, nearby, in the distance, beyond, in the forefront, in the foreground, within sight, out of sight, across, under, nearer, adjacent, in the background
Concession	Although, at any rate, at least, still, though, even though, granted that, while it may be true, in spite of, of course
Similarity or comparison	Similarly, likewise, in like fashion, in like manner, analogous to
Emphasis	Above all, indeed, truly, of course, certainly, surely, in fact, really, in truth, again, besides, also, furthermore, in addition
Details	Specifically, especially, in particular, to explain, to list, to enumerate, in detail, namely, including
Examples	For example, for instance, to illustrate, thus, in other words, as an illustration, in particular
Consequence or result	So that, with the result that, thus, consequently, hence, accordingly, for this reason, therefore, so, because, since, due to, as a result, in other words, then
Summary	Therefore, finally, consequently, thus, in short, in conclusion, in brief, as a result, accordingly
Suggestion	For this purpose, to this end, with this in mind, with this purpose in mind, therefore

With permission: Taraba, J. (2004). Transitional words and phrases. University of Richmond writer's web. Richmond: the Writing Center, Joe Essid, Director.

tion words, and explicitly draw students' attention to their use and communicative function, students will naturally become more familiar, comfortable, and likely to experiment with incorporating the new words and phrases into their lexicon.

Practicing Discussion Skills

Once students are prepared with the essential words and phrases they can use in any discussion, it is crucial to provide students with well-selected discussion topics for practicing their discussion skills. The best way to go about choosing and presenting topics to students is by asking for student input. Finding out early

> **Vignette: Carina and Sentence Starters**
>
> Carina, a young student from the Dominican Republic, was always apprehensive about participating in classroom discussions. Oftentimes she would come up to me later and share an idea or point relevant to the discussion, but when I would ask her why she had not spoken up in class, she would either dismiss the question with an "I don't know" or admit that she did not want to speak in from of the class. Even though I tried to get her to participate by encouraging her, or even calling on her sometimes, she remained quiet during class discussions.
>
> All that changed once I began introducing and modeling various discussion-specific sentence starters and transition words in class. Having a model to follow, a scaffold to support her, allowed Carina to feel more comfortable adding to the classroom conversation. The sentence starters and transition words both gave Carina an "in" to share her ideas and taught her a new way of thinking about and classifying the various comments she could make. For example, instead of telling a classmate, "I think you're wrong," Carina learned she could say, "I see your point, but what about . . . ," and that this phrase would help keep the conversation going rather than hurt anyone's feelings. The change did not happen overnight, but it became obvious that Carina enjoyed using these new phrases and sought out situations to use them. Every time students tried to use the new scaffolds, I would acknowledge their efforts; this encouragement motivated other students to use the phrases more frequently as well, and they gradually became part of the everyday classroom language.
>
> Erin Leininger

about what students are interested in will certainly benefit you in the long term. One way to do so is by conducting a simple survey in which you solicit this type of information. Keep in mind the various English levels of your students as you create questionnaires or inventories to gather information from them. For more beginner-level students, yes/no questions or using images and physical movement to express or ask about ideas are appropriate forms of inquiry, while fill-in-the-blank or open-ended questions are more suited for intermediate- and advanced-level students.

Some topics that, in general, work well as discussion topics for adolescent ELLs are those that deal with common experiences such as immigration, family, friends, personal preferences, school experiences, sports, work experiences, and childhood memories.

Getting students to engage in discussion about personal views and experiences is important and useful. By talking about what is personally relevant and important, students build confidence and fluency in both English language and discussion skills. But teaching students to engage in academic discussion, unarguably a more challenging task, is crucial for their academic development and success, so you will want to provide practice with a mixture of both types of discussions.

Acquiring Text-Based Discussion Skills

One of the most useful and concrete skills of academic discussion to teach students is text-based discussion. This skill is one that will benefit students across the content areas, and can be taught to ELLs of all levels. The purpose of text-based discussion is to increase students' understanding of a text, while not guiding them toward one particular understanding or interpretation. No matter what type of text you are working with, the main idea of text-based discussion revolves around students selecting a portion of the text that they feel is the most "important," "significant," "meaningful," "powerful," or other such adjective to guide students in their search for what they feel is a fitting piece of text.

Once students select their phrase, sentence, paragraph, or other excerpt, they then develop, orally or in a written format, their ideas about why they chose their specific excerpt and prepare to share their thoughts with the group. Typically, this type of activity works best with smaller groups because in this way students can share their thoughts and classmates can respond or ask questions. It is on these occasions that true text-based discussion really takes place: as students share their views about specific passages and other students engage in further discussion of the excerpt, thus contributing to the collective increase in understanding of the text.

Here are some strategies to teach your students about, and encourage them to adopt, as you facilitate text-based discussion:

- Listen actively
- Build on or add to what others say
- Patiently take turns while allowing conversation to flow
- Talk to and look at *each other* rather than through or at the teacher
- Ask questions to clarify if confused
- Monitor speaking time to allow multiple voices
- Continue to refer to the text, using page, paragraph, and line numbers whenever possible

Acquiring Questioning Skills

Another very important discussion and oral language skill is that of questioning. Inherent in questioning is a linguistic skill of how to form a question, as well as the more important skill of questioning as a part of critical thinking. For students at the more beginner levels, it is important to provide a strong foundation in forming and framing questions. One way to do so is by introducing students to the commonly used question format of "question word + verb + subject + verb" (Q + V + S + V, for example, "What did the protagonist say?"). This format works well for most simple questions that begin with one of the six question words—who, what, when, where, why, and how. For example, "Why do you think . . . ?" This format can also be modified for questions that start with a verb by simply removing the question word from the format, so that the pattern is "verb + subject + verb" (V + S + V). (V + S + V, for example, "Do you think. . . ?" or "Are you saying that . . . ?") Teaching students these formats and displaying visual models around the classroom will help students internalize the patterns and rhythms of basic questions, a process that will help them build the capacity to properly form longer, more complex questions as their language skills improve.

The underlying skill involved in questioning is that of critical thinking. Teaching students to ask questions and think critically is no easy task. In fact, some may argue that critical thinking cannot be taught (Willingham, 2007). Students *can* be taught, however, that they should be thinking about questions they can ask of a teacher, classmate, or text whenever they receive new information. All students can be taught to ask questions about information they doubt or challenge as they read texts or listen to peers and teachers. As they practice and refine this task of asking questions, questioning becomes more of a habit, and this habit of questioning is the basis of critical thinking.

It is often the case that ELLs are highly critical thinkers but unable to express the complexity and sophistication of their thoughts because of their limited English skills. In this case, teachers can ask either/or questions to help students clarify and express their ideas, and provide other such scaffolds for learners. For example, to help a student clarify his or her critical thinking, a teacher may ask, "Are you saying that . . . ?" or "Are you saying that you think . . . ?" In this way, students can say whether or not something the teacher has said is concurrent with their thinking, or take parts of what the teacher has said to try and express for themselves what they are actually thinking.

Some students, however, may have cultural barriers to asking questions of those in authority, that is, teachers. Some learners may have cultural training and life experience that works against stating their point of view or forming opinions that differ from mainstream views. Such cultural conditioning may serve as a challenge that teachers must overcome in order to help students participate in the ways that secondary classrooms expect and demand of students (Verplaetse & Migliacci, 2008). So teachers will want to appreciate this fact as well and give students time to adjust to the participation expectations in American classrooms.

Using Visual Scaffolds

We have talked a lot about different ways to provide students with various *verbal* scaffolds to facilitate their participation in discussion, such as sentence starters and transition words on posters, worksheets, word cards or other written means. Yet another way to provide students with oral language scaffolds is by providing *visual* scaffolds in the form of pictures, realia, maps, graphs, diagrams, and graphic organizers. Such scaffolds provide comprehensible input, make complex ideas more accessible to students, and make language more memorable as students learn to connect ideas and language to images.

Visual scaffolds greatly assist students of all levels because students are not only learning the new language, but also learning how to express and organize thoughts and ideas. Use of pictures and words to express meanings also supports the expression and organization of ideas, allowing students to feel confident about their experimentation with language and thus progress in their language learning and acquisition (Echevarría et al., 2008).

Giving Students Feedback

Perhaps some of the most difficult decisions a teacher of English language learners must make are those regarding how, when, and how often to provide students with oral language feedback (Rothenberg & Fisher, 2007). To a certain degree, the type and amount of oral language feedback each student should receive depends on the student, and it may vary considerably among students independent of their proficiency level (e.g., degree of security, self-confidence, personality, etc.). However, it is fairly easy to get an idea of how much and what type of feedback each student is comfortable with, either by asking students directly or by observing their behaviors and reactions to the different forms of feedback you the teacher give in class. Once you determine how and when each student prefers to receive feedback, there are a few fast and hard "rules" about the types of feedback to give adolescent ELLs, and guidelines for how to go about giving the feedback.

Feedback on Accent and Pronunciation

The older people get, the more difficult it becomes for them to make new sounds. This difficulty results in accented speech. Changing a person's accent, especially once the language learner has reached adolescence, is extremely difficult. We know that after puberty the likelihood of acquiring nativelike speech production is diminished (Brown, 2006), and it is difficult for many learners of a new language not only to hear the slight nuances of pronunciation of that new language, but likewise to produce such nuances themselves.

As students become more proficient in English, their ability to hear, and sometimes their ability to produce, the subtle nuances of the English language may become more attainable. It is unrealistic, however, to expect most students who are learning a new language as adolescents to adopt the pronunciation of native English speakers. Therefore, correcting a student's pronunciation simply for the sake of trying to help the student *sound* more like a native speaker serves very little purpose, and it may even be counterproductive in that it may only serve to frustrate and silence a student and lower his or her confidence and self-esteem with regard to the new language. For this reason, the general rule of thumb to follow when it comes to pronunciation correction is that such feedback should only be given if a student's pronunciation inhibits others' comprehension of what the speaker says (Rothenberg & Fisher, 2007). The reason for this is that the main goal of language is to communicate needs and ideas; so if students are being understood, then they are communicating their message effectively. Simply speaking, no feedback is required if you understand; if you are confused, feedback is needed.

Feedback on Vocabulary Usage and Grammar

Determining when and how to give your ELLs feedback about grammatical mistakes and word choice is tricky, but in a different sense than giving feedback regarding pronunciation. Giving ELLs feedback regarding word choice is essential in order for them to learn the patterns and idiosyncrasies of English, and so we want to help them correct the errors they make as they experiment with the language. However, the trick is to not overwhelm or intimidate your learners by bombarding them with feedback and corrections for every mistake they make. Keep in mind that they are in the midst of the intense process of learning another language and, as a result, will make many, many mistakes. But simply correcting every mistake a student makes becomes impossible: impossible both for you as the teacher—a seemingly endless and incredibly time-consuming process—and impossible for the student to make use of in any lasting way. Attempting to correct every mistake will most likely also frustrate and discourage students from attempting to communicate at all, if the only response they get is correction and critique. Therefore, just as in determining when and how to provide pronunciation corrections, there are a few rules about how to go about giving students feedback on errors of vocabulary usage and grammar.

One thing to think about when giving grammatical feedback is to try to limit your feedback and corrections to those that pertain to the current lessons or foci in the class. For example, if you are teaching about the past tense, it is a good idea to limit your written and oral feedback to those mistakes that deal only with the past tense. Students will be primed to receive feedback on their use of the past tense if the current topic of instruction is past-tense structures and usage. The context for such correction will be fresh in their minds, thus increasing the likelihood that they will effectively process and internalize the correctional feedback. This system of providing students with feedback serves to benefit both the teacher and the student, as the teacher can focus his or her attention on one type of correction, and the student will know what kinds of feedback to expect from the teacher and therefore be able to focus attention and learning on one or two specific language elements. This type of *focused* correction has the most long-lasting effect on students' language acquisition (Lyster, 2004).

Something to keep in mind in this area is words with multiple meanings, as this topic straddles the line between vocabulary usage and grammar learning (nouns versus verbs, use of phrasal verbs). There are so many multiple-meaning words in the English language that students are bound to be confused. Therefore, it is extremely important to teach students about the concept of multiple-meaning words, and then teach and expose them to a range of examples, especially across the content areas. Inherent in this practice is the teaching of basic parts of speech, so that students can better understand how words are used and how their meanings change depending on the part of speech. For example, one of us recently taught students the multiple-meaning word "shift." We talked about how the word exists as both a verb and a noun, and has multiple meanings within both of those parts of speech—for example: "Let's *shift* topics from music to politics" (verb, meaning "to change"); "It's important to remember to *shift* gears when you're learning to drive" (verb, meaning "to change" specifically in reference to cars); "As I was driving, the gear *shift* stuck, and made a loud noise" (noun, meaning "transmission part"); and "We experienced a *shift* in the weather when the temperature dropped from a mild 60 degrees to a chilly 40 degrees overnight" (noun, meaning "a change").

This discussion of multiple-meaning words can also easily be expanded upon when working with other teachers of ELLs across the content areas. When a teacher works on multiple-meaning words with other content teachers, students' language acquisition and retention skills will become amazingly stronger. For example, learning that the word "revolution" can be applied to both history (in terms of war and rebellion) and science (in terms of movement of an object), or that the word "axis" can be used in social studies ("axis of evil") and math (points on the *x*-axis and *y*-axis of a graph), allows students to become more aware of how language is used in different contexts and empowers them in their own personal expression.

One of the best ways that we have found to effectively teach students multiple-meaning words is by reducing the number of new vocabulary words we assign students within a certain time period in order to focus more intently upon, and explore more deeply, fewer words with multiple meanings. First, we gloss the texts we use in class, looking specifically for multiple-meaning words. Then, we create handouts for students that include the word, the parts of speech, and the various meanings we want to address in the lesson, and depending on the proficiency level of the students, we may include a separate example sentence for each meaning of the word. While this seems like a lot of information all at once about each word, it helps give students a bigger, more complete picture of words, and as a result they can attain a greater understanding of words and English and how to use new words in various contexts. (See also Graves, 2006, for ideas on vocabulary development for ELLs.)

Of course, the next step is providing students with multiple opportunities to practice the language they are learning and improve their language based on the feedback you provide. To facilitate the practice of multiple-meaning words, have students write sentences for each of the meanings as a class or in small groups or provide teacher-created original sentences with the focus word(s) missing for students to fill in the blank. You can also experiment with having students act out word meanings, visually illustrate their understanding of new vocabulary, or play various word games. Getting students to think about, use, and understand new words in a variety of ways will help them acquire a deeper, more lasting knowledge of the word.

Classroom Strategies for Vocabulary Learning

- *Shades of meaning:* In addition to teaching students words with multiple meanings, it is equally important to talk about *shades of meaning* among semantically related words, and which words are appropriate to different circumstances (Fisher, Brozo, Frey, & Ivey, 2007). There are various ways of presenting shades of meaning to students. Shades of meaning can be presented by talking about words in terms of scales, intensity, descriptive adverbs (such as *how* something is done), positive versus negative connotations, and slang versus Standard English.

  One of the easiest, but not very common, ways for students to grasp shades of meaning is with the use of a scale. Scales give a clear image and gradation of how words relate to one another. Take, for example, the following scale to describe temperature: boiling–hot–warm–lukewarm–cool–cold–freezing. Not only do students learn new vocabulary, they acquire a solid understanding of how the new words relate to the other new words, thus strengthening their understanding of all the words on the scale. A similar strategy to using scales to teach shades of meaning is talking about the intensity of synonymous words. For example, "throw" is more intense than "toss," just as "scream" is more intense than "yell."

  Another way to teach differences in meaning is by using adverbs to describe how the action of similar verbs happens. For example, to teach a related group of words such as "stalk, stroll, stumble, skip, and stomp," the teacher would instruct students about how each verb means a different form, or way, of walking. Teaching students a group of new vocabulary words that are semantically related makes it easier for students to learn and understand the words individually and collectively.

  Distinguishing between positive and negative nuances of meaning is a way of both building students' vocabulary and helping them strengthen their sociolinguistic competence, something ELLs develop over time. For example, knowing the difference between the adjectives "skinny" and "thin" or between the words "fat" and "overweight" helps students learn to be more selective and intentional in their language usage.

- *Slang versus formal vocabulary:* Another strategy for teaching about word meanings is by discussing private, or group-specific, language versus public English. English language learners will naturally be exposed to a lot of slang and street talk, either indirectly at school or in their neighborhoods, or directly though new native English-speaking friends. It is important to talk to students about what slang is, and stress when, where, and with whom it is acceptable to use slang, especially profanity. In fact, it is not uncommon for students to hear slang and profanity so often that they may not realize that such words have an inappropriate or profane connotation and should not be used in mixed company or in more formal social situations.

    Certainly we want to help our students navigate the various settings in which they need to participate and for which they will need specific vocabulary. Sometimes we need to let the community into the classroom so that we can help learners sort out how things are said in different contexts.

Conclusion

In this chapter you have seen that one of the primary challenges in getting students to speak in the classroom, to read then participate in a text-based discussion, or to offer their ideas pertaining to content they are learning is to make sure they understand what is being said to and asked of them. In order for students to be able to use their developing oral language skills in the classroom, they need our support and assistance. In this chapter you learned some key targets for your work and also some helpful strategies you can use in your classroom. The checklist that follows is designed to remind you of some of the key things you will want to be sure to do to promote oral language use and development.

Checklist

Twelve Ways to Support Students in Discussions in Your Classroom

- ☐ I provide clear expectations of classroom rules and routines to ensure that students feel confident in how to engage and participate in classroom activities involving oral language.

- ☐ I provide lots of opportunities to practice discussion skills in my classroom in a variety of grouping structures: small group, partners, and whole class.

- ☐ I start discussions in small groups and give students safe ways to practice before doing whole class discussions.

- ☐ I vary the pair and group arrangements so that students feel comfortable talking to everyone in the room.

- ☐ I provide needed background information so students can use their developing oral language skills most effectively in the classroom.

- ☐ I offer verbal scaffolds to students in the form of word banks, helpful phrases, and chances to get ideas out through the native language.

- ☐ I provide students with nonverbal scaffolding that supports oral language, such as visuals, graphic organizers, and sentence starters.

- ☐ I introduce needed vocabulary and phrases ahead of class discussions so that students have the language they need to join in.

- ☐ I present and review language forms students will need, and teach "scripts" and transitional words, so they can join in class discussions.

- ☐ I encourage students to share their ideas and give them the assistance they need to get their ideas into the discussion (expanding their ideas, clarifying their meanings, asking if I captured their meaning correctly).

- ☐ I choose topics students can relate to for practicing discussion skills in my class and try to give students real-world practice.

- ☐ I monitor students as they work and give supportive and focused feedback to advance learners' oral language as much as possible.

CHAPTER 6

Reading in a Second Language

Jean, Haiti, with Ms. Leininger

Secondary teachers are well aware of how important it is for students to be competent and critical readers. The ability to read well may be the most important and empowering tool teachers give their students. However, some teachers may not feel fully equipped to serve their English language learners (ELLs), though they desperately want to. The purpose of this chapter is to help you do just that: empower your ELLs by advancing their reading skills in English.

Guiding Questions

- What are the special challenges English language learners face when reading secondary texts?
- What criteria can teachers use to select books that secondary English language learners want to read?
- What reading abilities do English language learners have at the different levels of language acquisition, and what skills should they be working toward?
- What strategies are most effective in promoting reading development for English language learners?
- What strategies do good readers use, including second-language readers?
- Why do English language learners and other secondary students need to read every day?
- How can you use assessments to determine ELL students' literacy abilities in order to inform and guide your instruction, as well as for assessing students' reading comprehension?

Acquiring academic English was one of the major challenges identified in Chapter 1. Short and Fitzsimmons (2007, p. 22) have documented the research literature that shows a strong relationship between literacy level and academic achievement—a relationship that grows stronger as grade levels rise. Because our goal is for ELLs to successfully graduate from secondary schools, it is imperative that we teach them how to be proficient readers of academic English. In order to teach reading effectively to ELLs, we first need to understand some of the unique barriers that can stand in their way.

Unique Challenges for ELL Readers

There are a number of challenges ELLs face in achieving reading proficiency in a new language, namely,

- Acquiring the *background knowledge* necessary to understand texts in a new language and school context
- Acquiring high-frequency words and content-specific *vocabulary*
- Acquiring the *patterns and phrasing* of English to read fluently with comprehension

Background Knowledge

Adolescent ELLs have a steep learning curve ahead of them in order to acquire the background knowledge they need to understand the academic texts they encounter in school. Texts at the middle and high school levels assume a certain degree of U.S.-centric cultural capital on the part of the reader, the great majority of which ELLs do not have, since they have not been educated in the United States. Students' lack of U.S.-centric cultural background knowledge can seriously impede text comprehension, even if the text is not linguistically challenging. Indeed, a student new to the country may be able to understand every word of a text, yet be unable to grasp its meaning or significance because of this factor alone. For this reason, effective teachers of ELLs "frontload," or provide students essential background information at the beginning of a lesson or unit, about topics that are potentially unfamiliar to their students. Alternatively, to avoid the problem of lack of background knowledge, teachers can seek to select texts with concepts and themes familiar to the students as they advance students' abilities to develop important reading skills and strategies. More will be said about selecting texts for ELLs in this chapter.

The Challenge of Unknown Words

One of the greatest challenges for ELLs is acquiring all the vocabulary that their English-dominant peers have already mastered. Certainly, we know that vocabulary strongly influences the readability of text (Chall & Dale, 1995). Indeed, learning English vocabulary is one of the most crucial tasks for ELLs, because it is well documented that they have a substantially smaller vocabulary than their agemates (Graves, 2006; Nation, 2001). When every third word is an unknown word, comprehension is seriously compromised, and yet this is the situation for many of our secondary ELLs when they attempt to read age-appropriate text.

The Challenge of Unknown Patterns and Phrasing

As ELLs read, they also encounter patterns in English that are unfamiliar. The way thoughts are put together in their native languages may not be the way sentences or texts are constructed in English. Such differences can create barriers to understanding, as students seek to understand the relationship among words and phrases they encounter in the academic text they are reading, not because of the content, but rather because of the language constructions they encounter. There are many phrasings in English that are hard to interpret, such as a double negative to express an affirmative: "a not unwelcome outcome" or "there wasn't a day he didn't think of Susana." English language learners may see the words "not" and "didn't" and literally interpret only that part of the phrase, thus causing misunderstanding of the text. There are other English constructions that take time to learn as well, such as phrasal verbs. They may not understand the differences in meaning between *run into, run over, run through, run by,* and *run around.* To ensure their comprehension, stay alert for forms of English in text that can trip learners up, and introduce these forms to students in advance of their reading. Just a bit of focused instruction on these forms, or previewing and highlighting these forms in the text, can go a long way to ensuring more fluent reading and deeper comprehension.

As we work to address these common challenges faced by our learners when reading texts in English, we want to be guided by defensible principles of instruction, such as the following:

Principles of Effective Reading Instruction for ELLs

- Select books students can read, and want to read, and as needed, provide students with scaffolds such as glossed, adapted, shortened, or alternative texts that will support and help build reading comprehension skills.
- Actively teach vocabulary to ensure comprehension.
- Teach text structures and signal words to enhance comprehension.
- Teach and practice the strategies good readers use.
- Provide daily experience with authentic and real-world texts (newspapers, job applications) to ensure that students are exposed to a variety of text structures and genres, as well as to build fluency.
- Conduct formative and summative assessments to inform and guide instruction and assess reading comprehension.

Selecting Books Secondary ELLs Want to Read: Looking at Content and Proficiency Criteria

In order to provide effective reading instruction, a precondition is that we need to get students reading both in and outside of class. In the classroom, if we are to get students actively reading literature in a new language, we must find texts they can read.

Looking for Literature ELLs Want to Read

The challenge of finding literature that is relevant to all students in your class is a difficult one, but one that must take high priority, as students are not going to be engaged in reading literature that they find uninteresting or to which they are unable to relate. Choosing texts with appropriate content is the number one way to get students interested and engaged in reading. This statement is true for both accomplished and struggling readers. So, in choosing appropriate texts, consider the following four factors: (1) age appropriateness and relevancy; (2) cultural appropriateness and relevancy; (3) genre appropriateness and relevancy; and (4) authenticity.

Considering Age Appropriateness and Relevancy

First, it is very important to find texts with age-appropriate themes that fit the reading levels of your students. Most low-level reading texts are elementary in theme and are not interesting to adolescent students. Texts used for adolescent students must contain adolescent themes about which students will be want to read and talk. If students do not feel a connection to the speaker or characters in a text (age-related themes being an obvious connection through which teens feel united), they are less likely to be drawn into a text, or they may become completely turned off by the text. Some examples of effective adolescent themes are growing up, rights of passage, relationships, and puberty.

One resource for finding appropriate texts for adolescent ELLs (high interest/ low reading level) is National Geographic/Hampton-Brown ELD inZone leveled libraries. Books are organized by "zone" (Zone 1, 2, 3, or 4), and each zone corresponds to a Lexile Reading and Grade Level range. Zone 1 refers to grade levels 1–3, Zone 2 to grade levels 4–5, Zone 3 to grade levels 6–7, and Zone 4 to grade levels 8–9. These books can be ordered in sets; they include teacher resource guides; and some come with student journal activities. (See National Geographic School Publishing—http://www.ngsp.com/.) Another resource is to browse your library and those on the Internet for "high-interest/low-reading-level texts." Many schools and libraries in the United States have already done the work of compiling lists of books that work for adolescents of various reading abilities and interests.

Considering Cultural Appropriateness and Relevancy

Second, it is important to use texts with culturally relevant themes. Much of the known cannon of adolescent school-sanctioned literature features American and British characters whose mannerisms, ways of thinking, and backgrounds are unfamiliar to immigrant students. Using texts that feature adolescent immigrants or themes related to the vast array of immigrant experiences, including perspectives, histories, and contributions, is a good way to find relevant themes. Themes that resonate with teens include moving, fitting in, language learning, language loss, and separation of family. (See http://www.literacymatters.org/adlit/selecting/ literature.htm, a Web site of the Education Development Center in Newton, Massachusetts, for recommended adolescent literature lists organized by categories such as theme, gender, student recommendations, and more.) These topics will attract and hold students' attention, and also serve to show immigrant students that they are not alone in their experiences. Pride in bilingualism, biculturalism, and contributions of the various cultural groups your students represent can also be included. Providing students with culturally relevant texts will also have a positive effect on students' reading engagement and participation (Feger, 2006). Such texts not only will be of interest to ELLs, but also will be a source of reassurance and education for them as they negotiate and come to terms with living and learning in a new country and find a comfortable space informed by knowledge of their group's history and contributions within the larger U.S. culture. It is very important for classrooms and school libraries with large numbers of ELLs to have "text sets" (groups of between 5 and 15 texts of various genres and formats related to the same theme) of these themes available for students.

Considering Genre Appropriateness and Relevancy

Third, when evaluating literacy texts for use with ELLs, it is necessary to consider genre. Some genres and writing styles are easier for ELLs to understand than others because of culturally specific content. For example, students may be familiar with myths from their native culture but have a hard time understanding myths from a different culture because of the nature of myths' emphasis on culturally specific values, as well as the connections to specific religious and spiritual beliefs of a culture. Because language teachers want to expose students to a variety of genres, as well as prepare them for the genres they will encounter in mainstream classes and on standardized tests, it is important to explicitly teach the characteristics of the genres you use in class by making the features and patterns explicit. This teaching needs to be done before engaging students in the reading of the new genre.

Certain genres, topics, and narrative structures are more appropriate for students of differing proficiency levels as well as those from different cultures. When considering these factors, consider the language register in which the piece is written and the quality and quantity of metaphorical language in the text. Texts that are easiest to understand present familiar topics, use more informal registers, and contain a small amount of, or no, metaphorical language. Two examples of these types of pieces are short stories and short factual or informational pieces. Texts types that are most difficult to understand, such as myth, poetry, and some informational texts, present foreign topics, use more formal registers, and contain large amounts of metaphorical language.

One way to move students from reading personal to factual to analytic texts is through a thematic organization of the curriculum, where content area concepts are organized around a thematic center. As you progress through the thematic unit, gradually introduce more complex texts that match the theme. This strategy allows students to access more cognitively and linguistically demanding texts through one constant theme. Begin to point out the specific textual characteristics of expository and persuasive texts, and teach students how to identify these characteristics. As students' proficiency improves, continue to introduce a greater quantity of higher-level texts. As noted by Freeman and Freeman: "The best way for ELLs to develop the semantic cueing system is extensive reading of different genres at an appropriate level of difficulty" (D. Freeman & Freeman, 2007, p.129).

Authenticity

Finally, it is important to provide students with authentic texts in their original form, rather than simplify or edit such texts with the intention of making them easier for ELLs to understand. Oftentimes, such editing of a text may prove counterproductive to a students' learning of the new language (Ragan, 2006; Shrum & Glisan, 2005). In fact, using authentic texts has been shown to be beneficial to students, even at very early stages of language development (Gascoigne, 2002).

Authentic texts provide students with the opportunity to develop cross-cultural perspectives, as well as language proficiency (Donato & Brooks, 2004), while inauthentic texts found in many textbooks, "carefully control for length and vocabulary, which may actually prove to be much more difficult for students to comprehend" (Shrum & Glisan, 2005, p. 171). In fact, it has been shown that students will be able to more deeply comprehend and articulate their thoughts regarding a more linguistically complex yet authentic text of high interest than a less linguistically complex yet inauthentic text of low interest (Dristas & Grisenti, 1995). Therefore, it is not always the texts that need to be edited and glossed, but rather the activities and instruction used by the teacher to guide students' comprehension of the text.

It is important to note that some texts can be leveled, such as informational texts, while others, such as literary texts, need to be authentic. Selecting authentic texts that express shared cultural beliefs with which students can identify, as well as those that contain teen-relevant themes and genres to which they are drawn, is essential. Once selected, our task is to guide students through the text to insure a positive impact on their language acquisition and literacy skill development.

Proficiency Criteria for Literature and Content Texts: Looking at Range and Rigor

No matter how well ELLs are grouped in terms of proficiency level, in every class there will always be a wide range of abilities across the four academic domains: listening, speaking, reading, and writing. This observation is true not only of ESL classes, but also of mainstream classes, especially in schools that integrate the ELL population into mainstream classes. The difference in the abilities of the students in any one class presents a particularly difficult challenge for teachers in providing adequate and appropriate instruction for their students. Choosing texts with an appropriate proficiency level for each student is therefore a crucial differentiation strategy, one that is necessary to engage students in meaningful reading activities. In choosing texts for varying proficiency levels, it is important to consider both range and rigor.

Range

No matter what the criteria are for placing students in classes, not all students in any one class will ever be at the same proficiency level at the same time. Therefore, students need access to many age-appropriate texts in a variety of proficiency levels as they progress, improve, and move on to higher levels of reading ability. One way to provide this access is by selecting a variety of books on a similar theme that cover a range of proficiency levels.

Proficiency level and age appropriateness differ in that proficiency level refers to the complexity of the morphology, syntax, and semantics of a text, while age appropriateness refers to the overall theme or topic of the text regardless of the specific language used. The teacher can group students by proficiency level and then assign texts at appropriate levels to each group, and at the same time conduct broader, more theme-based lessons and discussions that tie together the texts for different levels that are being read in the class. As mentioned earlier, of course these materials need to be age appropriate and related through theme or topic.

Rigor

While recognizing the need to provide students with a variety of texts that corresponds with the varying proficiency levels in a class, it is also important to ensure that all students are held to a certain level of rigor, or high academic standards. Providing students with clear expectations, and teaching in a way that demonstrates and upholds such expectations, will encourage and motivate students to do their best and rise to the standards set for them. Establishing rigor means not only holding students accountable for content knowledge, but also developing their critical thinking skills and encouraging them to apply their new knowledge to real-life situations.

Of course, establishing rigor in a mixed-proficiency/mixed-age-level class of ELLs is a significant challenge, but it is nevertheless critical for the success of the students and the class as a whole. By setting a high standard for all your students,

TABLE 6.1   Reading Performance Indicators by Proficiency Level

Language Domain	Beginner	Intermediate	Advanced
Reading	Identify cognates and high-frequency words from texts on focused content.	*ELA:* Compare and contrast characters in a narrative text *Social studies:* Sort information and identify similarities and differences within the branches of government from history text	*ELA*: Evaluate a character's words, thoughts, and actions and make evidence-based predictions *Social studies:* Make connections between various relevant historical texts *Science:* Interpret scientific research data presented in text and tables.

you are challenging them and giving them a goal to work toward. Use Table 6.1 and the communicative functions discussed in Chapter 5 as examples of how to create rigor for students at various proficiency levels.

Once you have selected the texts you will use in your classroom, it is time to begin planning your language instruction to insure maximum reading comprehension by your students. The following sections provide English language arts and content-area teachers strategies for teaching important vocabulary and how to understand text structures that will prepare your students to actively engage with the text.

Making Vocabulary Instruction Routine

Vocabulary instruction for ELLs must be twofold. Students must learn both high-frequency words (words that occur most often in the English language) and lower-frequency, content-specific words (words that are key to understanding the text at hand). To ensure that instruction for both types of vocabulary development takes place, it is helpful to make vocabulary goals for each lesson (as advocated by Echevarría et al., 2008). For each new text presented, identify three to five words from the reading that fit into each category; for example "could" and "would" are high-frequency words, and "settle" (social studies) and "hatch" (science) are content-specific words. Plan activities and instruction to help students understand and master the identified words.

When considering which words to single out for instruction, it is best to choose words that are the most frequently used in a text, not necessarily the words that are the most difficult or unusual. Although it may seem useful to select the most challenging words, if the word appears so infrequently that students are not exposed to it enough to build a firm understanding of its meanings and usages, then that word is best explained in passing, simply as a way to help students get through a passage, rather than singled out as a focus of instruction.

English language learners also need to understand the idea of multiple-meaning words and learn as many examples of the words and their multiple meanings as possible. For example, the word "fault" can mean "blame" in an English language arts context, but mean "a break in the earth's surface" in a science context. Such words may cause confusion for ELLs who have not acquired this deeper, more refined knowledge of English semantics.

Idiomatic and metaphoric language can also be very problematic for ELLs who have difficulty distinguishing between literal and nonliteral meanings (D. Freeman & Freeman, 2007, p. 129), and often take words and expressions at face value. For example, the common American phrase "It's a piece of cake" functions as both an idiom and metaphor, and would most likely leave an ELL "in the dark" in terms of what it means. So vocabulary development, broadly interpreted, also involves exploring the meanings of phrases and idiomatic speech, not just words.

Certainly, in addition to doing vocabulary work in classrooms, we will want to teach adolescent ELLs how to independently build their vocabulary and language skills by consulting resources such as dictionaries and thesauri. Regular and skillful use of these tools helps our ELLs become more independent, successful readers.

Enhancing vocabulary development also means teaching students to look at the context of a word to understand its meaning. Word groupings and how words go together affect students' understanding of words in a specific context. Many times, students will be better able to interpret the meaning of new or ambiguous words if they are familiar with, or are able to understand, the context in which the words are presented.

Teaching High- and Low-Frequency Words

Vocabulary instruction consists of teaching students both high- and low-frequency content-specific words. High-frequency words are those that appear most frequently in the English language (see Table 6.2). In contrast, content-specific low-frequency words are the words that do not show up as often but that communicate specific and key ideas in a text.

The top 25 high-frequency words make up about one-third of all written material, and the top 100 words make up about half of all written material. In addition, each content area features its own set of high-frequency words (e.g., *life* or *cell* in a science text, *sum* or *product* in a math text). To best help ELLs acquire cross-disciplinary and content-specific high-frequency vocabulary, teach them to recognize and comprehend both. You will want to do so as a regular part of instruction, because research has shown that explicit study of high-frequency words increases ELLs' reading comprehension (Coady, Magoto, Hubbard, Graney, & Mokhari, 1993) and helps them perform the activities they are assigned in relation to a text. Because of the importance of teaching new vocabulary to students, the next section will focus on strategies for achieving that purpose.

Teaching Word-Learning Strategies

The following strategies help students acquire new vocabulary. These strategies can be used in combination or separately and can be tailored for students of different proficiency levels.

Word Wheels

Word wheels are a vocabulary acquisition strategy that can be used in any content area as well as in the study of literature. It is useful if teachers across the content areas adopt the same, or similar, tools for helping students learn new words so that

TABLE 6.2 High Frequency Word Lists

Fry, E.B. & J.E. Kress (2006). *The reading teacher's book of lists. Fifth edition.* San Francisco: Jossey Bass.

Produced by Edward B. Fry and Jacqueline Kress, this book includes many helpful lists for the teaching of reading; among them high frequency word lists developed by the first author (Instant words, primary students' most used words and content word lists)

Fry, E. (2000). *1000 instant words. The most common words for teaching reading, writing and spelling.* Westminster, CA: Teacher Created Resources.

Provides a numbered listing of 1000 words in English in groups of 5 words each. These are words that should be recognized instantly by readers and will give students greater fluency when reading.

Hiebert, E.H. (2005). "In pursuit of an effective, efficient vocabulary curriculum for elementary students." In *Teaching and learning vocabulary: Bridging research to practice,* edited by E.H. Hiebert and M. Kamil, 243–63. Mahway, NJ: Lawrence Erlbaum.

Identifies 6 zones of words and stresses the teaching of these zones according to how much they are featured in written texts so that the words, learned as sight words, may have the widest possible application as students read.

Scholastic. (No Date). *Essential Word Lists by Grade.* Article for teachers on the Scholastic website. Available at http://www2.scholastic.com/browse/article.jsp?id=3749477

Provides grade level vocabulary lists and frequently consulted lists like Dolch Word Lists, Academic Word List (Coxhead), Ogden's Basic English and Elfrieda Hiebert's Word Zones.

students know what is expected of them. Word wheels can take a variety of forms, one of which is shown in Figure 6.1. In this word wheel, students look up a definition, find a synonym and/or antonym, create an illustration, and write an example sentence (either their own or an example from the text). Word wheels are easily adapted to focus on whichever aspects of a word a teacher wants to emphasize.

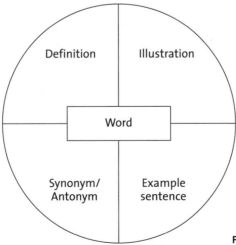

FIGURE 6.1 Word wheel

Note Cards and Flash Cards

Using note cards or flash cards is another way to help students both memorize word meanings and quickly review words independently. Likewise, using note cards will increase familiarity with the written word and its spelling. Two-sided cards provide students with a strategy to learn new vocabulary and quickly recall information. This is especially helpful when students are acquiring new content-specific vocabulary, as in the example of "Holocaust," a key word related to a historical event, or "mitosis," a scientific process, or "simile" and "metaphor," which are literacy devices. The first time you introduce note cards as a strategy, create a small set of cards with students in class and provide them time to practice using the cards with a partner and by themselves. Stress the importance of using note cards as a learning *and* a studying tool by assigning "flash card practice" for homework a few days before a test or other form of assessment.

Active Learning Approaches

A fun way to mix up vocabulary instruction is using movement and actions to teach and reinforce the meanings of new words. Here are several ways to use active learning to solidify vocabulary learning:

- Students create and act out with a partner or small group their own movements to match with new words. (See http://www.tpr-world.com/for a description of how to use Asher's Total Physical Response method, a well-known active learning method for ESL learners, in your classroom.)

- Students use gestures and hand motions along with words to remember the meanings. (For beginners, *high and low* could be demonstrated by holding the hand at a particular position in the air.)

- Students play games such as charades to act out meanings and relationships. Charades can be used to check for comprehension or as a way for students to quiz themselves on their own understanding and recognition of new words.

Synonyms, Antonyms, and Semantic Groupings

Semantic groupings are an effective way to teach many new words simultaneously, as such groupings help students learn multiple ways to express a similar idea (e.g., argue, bicker, fight, quarrel, dispute). Teaching words that are semantically related helps students learn and understand the nuances of English by exposing them to how different words are used to relate, describe, and communicate the same idea in distinct situations. Pairing new vocabulary words with basic synonyms and antonyms can also aid students in their understanding of new, more complex vocabulary.

Vocabulary Journals

Encourage students to become self-motivated, reflective learners by teaching them to take responsibility for their own vocabulary development. Recording new words in a vocabulary journal is one way to encourage and assist students in taking responsibility for building their own word knowledge. Vocabulary journals take many forms, and they can range from a more individualized, informal format to a very specific, formal assignment closely monitored by the teacher. Different forms of vocabulary journals will work well for different students. A more structured vocabulary journal assignment may be better suited for beginner-level students of all grade levels, or students of any proficiency who need more of a formal assignment to stay organized and motivated. And a more informal journal may work well for students who are already engaged in their own learning beyond the work assigned in class and for homework.

Teaching students to keep a vocabulary journal also involves incorporating lessons on how to use reference materials, such as dictionaries and thesauri. Although most students understand the basics of how to use a dictionary, do not assume that students are familiar with the more detailed aspects of dictionary entries. Taking time to explain entry details such as parts of speech, synonyms and antonyms, words in phrases, different forms of the word, and word origin will greatly enhance the quality of students' journals and their overall understanding of the words they investigate. It is also good to have student dictionaries available, as well as dictionaries especially designed for ELLs (e.g., *Longman Study Dictionary of American English,* edited by Cleveland-Marwick, et al, 2006).

Finally, in addition to teaching isolated words, it is important to give students basic instruction on English phrases as needed during reading instruction. Search instructional texts ahead of time with an ELL eye for language features that may create misunderstanding or compromise comprehension, such as idioms ("keep your shirt on" "break a twenty") and phrasal verbs ("break away," "turn into"). Once you find them, explicitly address such features during your instruction. Skimming your instructional texts for language that is potentially confusing for ELLs is not easy; you must attempt to remove all your prior knowledge and expertise in English in order to try and see the text from the perspective of an ELL. The more you practice this exercise, the better at it you will become. You might consider keeping your own teaching journal noting aspects of text that you did not catch the first time around—a word, a structure, a piece of background knowledge—but that presented difficulty for your students. By using this method you are more likely to catch potential difficulties in future readings.

Helping Students Grasp Vocabulary While Reading

Glossed texts (texts which provide definitions for already boldfaced or highlighted words) and cognates are two ways to help students make quick connections to unknown vocabulary while reading.

Glossed Texts

Glossed texts are texts that provide the definition of a word or phrase in L1 or simplified English, either in the margin next to the word or phrase, or in the back of the text (Nation, 2008). These types of texts can help students learn the meaning of new words and phrases while they read without having to stop and look them up in the dictionary. It has traditionally been easy to find glossed versions of classics, such as *Beowulf* and plays by Shakespeare, but now some publishers are coming out with glossed versions of more contemporary, adolescent-themed texts (see "Selecting Books Secondary ELLs Want to Read: Looking at Content and Proficiency Criteria" earlier in this chapter).

However, more likely than not, you may need to gloss the texts you are using in your classroom to help increase the comprehension level of ELLs. For most units, no matter the length or subject matter, you will want to gloss an unglossed text by preselecting content-specific words, expressions, and idioms to define for students. You will especially want to do so for words that are not very important to your lesson objectives, yet necessary to understand the passage. You can gloss a text before duplicating so that your students have this as a ready reference while they are reading. You can also provide a side sheet organized by the pages of the text to be read, so that ELLs can keep the glosses next to the text as they read, consulting it as needed.

Helping Students Notice Cognates

As noted in Chapter 3, cognates are one of the quickest and most accessible ways to bridge understanding with ELLs. For Romance languages like Spanish, it is estimated that 30–40% of all English words have a cognate (August, 2002). As a result, by making overt connections to cognates, students will engage with the material and connect to prior knowledge they may have already acquired in their native language. (See Chapter 3 for more details as to how to develop cognate awareness and use cognates to foster comprehension.) Show students that prior knowledge of words in their first language is one way to decode meanings of new words in English.

Teaching Text Structures and Signal Words

There are many different text structures that students need to be aware of in order to understand what they are reading. In fact, different content-area textbooks use different text structures. Research shows that making the text structure evident to readers, especially ELLs, helps them attain higher levels of comprehension (Coiro, 2001).

According to Fisher and Frey (2004), across the content areas, the most common expository text structures are the following:

- *Exemplification/enumeration (concept/definition):* used across a variety of content areas; names, tells, or gives examples that help define concepts presented

- *Description:* often used in social studies and science texts; used to describe people, places, or phenomena

- *Comparison/contrast:* – used in a variety of content area texts; used to compare and contrast two or more people, places, or phenomena

- *Cause/effect:* used in both science and social studies texts; used to show the causal relationships between phenomena

- *Problem/solution:* used in mathematics and sometimes social studies texts; used to show solutions developed from a problem or need

- *Sequential:* – most commonly used in math and science texts; used to show the order in which something occurs

As we mentioned before, the reason that text structure is so important is that research shows that the reading comprehension of students across the spectrum increases with the effective use of text structures (Coiro, 2001). Research has shown that when students are aware of a text's structure, they can use that knowledge to help them construct meaning, and, as a result, their reading comprehension improves (Dickson, Simmons, & Kameenui, 1995).

Teachers can use graphic organizers to teach text structure. When considering the use of graphic organizers, think about the purpose you want the organizer to serve and the structure of the text with which you will use the organizer. You will want to match the text structure to the graphic organizer; in other words, select the graphic organizer to mirror or match the text structure. For example, you may want to use a timeline with chronological texts (to show the sequence of events in a story, especially novels with flashbacks and history texts); Venn diagrams with texts about similar or opposing elements (to compare or contrast two characters in a story, or two species within the same family); and webs with texts with enumeration (to show all the things that are true about a character, or the reasons for the Revolutionary War). When students actively use graphic organizers that match the texts they are reading, they advance their comprehension and are able to process what they are reading on a deeper level. (See Table 7.3 for a list of graphic organizers and the specific functions they serve.)

Teaching Students to Use Signal Words to Detect Text Structure

One way students can begin to detect a text's structure is by recognizing the signal words. Teaching students to recognize these cue words helps them figure out what type of text they are reading and increases their overall comprehension.

Having knowledge of common transition words used in expository text will help students better grasp the larger concepts of a text, even if they have difficulty understanding some of the more content-specific vocabulary. Table 6.3 provides examples of signal words associated with the five most common text structures.

TABLE 6.3 Signal Words and Purpose

To Signal . . .	Signal Words
Chronological sequence	After, afterward, as soon as, before, during, finally, first, following, immediately, initially, later, meanwhile, next, not long after, now, on (date), preceding, second, soon, then, third, today, until, when
Comparison/contrast	Although, as well as, as opposed to, both, but, compared with, different from, either . . . or, even though, however, instead of, in common, on the other hand, otherwise, similar to, similarly, still, yet
Description	Above, across, along, appears to be, as in, behind, below, beside, between, down, in back of, in front of, looks like, near, on top of, onto, outside, over, such as, to the right/left, under
Generalization/principle	Additionally, always, because of, clearly, conclusively, first, for instance, for example, furthermore, generally, however, if . . . then, in fact, it could be argued that, moreover, most convincing, never, not only . . . but also, often, second, therefore, third, truly, typically
Process/cause	Accordingly, as a result of, because, begins with, consequently, effects of, finally, first, for this reason, how to, how, if . . . then, in order to, is caused by, leads/led to, may be due to, next, so that, steps involved, therefore, thus, when . . . then

With permission: "Words That Signal a Text's Organizational Structure", Somers Central School District; Available at http://www.somers.k12.ny.us/intranet/reading/signalwords.html

Teaching and Practicing the Strategies Good Readers Use

Help students become good, fluent readers by introducing and practicing effective reading strategies in your classroom. The conscious and reflective use of reading strategies is what beginning and emerging readers need in order to increase their reading comprehension. The following checklist is a quick reference that presents reading strategies, most often expressed as "Good readers [insert strategy] . . . ," that all readers can use before, during, and after reading a text with the goal of increasing their reading comprehension.

Good Readers Preview the Text

Students need to know different ways to preview a text depending on the content area. "Previewing the text" looks different in a literature class than it does in a science class. Previewing a literary text may involve reading the title and subtitle (if applicable); reading the back cover (of a novel); looking at the text's structure; reading chapter or section titles; reading the introduction or random pages throughout; learning background information about the author; looking at the publication date; reading reviews of the text, noticing names of main characters; and noticing the setting or topic of the piece.

Previewing a text in any content class, such as math, science, or history, or previewing informational texts, such as newspapers and reference materials, consists of a different set of strategies. Previewing strategies for textbooks used in content classes include reading titles; reading subtitles, subheadings, and sub-subheadings; looking at pictures and captions; reading graphs, charts, and timelines; and reading any beginning-of-the-chapter summary or "What's Important" prechapter summary. All these are extremely effective strategies for increasing comprehension for ELLs as they read textbooks in content classes.

Good Readers Apply Prior Knowledge and Build Their Knowledge Foundation

Helping students recognize what they know and apply that knowledge to what they are reading will not only help them comprehend the text that they are about to read, but also will help them make connections (another effective reading strategy) and retain the information they learn for longer periods of time. Having students ask themselves, "What do I already know?" is a good way to engage students in what they are about to read. Asking students to think, write, and talk about what they already know with regard to the topic helps them to begin thinking critically about the text. However, asking questions when they do not have the

Good Readers . . .

- Preview the text
- Apply prior knowledge
- Make predictions
- Code/talk to the text
- Highlight
- Make notes
- Reread
- Summarize
- Paraphrase
- Make inferences

background knowledge they need and searching out the information they are lacking to make sense of the text are also key skills of good readers. Helping students recognize what it is about a text that they do not understand—be it a word, an expression, or a reference—and where to go to clarify their confusion is the first step students take in managing their own education and being independent learners. For example, you might tell them to ask a friend, ask the teacher, or look it up on the Internet.

Good Readers Make Predictions

"What do you think will happen next?" is a simple question to ask, but answering this question forces students to reflect on what they have already read in order to make a reasonable prediction about what is to come. Making predictions involves the possibility that one's prediction may be incorrect, and so some students may feel insecure at first about publicly voicing their predictions. So, start small. First, ask students to make a prediction in their mind. Then, progress to asking students to write down their predictions on a piece of paper or in their journal. Explain to students that the learning is in the act of predicting, not the accuracy of their prediction. If students do not seem uneasy about making and sharing predictions aloud, it may be fun to have students voice their opinions aloud and record them on large pieces of paper to display in class. This whole-class activity of making, sharing, and recording predictions enhances the feeling of community in the classroom. Students can build upon their classmates' predictions with their own prediction variations. As the text is read, the class should review and revise predictions as a way to check for understanding.

It is important to note that making predictions may be a culturally distant practice for students from cultural groups where "guessing" is not valued. For these students, making predictions may feel foreign or uncomfortable. In some cultures, students are only to speak if they have knowledge; otherwise they are to listen. However, in the United States we value making guesses as an educational strength, and students need to be aware of this new behavior to properly acculturate.

Good Readers Code, or Talk to, the Text

Instructing students on how to code, or "talk to," the text will help them stay engaged as they read. Techniques may differ among subjects, mainly between English language arts and the content areas. English-language-arts techniques include *stop and jot* and using *reader response stems*. Content-class techniques include highlighting the text, writing in the margins, asking questions of the text, making comments, and making connections.

The process of coding, or "talking to," the text is very similar to the process of "talking to your notes," that will be described in Chapter 7. Although talking to the text may take different forms, it is helpful to introduce this strategy using a strict format. Start by giving students two or three ways in which they are to code/talk to the text. Create specific "codes"—letters or symbols—to correspond with different tasks, such as "?" for question, "C" for comment, and "↔" for connection. Be sure to model how to use the codes using the same or similar text as that which students will be reading and coding. For more beginner level students, it may be necessary to provide an already coded text with sample questions, comments, and connections so that students have a better idea of what they are being asked to do (ELA/Department for Learning and Educational Achievement, 2008).

As students begin reading, they code the text using sticky notes, dots, or labels, or by writing lightly in the margin. As a way to expand the activity and provide an opportunity for further writing practice, you may ask students to elaborate, or continue their "discussion" with the text on another piece of paper. For example, say a student has a question on page 3 of the text. She or he codes the text with the appropriate code—in this case, "?"—and on a separate piece of paper writes the code, the page number, and the full question. The teacher can then begin a discussion of the text through codes by asking students, for example, "What questions do you have?" The primary focus with coding the text is to teach students to actively process and interact with text as they read. This practice is something good readers inherently do as they read, so you are simply making it explicit and showing your students how to do it—essentially scaffolding the strategy until they begin to use it on their own (ELA/Department for Learning and Educational Achievement, Jefferson County Public Schools, 2008).

Good Readers Highlight

Highlighting is an important skill, applicable to all content areas. Many students like the idea of using a highlighter to mark up their text, but they end up highlighting entire paragraphs or pages because they are unsure of what they should and should not highlight. Show students different highlighting techniques and give them practice in using the techniques. One highlighting technique is to highlight only one text element, such as the topic sentence in each paragraph or one character's thoughts and actions. Another technique is to use different colored highlighters for different meanings or uses. For example, use one color to highlight new vocabulary, another for aspects of the text the students do not understand, and a third for main ideas and supporting details. Showing students different ways to use the technique of highlighting will allow them to experiment with and find the most effective highlighting style(s) for them.

Good Readers Make Notes

Making notes while reading helps increase comprehension *and* provides study material for future reference. (Chapter 7 discusses note taking, which is writing down points while someone speaks.) If the text belongs to the student, is it very effective to have him or her make notes by writing directly on the text—either in the margins or in the available white space. If making marginal notes is not an option, making notes on a separate piece of paper or in a notebook, in a style similar to "talking," or "marking up" the text, can be just as effective. Planning an organizing strategy for note making, such as two-column notes—where the text page is listed in the left-hand column and the note in the right-hand column—can help students maximize the usefulness of their notes. Emphasize the importance of reading a text multiple times as a way to select specific or different information during each read-through. This idea leads us to our next strategy: rereading.

Good Readers Reread

Struggling readers are often reluctant to read most texts once. Impressing on students the value and importance of rereading the same text multiple times therefore takes patience, consistency, reinforcement, and a lot of support. Modeling for students how rereading texts multiple times can reinforce comprehension will help them see the value of rereading. One way to model this is by focusing on different textual elements during each reread. During the first read-through, the focus may be on point of view. During the subsequent read-throughs, focus may shift to specific content, such as various characters or details; to text structures, such as cause and effect or flashbacks; or to literary devices, such as similes or personification. Demonstrating how rereading allows the reader to focus on different aspects of the text, and therefore understand more of the text, will show students both *how* to reread and *why* it is so important to do so.

Good Readers Summarize

Summarizing is a skill teachers frequently ask students to use in order to demonstrate comprehension and understanding. However, summarizing is quite difficult to do, especially for ELLs who lack vocabulary and often resort to simply copying for lack of a better option. Moreover, summarizing takes on different meanings in different content-area classes. For English language arts classes, summarizing involves showing an understanding of the plot line—of characters, setting, conflict, and resolution. For content-area classes, summarizing may involve any number of textual elements such as theses, main ideas, and details. Students are attempting to find the answers to the five W's + H—who, what, when, where, why, and how—within these text elements. For more information on summary strategies, see Chapter 7 and the "Summary" section of Chapter 8.

Good Readers Paraphrase

Paraphrasing is similar to summarizing in that it involves the communication of information in one's own words and language. Where paraphrasing differs from summarizing is that paraphrasing is used to communicate more than just main ideas. It is a rephrasing of the text rather than a condensing or shortening of information. Paraphrasing is used to show understanding of shorter excerpts by communicating another's ideas using one's unique and personal way of communication. For a quick reference, see the following box, which shows the basic distinguishing characteristics of summarizing and paraphrasing. Use this chart to aid in class discussions and other forms of oral communication. (For information on writing summaries and paraphrasing, check out the "Summary" section of Chapter 8.)

Summarizing versus Paraphrasing

Summarizing is . . .

- Only the most important points
- Communicating the main ideas
- Condensing a larger amount of information into a smaller amount
- Using one's own words
- Providing a reference

Paraphrasing is . . .

- Someone else's ideas in your own language
- Completely changing the original text
- Using new words and sentence structure
- Providing a reference

Source: Mr. Gonzalez's class Web site, Chimacum Middle School, Chimacum, Washington (no date); available at http://educatoral.com/paraphrase-vs-summarize.html

Good Readers Make Inferences

Making inferences is different from making predictions, because with predictions, the reader makes guesses about the text, whereas with making inferences, the reader is filling in gaps in the text, making a conclusion about information that is not supplied. The first step to teaching students to make inferences involves having them practice making conclusions, or deductions, about the actions of their friends and classmates in everyday situations. Students make inferences all the time about the people around them and the actors they see on television and in movies. Helping students make the connection between the inferences they automatically make every day and what they are being asked to do with regard to characters and plot development in a text will empower them to interact more independently and authentically with texts.

As students learn and gain practice in applying the "Good Readers. . ." strategies that we have discussed, they will be able to interact more skillfully and independently with the endless supply of authentic and real-world texts they will encounter outside the classroom.

Providing Daily Experience with Authentic and Real-World Texts to Enhance Reading Fluency

So far, we have discussed some of the important, comprehension-enhancing tools to teach students. Now, we are going to focus on ways you can provide students with multiple opportunities to read. Engaging students in multiple and meaningful reading experiences is one of the most important activities you can promote in helping students advance their reading abilities (Krashen, 2004).

Regardless of how teachers ask their students to engage in reading—whether it be reading aloud in front of the class, reading silently, reading with a partner, or reading independently for homework—the ability of students to comprehend text depends greatly on their level of reading fluency. Some may think that the structuring of various reading activities will have an effect on students' reading comprehension, but if students do not have an adequate level of reading fluency to understand while they read, then the way in which they read and with whom they read are irrelevant. Equally important is understanding that reading fluency affects students' feelings of self-confidence and comfort, especially when reading in a new language.

In order to help students feel at ease with reading in English and to feel they are skilled and fluent readers, they must read on a daily basis, and they must read a variety of texts with a variety of purposes. Wide, daily reading gives students multiple opportunities to practice the reading comprehension strategies they are learning, advances their vocabulary knowledge, and exposes them to the predominant language patterns of English.

Daily Reading

Encourage your students to engage in independent reading and to read English as much as possible. Start this process by structuring independent reading in your class as a daily activity—either by reading a text aloud to the class or asking students to choose their own text to read silently. Create the time and space for inde-

Research on out-of-school reading habits has shown that even 15 minutes a day of independent reading can expose students to more than a million words of text in a year (Anderson, Wilson, & Fielding, 1988).

pendent reading in your classroom, and then go a step further and hold students accountable for what they read with comprehension questions or reader response journals. Plant the seed of daily reading in the minds of your students. The more you reinforce the idea and importance of independent reading, the more likely your students are to see the value themselves and move toward their own daily reading practice.

In many classes, there is a common textbook or core novel that is the focus of an instructional unit for a set amount of time. This thematic reading is usually done in class and, depending on the level of difficulty of the text, is done as a class or individually. Thematic reading is an excellent opportunity for teachers to instruct students on various prereading, during-reading, and postreading comprehension strategies. By making such strategies overt to students and revisiting them often, students will become increasingly familiar with ways in which they can monitor their independent reading, thus increasing their reading proficiency.

Reading Student/Peer Work

While learning to read academically challenging and content-specific texts is crucial in a student's reading development, reading student work is likewise important in building reading fluency. Reading student work helps students increase their fluency because they likely are reading text that is at their own reading level, thereby likely reducing the number of times a student encounters an unknown word or word phrasing. Reading student work can also improve students' reading skills because most often when students are reading their peers' work, they are engaged in peer editing or evaluation and are responsible for looking for the presence or correctness of specific language elements in the text. This focused attention encourages a deeper interaction with the text, as well as a conversation with their peer, the author, about the language and content of the text. Reading student texts provides students a more personal experience and oftentimes results in learning and connections that may not always happen when students read published texts.

Keep Them Reading in L1

As discussed in Chapter 3, there are many ways to support students using their native language. One way to use L1 is by promoting independent reading in the native language while the students are learning to read in their new language. In this way, they are actually reading twice as much, and they are gaining literacy skills that can transfer back and forth between languages. Helping students gain access to reading materials in their native language can be a major motivating factor in getting them to start reading. English language learners, especially newcomers and beginner-level students, may view reading in a new language as an impossible challenge. Providing students with reading materials in their first language can serve to break the ice for students who are afraid of, or intimidated

Vignette: Josmery and Peer Reading

Josmery, originally from the Dominican Republic, was a very vocal student, both in English and in her native language, Spanish. She always had something to contribute to the class discussion and was constantly practicing her oral English skills with her teachers and peers, even with her classmates who shared Spanish as their native language. Though she worked hard at speaking English, her literacy skills, especially her decoding abilities—correctly sounding out or pronouncing words when reading—were weak. Nevertheless, Josmery would volunteer to read aloud at every opportunity no matter what text we were working on. She recognized that reading and decoding were areas she needed to strengthen, and she took advantage of any opportunity to practice and improve.

One day, students were working in pairs, reading aloud each other's memoir as part of a final editing stage of the writing process. All of a sudden I heard Josmery exclaim from across the room, "Oh, I didn't know that was how you spelled laugh!" Josmery had asked her partner what the word "laugh" meant in her partner's text, not realizing what the written form of the well-known word "laugh" looked like. I knew for a fact that Josmery had read the word "laugh" at least three or four times in the last month, and I remembered teaching students the sound of the -*gh* word ending. But of course, students need multiple exposures to words to learn them deeply. On this day, it had finally clicked for her; a word she clearly knew the meaning of, and had certainly used in conversation many times, and probably in writing as well (though most likely misspelled), finally became part of her vocabulary repertoire through simply reading a peer's piece of writing.

Erin Leininger

by, reading in English. First-language texts will allow students to continue to acquire vocabulary and comprehension skills that will transfer and support their reading in English later on.

There are a few ways to go about trying to obtain native language reading materials for your students. The most convenient and accessible option is to team up with your school's librarian. Whether or not your school library has any relevant texts in stock, ask the librarian about other resources, such as the city library or other school libraries, and whether there are financial resources to order such texts for the library. Depending on the language you are searching for, there may be downloadable materials online. Refer to Chapter 3 for more ideas on how to locate human and material resources in the primary languages of your students.

Conducting Formative and Summative Assessments to Guide Instruction

Assess L1 Literacy

We saw in Chapter 3 that students' literacy in their native language is a strong contributor to their ability to build literacy in English, their new language. Students with high literacy levels in their native language will be able to transfer much of their underlying knowledge about language—from semantics to text structure, to the rules that govern word formation and syntactical structures—to their acquisition of English. At the same time, students with low literacy skills in their native language may encounter more difficulty in becoming literate in the new language. Therefore, it is very important to know the L1 literacy level of your students when they enter your class.

If your students are literate, you should use their L1 literacy to encourage wide reading outside of school as well as promote maintenance of literacy skills in their L1. Emphasize the fact that keeping up with and improving their first language will not detract from their English development (as long as they continue to make an effort to acquire literacy in English) and will be an invaluable asset in their educational and professional lives.

Assessing Stage of Proficiency in English

Communicative functions—essentially the purposes that communication serves—were introduced in detail in Chapter 5. As noted in Chapter 5, communicative functions are helpful tools for planning instruction and assessment. These tools provide teachers with guides for the linguistic skills students should be able to perform at different proficiency levels. Of course, this approach necessarily requires that you identify the proficiency level of each of your students. Therefore, another important language aspect to assess is students' current stage of English proficiency. Once you have this information, you can assign different level-appropriate literacy activities for each student, depending on his or her proficiency level (see chapter 5).

For examples of the types of literacy activities (reading and writing) you might expect of your students at each proficiency level, see the box below.

Classroom-Based Assessment Strategies

There are many ways teachers can conduct in-class assessments of their students' knowledge and understanding. When making decisions about types of assessment, consider the proficiency level of the students and the language and content goals of the assessment.

In-Class Discussions and Check-Ins

In-class discussions and check-ins are informal assessments done while reading as a class or while students are reading independently. To do an in-class discussion, first ask the whole class a question related to the reading. Then ask students to respond. The way you ask students to respond should vary depending on the proficiency level of the students. With lower-level beginner students, ask students to all respond in one specific, familiar way. For example, you can ask students to participate by raising their hands, showing thumbs up/thumbs down, or giving one-word responses to your questions. Asking students to share or respond in a simple, straightforward manner reduces students' affective filter and makes them feel more comfortable and confident.

Assessment Strategies for Reading Comprehension

- In-class discussions
- Check-ins
- Reader response journals
- Art and illustration
- Quizzes and tests

When conducting in-class discussions or check-ins with intermediate- or advanced-level students, give options for ways they can to respond to your questions. For example, ask students to give their opinion, explain how they arrived at an answer, or pose their own question to the class that is related to the focus text.

Keep in mind that these check-in strategies can be used with the class as a whole or with individual students, depending on your goal. Obviously, whole class check-ins will give you a more general idea of where the class stands as a whole in terms of text comprehension, as opposed to specific individuals' comprehension levels. Individual check-ins will obviously provide you with more detailed information about each student's personal level of comprehension.

Reader Response Journals

Reader response journals are an informal way to effectively assess students' understanding of a text and writing skills. Reader response journals can take on a variety of forms, depending on the focus and purpose. However they are used, student response journals are one way for teachers to address the challenge of helping each student on an individual level. The following is a list of common ways teachers use reader response journals in their classes:

- *Dialogue or double-entry journal:* Students copy an excerpt from the text and respond in some way (personal response, connection, question).

- *Textual characteristic identification journal:* Students take notes on a specific textual characteristic. This could be any characteristic on which you want students to focus. You may choose a grammatical focus, such as parts of speech; a content focus, such as characteristics of mammals in a science class or of European settlers in social studies; or a stylistic focus, such as literary devices or use of dialogue.

- *Student teacher dialogue journal:* Teachers can use journals as an opportunity to create dialogue with students. You may choose to respond to a student's writing with comments, questions, or suggestions related to the topic or to a student's individual writing skills.

Oftentimes, teachers will find themselves giving similar or identical feedback to multiple students. When this happens, it is helpful to type up the feedback and print out multiple copies on sticky labels. Instead of repeatedly writing the same response, apply a feedback sticker to a student's work. This strategy saves time and helps teachers become more aware of the common strengths, weaknesses, and general trends of their students. This awareness allows teachers to better respond and adapt instruction to meet the needs of all students. For more discussion on giving feedback and understanding student needs, see also Chapter 8.

Art and Illustration

Using art or illustration to convey the understanding of words, concepts, ideas, or characters is a great way to quickly assess students' basic understanding of such ideas. Surprisingly, many students, when asked to show their understanding through visual or illustrated representation, respond by saying, "But I can't draw!" This response usually means one of two things: either a student feels insecure about illustration or art, or the student does not understand the word, concept, idea, and so on. Either way, it is important to encourage students to do whatever they can, to have fun with it, and to be aware that becoming the next Van

Gogh is not the goal of the activity. As they practice this strategy and it becomes more routine, students become more comfortable, and they may even come to appreciate how it allows them to communicate without struggling to put their thoughts into words in English.

In-Class Exams and Projects

There are many different ways to use exams to assess what students are asked to read and understand. It is important to choose appropriate strategies for varying proficiency levels. Usually the best approach is to use a combination of multiple-choice, matching, true/false, and short-answer questions, although this will always depend on your student population.

Matching and true/false activities are well suited for beginner-level students who are still in the early development stages of English and not yet ready to clearly articulate their knowledge and understanding through their own production of the new language. As students gain proficiency, teachers can incorporate activities that require a wider, more solid grasp of English, such as multiple choice and short answer. Essays are generally not a fair or accurate assessment until students reach more advanced levels of proficiency, unless scaffolds such as templates and writing guides are provided.

Projects are another way to assess students' knowledge and comprehension. The benefits of projects are that they can be conceived in a way that deemphasizes the memorization of facts and new, potentially confusing and complicated language, especially for beginner students. It is important to choose assessment strategies that fit your assessment goals, whether they are language based, content based, or both. As you well know, you need to make sure the focus of your instruction matches the focus of your assessments.

High-Stakes Tests

Though the intent of this chapter is to provide teachers with strategies for helping ELLs improve their reading skills, it is worth mentioning a couple of useful tips for teaching strategies for taking high-stakes tests.

First, it is of the utmost importance that students understand how to properly read and interpret test-taking directions. Many students have become accustomed to listening to the teacher's directions rather than reading the directions for a writing assignment or activity. Others do not have the technical or content-specific vocabulary necessary to understand formal, written directions. Either way, stressing the importance of reading the directions and helping students practice this skill frequently in class will benefit them in any standardized testing situation.

Second, it is likewise crucial that students learn and practice how to use textual citations and examples to support their understanding and arguments. It is important to stress the difference between plagiarism and using properly cited textual support. Oftentimes, students do not realize that copying is perfectly acceptable and even encouraged, as long as proper citation is used. Show students how to correctly use quotation marks and provide the page, paragraph, or line number in parenthesis after the final quotation mark but before the period. There are some slight variations depending on the text being cited, but a general example of proper citation, taken from the novel *Romiette and Julio* (Draper, 2001) is provided in the box.

Using Quotation Marks

Romiette describes herself as "brown, like the earth, tall and slim like a poplar tree, and outspoken, like the wind on a stormy day" (p. 4).

Conclusion

In this chapter we have discussed the special challenges that ELLs face when reading secondary texts, and the aspects of English that are important for you to understand in order to help ELLs develop their reading skills. In addition, it is important to encourage ELLs to engage in daily reading, in and out of the classroom, and to practice the strategies good readers use, as these activities are critical to their success as readers. Encouraging and supporting wide reading and the practice of reading strategies is best accomplished when we offer books that secondary ELLs want to read and match those books to students' differing proficiency levels. Finally, you will want to routinely use formative and summative assessments to determine ELLs' literacy abilities to inform and guide your instruction.

Checklist

Ten Ways to Support Students in Reading Development in the Classroom

☐ I provide exposure to many authentic, real-world texts to build practice with a variety of text structures and genres.

☐ I teach both high- and low-frequency vocabulary and grammar structures to increase reading fluency and comprehension.

☐ I instruct students on the various text structures across and within the different content areas.

☐ I instruct students on signal words such as transitions and content-specific meaning cues to enhance text comprehension.

☐ I actively teach and model strategies good readers use and allow students many opportunities to practice these skills.

☐ I offer scaffolds to students in the form of glossed, adapted, shortened, or alternative texts to support them as they build reading comprehension.

☐ I choose texts with topics students are interested in and can relate to.

☐ I encourage wide, independent reading in both English and the student's native language.

☐ I monitor students as they work and give supportive and focused feedback to advance learners' reading fluency and comprehension as much as possible.

☐ I conduct informal and formal reading assessments to monitor student progress as well as guide instruction.

CHAPTER 7

Academic Listening and Note Taking in a Second Language

Veronica, Guatemala

It's so hard to keep up. I'm trying to understand what the teacher is saying, while reading what is on the board, and then writing it down myself. I just can't do it. It was hard in Spanish, but in English it's just impossible!

Nayely, 18, Dominican

Guiding Questions

- What does note taking look like at the secondary level, and why is it so important?
- Why is note taking so difficult for English language learners?
- How can educators guide English language learners toward becoming successful note takers in all subject areas?
- How can the use of note taking facilitate the processes of summarizing and paraphrasing; two difficult tasks for second-language learners?

Nayely is not alone. English language learners (ELLs) at the secondary level have an extremely difficult time in school—attempting to learn both a new language and a new culture (Hill & Flynn, 2006), while learning challenging academic subject matter through the new language. At the secondary level a whole host of skills are required for students to be successful in school. Two of the most challenging ones are listening and taking notes simultaneously—a monumental task for an ELL, as the student quote demonstrates. This chapter is written to help you make the note-taking process more doable for your students.

As we begin our discussion we will also recommend the following set of teaching principles to focus and guide your work in the important area of academic listening and note taking.

Teaching Principles

- Because the foundation of note taking is listening, provide students with multiple opportunities to practice listening on a daily basis, both individually and collaboratively.
- Because note taking has so many practical uses in higher education and life, be explicit with students about why they should work on their note-taking skills.

- Because note taking is so difficult, provide students with knowledge of how to format their notes, use abbreviations and symbols, and recognize important signal words.

- Because note taking, summarizing, and paraphrasing are complex skills, break them down into easier to perform, step-by-step tasks.

- Because ELLs are capturing information at a slower rate in English than their mainstream counterparts and have more limited vocabularies than their mainstream counterparts, at the same time you teach academic listening and note-taking skills, alter your speech, delivery, and vocabulary to support second-language (L2) learners when lecturing in class.

- Because listening in a second language is difficult, use visual aids whenever possible.

- Because note taking is such an arduous task for ELLs, ensure that at the beginning students are given varying forms of partially completed notes to facilitate the process.

- Because students respond to incentives, make note taking an integral part of their grade and consistently evaluate both their notes and ability to revise their notes.

- Because you use assessments to inform instruction, use students' notes as an opportunity to reflect on your teaching effectiveness and modify your instructional practices as needed.

Note Taking versus Note Making

Taking notes and making notes are both critical skills that are constantly used in both secondary and higher education. Although these terms are often interchanged, they are in fact two distinct skills, and it is important that we understand the differences. Note taking refers to "students' written notes as taken from a lecture or class discussion," while note making refers to " the slightly different phenomenon of recording notes from printed materials" (Fisher & Frey, 2004, p. 86). Therefore, students typically take notes during teachers' lectures, as they are trying to record information while listening, a very challenging task. In contrast, students tend to make notes while reading, responding to, or summarizing the text in some fashion. This process is self-paced and more in the students' control. This chapter will focus on taking notes, whereas Chapter 6 has already provided note-making strategies in its larger discussion on reading.

The Importance of Listening and Note Taking

Listening and taking notes is a skill—one that is difficult for both adolescents and adults. That said, it is a necessary skill—one that is used daily in both educational and work contexts. Whether in college trying to furiously take down a professor's lecture or on the job trying to record a boss's instruction, for their futures, students will need to know how to listen and take notes that are useful to them.

Note taking becomes especially important to students as they advance in their education and encounter teachers who rely on lecture as a way of conveying important information. In upper-level high school courses in mathematics, English, history, and science, many secondary teachers often couple their hands-on activities with lectures. Perhaps this approach is important to your teaching. As you know all too well, students who are not adequately equipped to take notes during lectures are put at an extreme disadvantage, no matter how effective and engaged they may be during hands-on activities.

Note taking is particularly challenging for secondary students because it is so multifaceted. Students are required to display receptive skills like listening to and processing information, but also expressive skills such as actually writing the notes and organizing them effectively—all at the same time. This is a lot to juggle for an English-dominant middle or high school student, much less an ELL. Every single step presents a unique challenge for our secondary ELLs.

Unique Challenges for ELLs

As has already been stressed in this chapter, note taking begins with listening. As many others have done, we want to emphasize the contrast between listening and simply hearing. Much like note taking and note making, these two terms are often interchanged even though their meanings are quite different. Hearing is nothing more that the act of perceiving sound performed by the ear. If you are not hearing-impaired, hearing simply happens. Listening, however, is something you have to do consciously. Listening requires concentration so that your brain actually processes meaning from words and sentences. For example, I can say, "I *hear* that you are talking although I have no idea what you are saying," or I can say, "I am listening to what you are saying and actively trying to comprehend what you are saying." The distinction matters because the passive activity of hearing is not sufficient; we are interested in listening: an active process that leads to learning. Therefore, our job is to focus on teaching students effective ways to listen and process information (Hadley, 1993), an act that, for ELLs, takes place in a language they are still in the process of learning.

During the school day, students are constantly challenged to use many different language skills, although none as frequently as listening. As Joan Morley writes, "Listening—compared with speaking, reading or writing—is used far more than any other single language skill in our daily lives. We listen twice as much as we speak, four times as much as we read, and five times as much as we write" (1999, 16). It is therefore imperative that our ELLs become effective listeners, not only in their primary language but also in their second language, English. Unfortunately, listening is often taken for granted, and there is little focus on instructing students on effective listening strategies (Carrier, 2003). However, all students, including ELLs, need to be taught how to effectively listen to English, especially academic English. So what should you work on to help them along?

Capturing Speech

Listening in a second language is important to note taking because students are actively constructing knowledge from orally inputted information (Bentley & Bacon, 1996). Additionally, listening in a second language is extremely difficult because it presents challenges in capturing, comprehending, and following along—all in "real time"—as speech is received. Indeed, experts remind us that listening is an interactive process in that it involves both top-down factors such as background knowledge and semantics and bottom-up factors like acoustic features, stress, rhythm, and syntax (Rubin, 1994).

Individuals who are listening in their primary language may be able to zone out for a minute and still be able to follow a lecture or conversation, whereas zoning out may not be an option for second-language learners, forcing the simple act of listening to become a truly active and, at times, nerve-racking experience. Students may experience nervousness when they do not understand something, and this anxiety may well cause them to understand even less as they expend energy worrying instead of listening. Any number of factors can affect a student's ability to capture what a teacher is saying, ranging from instructors' accents, to the speed at which they are speaking, to the volume at which they are speaking, to background noises, to peers speaking and distracting other students. As soon as any of these speaker or environmental factors take hold and cause students to feel lost, they may give up and decide that what is being asked is impossible for them to do.

Processing Oral Language

Active listening is only the first step in note taking, however. Processing the language they hear presents yet another difficulty for ELLs. Even those students who are quite adept at catching the words and phrases may not know how to write the words and phrases they are hearing, or they may capture words and phrases for which they have no meanings established.

So in the end, if students cannot at least feel confident that they comprehend the main idea of what is being said, they will most likely tune out. It is for this reason that we recommend that, at the beginning, you help your students work on writing down the gist of what is being said, and as their proficiency increases, you help them capture a more accurate detailed recall of the information being transmitted. More will be said about this topic a little later in the chapter.

Writing Down Your Notes

Capturing and processing speech are still only the beginning of note taking. The actual skill of taking notes requires putting a pen to a page, which, again, presents unique challenges for ELLs who struggle with spelling and other aspects of English grammar. As Patricia L. Carrell (2007) writes, "Even highly proficient L2 learners may find the simultaneous cognitive tasks of comprehending the incoming lecture and producing effective, efficient, and well-organized notes cognitively overloading" (p. 45). Additionally, many of our secondary students allow minor issues to interfere with their note-taking process. For example, they may be unwilling to misspell a word in English, causing them to pause to try and get the correct spelling, falling minutes behind in what is taking place in the classroom. At the same time, we recognize that note taking also provides a wonderful opportunity for both teaching spelling and revising spelling, just not at the same time notes are being taken. We will say more about this topic later on in the chapter.

But for now, suffice it to say that simultaneously listening, processing information, and writing in a second language is an extremely arduous task for students learning a second language. As Carrell (2007) writes, "It may be unrealistic to expect any but the most advanced L2 learners to produce quality notes in the face of the listening comprehension processing they must undertake with limited controlled processing capacity" (2007, p. 45).

Personal experience verifies the research. Those of us who have received education in other languages and experienced the demands of taking notes in an L2 know firsthand that even though you may be a highly competent student, well versed in note taking, highly proficient in your primary language, and moderately proficient in the target language, you still struggle when listening to lectures in another language, trying to both comprehend what is being said and write it down. The attempt leaves you feeling lost, frustrated, and inadequate. One can only imagine how students with less education, lower levels of literacy, lower levels of their second language, and a lack of strategies and tools feel trying to take notes in their secondary classes. As teachers, we can empathize with the feelings students are having when trying to take notes in a second language, and then we can provide them with the necessary tools and strategies to become confident and effective note takers. The rest of the chapter is designed to help you do just that.

Note Taking Matters, and Students Should Know Why

Like all areas of education, it is helpful to begin instructing students on note taking by explaining to them why it matters. If students see no value in taking notes, they will most likely find little impetus to get better at it. When thinking about how to frame note taking for your students, you should consider stressing what note taking is. Note taking is

- Required in all disciplines.
- A developmental process: the more they practice, the better they will get at it.
- A skill that most of them are not proficient at, since many teachers do not teach note taking—so being good at it will give them an advantage over other students.
- A skill that helps them eliminate unnecessary information so they have less information to process.
- A skill that helps them organize information, making it easier to understand.
- A skill that creates aids that they can use to study for quizzes, exams, papers, and projects.
- An opportunity to practice multitasking in English while building proficiency in reading and writing (adapted from Boch & Piolat, 2005).

The reality is that all students, especially ELLs, must become effective note takers if they hope to acquire necessary information provided in lectures. According to Françoise Boch and Annie Piolat (2005),

> The average writing speed of a student is around 0.3 to 0.4 words/second, whereas a lecturer speaks at a rate of around 2 to 3 words/second. Unless everything is said at dictation speed, or students develop exceptional shorthand skills, teachers will never speak slowly enough for students to write down everything that is said. (p. 102)

Therefore, students must develop useful ways to record the content of teachers' lectures—to get the gist of the content and to capture as much detail as possible to support an accurate understanding of the topic at hand.

Note Taking Begins with Listening

The first step to taking useful notes is becoming an active listener. The first step we can take toward aiding our students in becoming more proficient listeners is integrating listening activities into our daily instruction in the classroom. There are a number of activities and exercises that we can use. Here are six activities you might try—all conveniently named using song lyrics.

Listening Activities

1. *You Met Your Match:* Pairing images with words.
2. *We Belong Together:* Pairing concepts with statements.
3. *Stand by Me:* Pairing large pictures with characters.
4. *This Is the Picture:* Drawing what you hear.
5. *Put Your Hands Up:* A whole class physical response using simple motions in unison to answer yes/no questions.
6. *Stop, Collaborate, and Listen:* Using the preceding strategies with teams or pairs of students to provide more modeling and practice.

Remember, you can use these listening activities when you are the primary transmitter of information, but any of these activities can and should be done also when information is provided through media—podcasts, DVDs, music, radio, and videos. As we all know, it is important to vary the speaker to give our ELLs an opportunity to hear other voices. Additionally, as educators in the 21st century, we all understand how important it is to show students educational uses for all the technology that most of them already use on a daily basis. So you will want them listening to real-time teachers' voices and also recorded presentations of information.

You Met Your Match

Used for: Building new vocabulary   *Levels:* Beginning, intermediate

Allow your students to engage in a matching exercise that forces the students to correctly pair images with corresponding words or terms. If, for example, you were to spend ten minutes reviewing key terms related to a new unit on photosynthesis, you could evaluate students' listening comprehension by providing them with ten note cards: five pictures and five key terms. Students would match them according to their understanding based on their prior listening. Of course, when dealing with beginner students, because of their limited proficiency, be sure to limit both the number of words being chosen and the difficulty of the words and or terms.

We Belong Together

Used for: Building conceptual   *Levels:* Beginning (with visual aids),
          understanding   intermediate, advanced

After reviewing several concepts, you can provide two carefully and simply worded statements you know your ELLs can read and process—one correct and one incorrect—for the students to choose from. One statement represents the concept being taught; the other does not. The students will have to determine which one to choose. For example, if a social studies teacher lectures on democracy, he or she can put up two sentences:

1. Ellen Johnson (a president of Liberia) gets fewer votes than George Weah (her opponent), but instead of letting George Weah become president she encourages her followers to overthrow George.

2. Felipe Calderon runs for reelection in Mexico and gets fewer votes than Andres Manuel Lopez (his opponent). Felipe congratulates Andres and allows Andres to become the next president of Mexico.

The teacher asks the students to identify which statement is an example of democracy and which one is not. In this way, they are not simply learning definitions but also learning concepts. Students are now engaging in higher order thinking by having to synthesize the information they are listening to, and not merely repeating it or identifying it. These statements can and should be accompanied by visual aids when the teacher knows they are necessary for a student's comprehension.

Stand by Me

Used for: Building subject-specific
           vocabulary

Levels: Beginning, intermediate

Another strategy that you can use to evaluate a student's ability to listen is to have large numbered pictures of definitions on display throughout the room. As a teacher explains, he or she can pause every few minutes and ask students to (1) physically get up and stand by the picture, (2) point at the picture, or (3) write down the number of the picture that accurately depicts the information being orally expressed. For example, if an English teacher is reviewing Greek mythology, covering the important traits of Greek gods and goddesses, the teacher could have 15 drawings up of Greeks gods and goddesses depicting these traits, each with its own number. After discussing several, the teacher could pause and ask the students to identify Zeus through one of the three response modes. All three modes (standing, pointing, writing down the number of a picture) reduce students' anxieties about being wrong by either allowing all students to answer at the same time or by allowing them to answer privately. The first two modes have the disadvantage of possibly allowing peers to influence each other's answers, but all three modes are nonthreatening strategies to evaluate a student's ability to listen.

This Is the Picture

Used for: Building subject-specific
           vocabulary
           Summarizing

Levels: Intermediate, advanced

This exercise is similar to the first three in that it forces students to listen, but it differs in that students are forced to do the drawing themselves, instead of choosing from options provided by the teacher. The first two matching strategies are more likely to be used with beginning and intermediate students, as they provide the extra scaffolding of provided drawings, while "This Is the Picture" will have more success with intermediate and advanced students. Using the same example as before, students listen to a brief lecture on the traits of Greek gods and goddesses, and, after a few are stated, the teacher asks them to draw one, checking the students' comprehension of what was being orally expressed as demonstrated by their drawings.

This strategy can also be used when reading literature out loud. After a teacher reads a paragraph or page (depending on proficiency level) students can be asked to draw a summary of what they think took place—essentially a picture of what they just heard. Once again, in forcing the students to draw and not write, the focus is placed purely on students' ability to listen and comprehend, not reproduce information in any written form on their own. Allowing ELLs to draw is a nonthreatening way of ensuring that they are actively listening and processing information in their second language.

Put Your Hands Up

Used for: Checking message comprehension

Checking effectiveness of teacher delivery

Levels: Beginner, intermediate

With this strategy students can respond together using simple thumbs up, thumbs down, or thumbs sideways to display their answer. For example, if a social studies teacher just finished a presentation on the main attributes of the Sioux Indians, the teacher could then have an oral evaluation where he or she would assign answers to different thumb positions and ask students to simultaneously make the hand sign that they think is correct. Students could put their thumbs up if they think the Sioux Indians lived in the East, their thumbs down if they think the Sioux did not live in the East, and their thumbs sideways if they are unsure. In this way, teachers can understand how much of the information they are presenting orally is actually being understood by their students. When you use this type of informal evaluation, you will be able to evaluate the effectiveness of your own teaching as well as show students they are being held accountable for the information provided during your mini-lectures. Every student is answering at the same time, nonverbally, creating a nonthreatening vehicle through which to understand student's comprehension.

Stop, Collaborate, and Listen

Used for: Negotiating for content understanding

Levels: Intermediate, advanced

In addition to the individual listening activities presented, you may want to consider allowing students to participate in listening activities in teams or pairs. First, pairing or placing students in teams may eliminate the stress and fear of listening by oneself—especially when beginner students understand very little, a situation that can cause high anxiety levels and fatigue (Gibbons, 1991; Kagan, 1995). Second, forcing students to listen in teams or pairs provides opportunities for the students to participate in additional and different listening exercises. When students are listening to a teacher lecture, they are only engaged in unidirectional listening—they are only receiving information from one source (Morley, 1999). This practice is important, as this type of listening occurs every day in real life through such mediums as radio, television, automated phone messages, or even religious services (Morley, 1999).

However, placing students in teams or groups allows the students to engage in bi- or multidirectional listening, which forces the student to be both the listener and the speaker. Students are forced to both listen to their partner or team member and respond; practice which aids them in modeling another listening task that takes place every day: conversations (Morley, 1999).

Besides the bonus of having to listen and respond to their classmates through participating in multidirectional listening, students are being exposed to voices other than their teachers'. This exposure can also be provided in class discussion, with students raising their hands and participating in a bidirectional process with the teacher, allowing other students to listen. This is important, as some students will become quite adept at understanding their teacher, adapting their listening to the teacher's speed, cadence, and accent. When other people speak they may find it extremely difficult to follow. These interactions make students negotiate with other students to gain understanding. In addition to having students interact with each other, we can also bring technology into the classroom and allow our students to listen to voices from radio, television, or cinema.

In North America, by participating in multidirectional listening, students are actually accomplishing two very important tasks: they are checking their own comprehension against that of their peers, and they are also exposing themselves to different accents and styles of speech in English. Given the linguistic and cultural diversity in the United States, the more exposure they have to the many dialects and varieties of English, the more success they will have outside of the classroom.

When doing listening activities in small groups, you can also expand on the activity by giving students the advantage of their peers' knowledge as well. For example, with "This Is the Picture" the teacher may also ask students to collaborate in forming a caption for the picture. Or in the case of matching, the teacher might ask them to identify the correct picture or note card and provide a one-sentence explanation as to why they chose that answer. Allowing the groups to come up with this response together and giving them the time to do so forces them to listen to each other and learn from each other when one may not know the answer but another may have the necessary vocabulary to answer the questions. This type of interaction is extremely important for students to practice, as it mimics natural communicative demands—students are now being required to express information to show understanding of a subject.

These activities are best done in heterogeneous groups, allowing those with more knowledge to educate those with less. That said, however, you also have to be vigilant during heterogeneous grouping to a phenomenon known as *hitchhiking* (Johnson, Johnson, & Smith, 1998)—where students stay silent and allow other students to do all the work. To avoid this, do your best to ensure a true cooperative learning structure where every student has a specific task, whether it be leading, transcribing, looking up words, or other tasks that may be activity specific. To ensure that students actually adhere to the rules and roles you establish, circulate and give students a grade for their participation. Grading is best accomplished with a cooperative learning participation rubric (Figure 7.1) that you can use consistently throughout the year when students are working in teams.

At the same time, it is important to know that the phenomena of lower-proficiency students "piggybacking" on higher-proficiency students (e.g., saying "I agree" after a higher proficiency student utters a long or complex sentence) is natural until they themselves gain a higher proficiency, so make good decisions about

FIGURE 7.1 Cooperative learning participation rubric

Criteria	4 Exceeds Proficiency	3 Meets Proficiency	2 Approaching Proficiency	1 Substantially Below Proficient	Comments
Getting to Work Do you start working right away? Do you have all of the materials you need?	You move *efficiently* and *quietly* into your group, ready to work. You have *all* necessary materials.	You move *reasonably well* into your group and are ready to get to work. You have *most of* the necessary materials.	You move *too slowly* into your group. You are *unsure* of where to go. You have *some of the* unnecessary materials.	You are *noisy, do not* move into your group quickly, and *interfere* with other groups. You *do not bring any of the* necessary materials.	
Listening and Speaking Do you actively listen to your peers? Do you listen as much as you speak?	You *always* actively listen to your peers and *never dominate* the group with your voice.	You *almost always* actively listen to your peers and *almost never* dominate the group with your voice.	You *sometimes* actively listen to your peers and *sometimes* dominate the group with your voice.	You *almost never* actively listen to your peers and *almost always* dominate the group with your voice.	
Being Cooperative Do you support and help each other? Do you seek help from the teacher?	You *always* support and help each other. You *always* ask the teacher for help when you need it.	You *almost always* support and help each other. You *almost always* ask the teacher for help when you need it.	You *sometimes* support and help each other. You *sometimes* ask the teacher for help when you need it.	You *almost never* support and help each other. You *almost never* ask the teacher for help when you need it.	
Staying on Task Do you stay on task? Do you complete your specific task?	You are *always* on task. You *fully* complete your specific task.	You are *almost always* on task. You *mostly* complete your specific task.	You are *sometimes* on task. You *partially* complete your specific task.	You are *almost never* on task. You do *very little* of your specific task.	

when to allow piggybacking and when to ensure that students are not overly relying on others. Be sure all students are engaged in both listening and speaking, as this practice is essential for building the skills your learners need.

Facilitating Note Taking in Class

All the strategies mentioned thus far have been solely concerned with listening and comprehending orally expressed information. As mentioned in the beginning of this chapter, note taking involves numerous coordinated skills. The first step toward note taking is being an effective listener; it was for this reason that the last section detailed many activities to help students build listening comprehension skills. Similarly, as you read the following section on promoting effective note taking in the classroom, make sure to think about multiple ways in which your students can practice all the subskills required to take notes. The following strategies detail what you, as a teacher, can do to foster the practice of effective note taking in your classroom. These nine strategies are split into three different categories: (1) *before* note taking, (2) *during* note taking, and (3) *after* note taking, where we are defining note taking as the actual process of scribing notes during a teacher lecture or presentation. Although at first you will want to follow all nine steps to help your students become effective note takers, as they get better at it you will likely begin to choose which steps are still necessary and which you would rather leave out.

Nine Steps Toward Helping Students Take Better Notes

Before a Note-Taking Exercise

1. Provide students with a standard system of heading their notes.
2. Provide instruction on shorthand and abbreviation techniques.
3. Instruct students on how to recognize a teacher's signal words.

During a Note-Taking Exercise

4. Alter your speech, delivery, and vocabulary.
5. Use visuals.
6. Provide already or partially completed notes.
7. Monitor student progress.

After a Note-Taking Exercise

8. Model how to talk to your notes.
9. Allow students to revise and edit notes.

Before a Note-Taking Exercise

Step 1: Provide Students with a Standard System of Heading Their Notes

Although every teacher should decide what is best for himself or herself, it is helpful to ELLs to standardize the way that they head their notes, such as including their name, the date, and the topic in the top right-hand corner of their notes. As secondary teachers of ELLs, we must be cognizant of the fact that our students, because of their diverse backgrounds, bring with them varying ways of heading their class work. When they are provided with a model and allowed to practice consistency, they will gain comfort with a uniform way of heading their notes.

Step 2: Provide Instruction on Shorthand and Abbreviation Techniques

The second step is to assist students in using abbreviations and symbols when taking notes so that they can more easily keep pace with your delivery of information. Although it is impossible to teach your students all the symbols that could be helpful, providing them with a chart may be useful to get them started. Table 7.1 can serve as a good starting point for you and your students.

As a seasoned educator, you know that providing students with a list of abbreviations is only as useful as you make it. Therefore, if you use this list or another like it, make sure to encourage the students to have it available as they take notes, and give them opportunities to work the abbreviations into their notes. Additionally, you should consider providing a content-specific list that is applicable to the material that is about to be covered, as these will be higher incidence words in your lecture or presentation. If you have the time or desire, you might also consider doing a separate lesson on how abbreviations can be formed through eliminating ends of words or eliminating vowels, or you might simply provide examples, such as the following:

Eliminating Ends

- *regular* becomes *reg*
- *information* becomes *info*
- *Wednesday* becomes *wed*

Eliminating Vowels

- *hours* becomes *hrs*
- *normal* becomes *nml*

These models provide your students with two strategies to form abbreviations without giving them a prescriptive list to memorize, and therefore some students might find it more useful than a list. Essentially students need to understand that

TABLE 7.1 Useful Symbols

Common Symbol	What It Stands For
& / +	and
=	is or equals
#	number
×	times
➧	leads to
1st	first
>	more than
<	less than
w/	with
w/o	without
@	at
b/c	because
/	per

abbreviations are best when personalized and that they can do whatever they like as long as they can figure out what it means when they are reviewing their notes later. Allowing students time to create abbreviations from commonly used words in your discipline may very well be a worthwhile activity and serve as a useful reference list throughout the year. In other words, why not make a list together for use in your discipline? You could even make it a working list that you add to throughout the year and keep on a large poster board in your classroom that serves as a reference point for students.

Step 3: Instruct Students on How to Recognize a Teacher's Signal Words

The third step is to help students recognize signal or cue words used by teachers in presentations that tell them which information is important and which can be ignored. Table 7.2 summarizes common signal words that teachers use and how students can interpret them. It may be useful to hand this out to your students and review it with them. This chart is merely a starting point that you can revise to cater more specifically to your classroom, your content, and your teaching style.

TABLE 7.2   Signal Words and How to Interpret Them

Signal Word Categories	Signal Words	Interpret This As ...
Emphasis	mostly, main, important, especially, most importantly, specifically	This is *very* important. Write this down!
Contrast	but, although, on the other hand, conversely, though, however, on the contrary	A contrasting point to note. Write this down!
Cause/effect	because, as a result, the reason for, due to, led to, created, brought about, hence, consequently, therefore, as a result of this	A detailed explanation that is making connections. Write this down! Make sure you know how it connects to information already provided.
Ordinal/sequential, numbers/list	first, second, third, last, finally, ultimately, next	Providing a sequence or timeline. Write each point down! If you miss a point, ask for the teacher to repeat that point.
Specifics/elaboration	for example, such as, the following, that is to say, furthermore	Only write this down if you need examples or something to clarify the point.
Summary	basically, in short, in brief, in conclusion	Pay attention because this is the big idea (gist). Write this down only if you do not have this in your notes already.
Repetition	in other words, in addition, let me put that another way	Reinforces a point made, so pay attention. You do not need to write this down.
Hints to write information down	Here is something you should know. I wouldn't forget this point if I were you. Remember this. This is particularly important. There are five things you have to know.	This is *very* important. Write this down! Ask the teacher to repeat if you do not catch everything! Make sure you have it recorded correctly!

During a Note-Taking Exercise

Step 4: Alter Your Speech, Delivery, and Vocabulary

Effective teachers of ELLs actively alter their speech, delivery, and vocabulary. Because ELL students are capturing information in a second language, they need us to speak at a slightly slower rate than their mainstream peers would. Speak slower and more clearly so that ELLs can keep up (Reiss, 2005). You can also recycle information so students are given multiple chances to capture the message. This approach is helpful for advanced students, as they still struggle to capture native speech velocity and cadence. But with beginner students this adaptation is critical. Students need extra time to listen and process information in a second language—plain and simple.

Like all students, ELL students need to feel confident that they can follow along, albeit with assistance. In addition to altering your speech, pick your vocabulary wisely, avoiding words and phrases that may confuse students. Try to stick to simple speech, avoiding complicated vocabulary, idiomatic expressions, or slang. Keep terms constant for reinforcement and to allow students to both be able to follow along and feel that they understand a large percentage of the vocabulary being used. As secondary educators we have all experienced that confident students tend to be more active students.

When you practice note taking, you can offer these speech modifications to your students; but when they are in other classes they may have to ask the teacher to slow down, repeat something, or ask if they understand the meanings of key terms. Make sure they know it is okay to do so. Or you may want to teach them to record lectures by teachers who talk quickly so they can listen multiple times at home to get all the notes.

Step 5: Use Visuals

It is extremely important to reinforce orally expressed information with visuals. Visuals are another medium through which ELLs can acquire content. If students lack comprehension, they may be able to recover some knowledge through visuals. The easiest and most effective method is to use an overhead projector and make overheads of important visuals before starting your lesson.

A music teacher, for example, presenting the Afro-Cuban jazz movement, would want to have pictures of the artists playing their instruments as he or she discussed the history of each one. While presenting Dizzy Gillespie, the teacher could have a picture of him playing the trumpet as well as a map of South Carolina—his home state—on overheads, with appropriate captions. In having information visually available to students as you present, you are both making the information real and reinforcing the material being covered.

Again, when teachers do not offer visuals to students in the future, teach your students to ask these teachers for things that could help them capture the notes better; to advocate for needed "scaffolds" that help the verbal information get through. We all know that in many cases the only advocates that students have are themselves, and it is our job to help them become confident enough to self-advocate outside of our classes.

Step 6: Provide Already or Partially Completed Notes

Provide already or partially completed notes to ELL students so that they have the orally expressed information being reinforced not only through visuals but through printed text as well. For beginner students the mere action of following along is an engaging and mentally difficult activity (C. H. Swanson, 1997). With beginner students, you may want to begin the process of note taking by providing already completed notes that will both serve as a model for students and allow students to see what is being said. Eventually you will move toward partially completed notes and then blank graphic organizers where students take all the notes, but it is important to provide students with both models and scaffolding at the beginning. Both the types of outlines and graphic organizers and the ways in which they can be partially completed will be explained and modeled later in this chapter.

Providing partial notes does take some effort on the part of the teacher, but if you start with a set of completed notes, you can then turn these into partially completed notes and finally just a template for recording information with very few or no cues provided. Figure 7.2 is an example of partially completed notes.

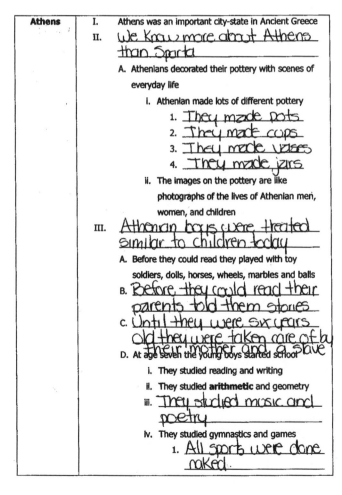

FIGURE 7.2
Portion of partially complete world history notes

Step 7: Monitor Student Progress

Monitor the progress of students as they take notes by both taking breaks and walking around the classroom to check their progress. It is important to provide ELL students with breaks so that they have chances to catch up or fill in missing information. Walk around to both monitor students' progress and try to help them fill in any gaps that you see in their information. When you feel that the majority of students are at the appropriate place, continue with your lecture or presentation. It is important not to let your monitoring period linger too long, however, or the students may begin to engage in discussion and other activities that are not on task.

For beginners, low intermediates, or those simply new to note taking, you might also break the note taking into segments—first two points, next two points, and so on, with time in between to see if students have the notes they should have. By comparing and contrasting their notes with a partner, they can see what they captured and missed; what is important, what is not important, and so on. This approach gives them small chunks of note taking with time in between for feedback, rather than one long continuous note-taking experience that could cause fatigue or make students completely give up when they feel overwhelmed.

After a Note-Taking Exercise

Step 8: Model How to Talk to Your Notes

It is important to treat note taking as an ongoing process, not something you do and then put away never to be looked at again. To make note taking real, students need to see their notes used, referred to, and engaged with. One way to achieve this purpose is to encourage students to talk to their notes. This is a wonderful opportunity to insert some levity into the note-taking process and show students that notes are resources.

To introduce this concept, you can get as lighthearted and playful as you choose. You can have students hold their notes up to their face and have them ask questions like "How are you doing?"; "What did you do this weekend?"; and so on. Then they can take their notes and hold them up to their ears, and invent responses. Often this is a much needed break from the difficult and draining process of taking notes. Although some high school students may find this silly, they will tend to follow your lead. Explain that they need to truly interact with their notes to make them useful.

Although there are many ways in which students can talk to their notes, starting with three different processes is a good idea. First, students will ask their notes a question—attempting to clarify something they do not understand. Second, students will make a comment—providing an opinion on something they have heard. Third, students will make a connection between their notes and their own life. With each process they draw an arrow from their notes to the margins where they are writing their questions, comments, and connections. Before writing, they will draw a box that contains a symbol defining what they are writing as a question [?], comment [C], or connection [←→].

The idea is to have students reading and engaging with their notes. In doing this activity, as is often the case with ELLs, it should be both modeled and scaffolded. One way to scaffold the activity is to provide students with sentence starters for questions, comments, and connections. So, once students understand what

Vignette: Talking to Your Notes

Isata was a Liberian refugee who had been in the United States for two years. Her literacy levels were lower than those of her peers though she possessed a much higher oral proficiency because she had grown up speaking English. As a result of her lack of formal education she struggled to pay attention in class, constantly distracted by her peers and frustrated by her lack of literacy. During reading exercises Isata would get lost, and in group work she simply could not concentrate, too interested in socializing.

One day, while studying ancient Greece, I decided to teach my students how to take notes while I lectured—or in this case, simply read prepared notes. I provided them with a partially completed version of what I would read, and asked them to listen carefully, and fill in the missing information. Isata, like so many other students, started to pay attention. She found the task of only filling in pieces of information achievable, so she was actively listening to obtain it. She knew that if she listened carefully she could fill in most of the missing information. She also knew that she could breathe while I read the notes that were already provided.

We finished taking notes, and I provided every student with the complete version of the notes that I had read. Students were given some time to go through their notes and revise them with a different colored utensil, based on the completed notes. Once again she was engaged. This was an easily comprehensible task and one she could complete successfully. If Isata took her time she could find her mistakes. She was engaged.

Then we got to "talking" to our notes, and Isata could not get enough. She loved pretending that her notes were alive and asking them how they were doing, putting them up to her ear, and laughing as she awaited a response that would never come. It was finally an opportunity for her to act silly without getting in trouble for it. Other students followed suit, seeing how much fun she was having with it.

When it came time to "talk" to her notes in a more academic way, Isata found this a little more difficult, but was willing to try, because she had seen it modeled on the board, and she had sentence starters to help her out.

Isata was finally academically engaged in a way I had never seen before.

Judah Lakin, Hope High School

they are doing, they can read through their notes and write on their notes as modeled in Figure 7.3. After students have finished, teachers can lead a discussion where students share their questions, comments, and connections, which serves as a further review of the materials and provides a nonthreatening environment for students to clear up any misconceptions they had while taking notes. Figure 7.3 is an example of what students' notes can look like after they have "talked to" them.

In addition to "talking" to their notes through writing questions, comments, and connections, students can also mark up their texts in other simpler, although just as useful, ways. If they do not understand a word, they can circle it, or if they think a concept is really important, they can underline it or put an asterisk next to it. If they find something surprising, they may want to put an exclamation point next to it. As educators, you will decide how important these strategies are to you and how much time you want to spend teaching them to students. The point is to

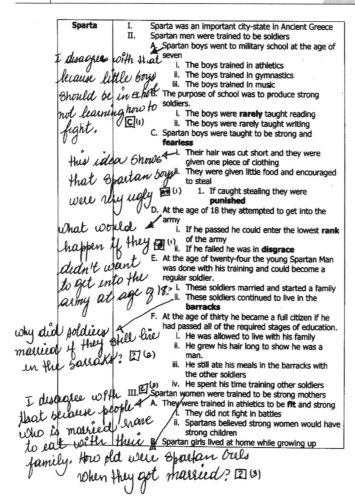

Sparta	I.	Sparta was an important city-state in Ancient Greece
	II.	Spartan men were trained to be soldiers
	A.	Spartan boys went to military school at the age of seven
		i. The boys trained in athletics
		ii. The boys trained in gymnastics
		iii. The boys trained in music
	B.	The purpose of school was to produce strong soldiers.
		i. The boys were **rarely** taught reading
		ii. The boys were rarely taught writing
	C.	Spartan boys were taught to be strong and **fearless**
		i. Their hair was cut short and they were given one piece of clothing
		ii. They were given little food and encouraged to steal
		1. If caught stealing they were **punished**
	D.	At the age of 18 they attempted to get into the army
		i. If he passed he could enter the lowest **rank** of the army
		ii. If he failed he was in **disgrace**
	E.	At the age of twenty-four the young Spartan Man was done with his training and could become a regular soldier.
		i. These soldiers married and started a family
		ii. These soldiers continued to live in the **barracks**
	F.	At the age of thirty he became a full citizen if he had passed all of the required stages of education.
		i. He was allowed to live with his family
		ii. He grew his hair long to show he was a man.
		iii. He still ate his meals in the barracks with the other soldiers
		iv. He spent his time training other soldiers
	III.	Spartan women were trained to be strong mothers
	A.	They were trained in athletics to be **fit** and strong
		i. They did not fight in battles
		ii. Spartans believed strong women would have strong children
	B.	Spartan girls lived at home while growing up

Handwritten annotations:
I disagree with that because little boys should be in school not learning how to fight.
this idea shows that Spartan boys were very ugly
what would happen if they didn't want to get into the army at age of 18?
why did soldiers married if they still live in the barracks?
I disagree with that because people who is married have to eat with their family. How old were Spartan Girls when they got married?

FIGURE 7.3
Portion of "talk to" world history notes

show students how to use the notes and make them useful in the student's learning process and as a tool for quiz and test preparation.

Step 9: Allow Students to Revise and Edit Notes

It is important, in demonstrating that note taking is an ongoing process, that you allow students the opportunity to revise and edit their notes. As the concept of note taking is introduced, students will initially struggle, since they are doing this in a new language. It is important to recognize students' struggles and encourage them by allowing them the chance to revise and edit their notes, as suggested previously in the description of the note-taking process. After notes have been taken, editing can be accomplished through various methods.

First, after the students have finished a note-taking session you might want to pass out your notes, or a student model, allowing the students to compare and contrast notes. After reviewing your notes, students can use a different colored pencil or pen to fill in what their notes are lacking. In this way the student can have complete notes, and the teacher can evaluate how much information her students are able to get down by looking at the difference in color.

After having the students do this assignment, they can be grouped and engage in conversation surrounding whether or not they missed information or simply thought it was not important. In those cases where students think information is not important, they can then discuss the issues of relevance and importance either in small groups or as a class. In this way students are not only practicing note taking but also engaging in metacognition by thinking about their own note taking and evaluating information and its importance.

In addition to comparing content, students should be encouraged to look for abbreviations and signal words that they may have missed, once again filling them in with a second color. When evaluating notes, it is important to hold students accountable for their ability both to take notes and to revise them; one way to do so is through giving credit for notes students have taken the time to study and revise.

Helping Students Summarize Information

Often the goal of having students take notes is to take a set of information and reduce it to its essentials, whether it is for the purpose of studying or for creating a written document. In content courses, especially material like history, there is simply too much information to cover, so it is essential that students have the capacity to reduce the amount of information with which they need to work, regardless of the end goal. This skill becomes imperative with ELLs, as the language obstacle causes even more difficulties in dealing with large amounts of material. The students' synthesis of the information adds to their conceptual understanding of the material.

The most effective way to begin ELL students on this process of eliminating unnecessary information is to scaffold their note-taking process with note-taking formats and graphic organizers. You can choose these by the content or skill being covered, and as discussed earlier these could be already complete, partially complete, or completely blank depending on the proficiency level of the students you are working with. Table 7.3 contains a list of note-taking formats and graphic organizers along with the specific functions they serve. In addition, Figures 7.4 and 7.5 display samples completed by ELL students and educators at the secondary level.

When dealing with a given set of information, it is important to stress to students that the goal of taking notes, irrespective of the note-taking format or graphic organizer being used, is to get the basics: the essential information and concepts. "Getting the basics" should be a dominant theme through the class when dealing with note taking. An effective way to broadly define "the basics" for student comprehension is to use five basic questions: Who, What, Where, Why, and When. These questions work very nicely in social studies and language arts, although they may need to be slightly altered or adapted for content areas like science and math depending on the material being covered.

It is useful to lead your students through the process of finding this information in their notes, especially the first time around. Creating a summary from this information can be done in six simple steps.

Step 1: Create graphic organizers that contain the following five questions: Who? What? Where? When? and Why?

Step 2: Provide both sets of the notes being used so that students have both their revised notes and the teacher's notes at their disposal.

TABLE 7.3 Note-Taking Formats and Graphic Organizers

Notation Formats	What It Is	Why It Is Needed	When to Use It
Cornell Notes (landmark notes)	A two-column chart where big ideas are presented in the left column and the right column is reserved for filling in the necessary information to understand that big idea	To help students with information that is presented in a linear fashion	Linear presentations of information including historical time periods or literature summaries; additionally, when you have a main idea and supporting details
		To help students split large amounts of information into small, manageable sections—the left column	
T-notes	A two-column chart that looks similar to the Cornell Notes in structure although it does not utilize the columns in the same way	To provide students with a way to divide information in a meaningful way	Dualistic presentations of information such as reviewing the causes and effects of the American Revolution
Simple outline	Roman numerals, letters, and numbers indented differently on a page	To help students understand the concept of main ideas and supporting details	When reviewing factual information that clearly has overarching ideas and supporting details as in English and social studies
Venn diagram	Two or more intersecting/overlapping circles	To visually show students how subject matter can be compared and contrasted	Comparing and contrasting information—e.g., reptiles and mammals
Web (semantic web; branching egg; spider web)	A centered cell with surrounding cells	To provide students with a structure to generate ideas	When brainstorming ideas on essay topics in English or geometric principles in Mathematics
Fishbone	A line with angled lines from the center line up and from the center line down at parallel intervals (in the appearance of a fish bone)	To provide students with a way to show simultaneously occurring events	Useful in science and social studies when two things occur at the same time—e.g., events in the South and events in the North during the Civil War
KWL chart	A three-column chart where the three columns are headed "Know," "Want to Know," and "Learned"	To help students focus on the learning process, which centers on activating prior knowledge, actively forming questions, and understanding what they have learned	When starting new topics like fractions in mathematics, ancient Egypt in world history, or *The Great Gatsby* in English

Different Parts of the Cell

ER (Endoplasmic Reticulum) 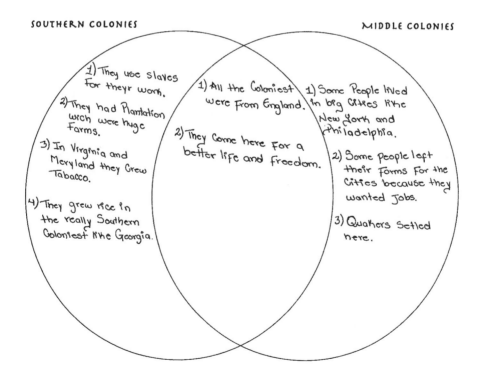	Two types
	      Rough Endoplasmic Reticulum
	            <u>Structure:</u> Studded with ribosomes
	            <u>Function:</u> Produces protein, which can
	                  Become as a part of a plasma membrane
	                  Be released from the cell
	                  Be transported to other organelles
	      Smooth endoplasmic reticulum
	            <u>Function:</u> Production and storage of lipids

Vacuole	<u>Structure:</u> Sac-like <u>Stores</u> food, enzymes, and waste products temporarily Plant cell has one big vacuole and 1-2 small vacuoles. Animal cell has many small vacuoles.
Lysosome	<u>Function:</u> Digest food, worn out organelles, virus and bacteria with the help of enzymes Example: Tail of a tadpole is digested by lysosome

FIGURE 7.4
Portion of Cornell Notes given to beginner and intermediate ELLs in Ms. Nandi's biology class

SOUTHERN COLONIES   MIDDLE COLONIES

1) They use slaves for theyr work.

2) They had Plantation wich were huge farms.

3) In Virginia and Meryland they Grew Tabacco.

4) They grew rice in the really Southern Coloniest like Georgia.

1) All the Coloniest were From England.

2) They Come here For a better life and Freedom.

1) Some People lived in big Cities like New York and Philadelphia.

2) Some people left their Farms For the Cities because they wanted Jobs.

3) Quakers Setled here.

FIGURE 7.5   U.S. history Venn diagram

Step 3: Lead students toward finding the required information in their notes, beginning with the three basic questions: Who, Where, and When, since it is easy for students to identify names, places, and dates. It is useful to give students a way of differentiating the information as they look for it, such as five differently colored highlighters, colored pencils, markers, or different shapes (circles, squares, triangles, clouds, and upside-down triangles). You can mirror this activity on the overhead step by step. Remember, having models and demonstrations is very helpful to ELLs, particularly those at the lowest proficiency levels.

Step 4: Lead students through a process of ordering the information, looking for connections between ideas, and writing the summary. Our experience leading students through this process shows that it requires some decision making on the part of the teacher. There really is no formula that will fit a given set of information. Choose a logical starting place and go from there—perhaps one time you will start with "what," another time with "who," because on each occasion a particular question word holds more importance to the concept you are teaching.

Step 5: Have students share their summaries. The first few times this process will be modeled by the teacher, and the students will merely write down the summary that the class has created together. The next step will be to allow students to undergo this process in groups. Heterogeneous groups of triads and dyads will work best, as this group size forces every student to become involved (Kagan, 1995). Students will write their collective summaries on large pieces of paper by picking and choosing sentences from individual summaries and combining the information into one coherent summary. Last, the groups will hang their summaries around the room, and then each group will circle the room reading and evaluating the other groups' summaries—a carousel procedure.

Step 6: Have students analyze each other's summaries. Students can either choose one summary that they think is best and talk about why. Or, students can choose parts of each summary that they think are strong and use those parts to create a new improved summary that includes the best part of each group's summary. Eventually, students will write these summaries by themselves, and they can be shared in small groups with students engaging in a discussion about why one's student summary is better or worse than another's. In this way, students are not only engaging in the act of summarizing but are also participating in metacognitive exercises by evaluating their own and others' learning processes. As you might imagine, students need to practice, practice, practice, if they are to get better at writing well-formulated summaries. So make the time investment because it will really pay off, not just for your class, but also for many classes taken by your ELLs.

A *criteria checklist for summaries* is a tool that students can use on their own summaries before handing them into the teacher in the spirit of participating in metacognitive thinking.

Criteria Checklist for Summaries

- I used both my revised notes and the teacher's notes to make this summary.
- I have information in my summary that answers Who? What? Where? Why? and When?
- I do not have any information that is not needed.
- I attempted to order the information in a way that makes sense and puts connected ideas together.
- I read other students' summaries and used their work to make mine better.

Sometimes, one or another question word will not apply, but the process would remain essentially the same minus the question word that has no application in the information to be summarized.

Paraphrasing: Putting Things in Your Own Words

Note taking and summarizing provide wonderful opportunities for students to practice paraphrasing—an extremely difficult task for an ELL but an important one to learn. These students struggle with paraphrasing for several reasons. First, many of them culturally may not understand why they cannot simply copy what someone else says (Odean, 1987). Second, paraphrasing requires putting ideas and concepts into other words, which for ELLs with very limited vocabulary presents a unique challenge, since they may not have the "other" words to use. When presented with the obstacle of paraphrasing, ELLs may simply say, "I do not know how to say that any other way," and be completely telling the truth. In order to help students become better at paraphrasing it is a good idea to break it down into three steps.

Step 1: The first step in paraphrasing is ensuring that students fully understand what they are hearing or reading. It is simply not possible to paraphrase information that is not understood. If you speak the native language of the student, it may be worth checking comprehension in the student's primary language.

Step 2: The second step in paraphrasing is allowing students to write down what they understood from what they listened to or read. Without looking at their notes, reading a document, or hearing anything, they are simply to write down what they understood. They should do so by writing down the phrases and key terms that they grasped.

Step 3: The third step in paraphrasing is allowing students to look at their notes or listen again to the information and make sure that what they say is not missing any information and does in fact contain different words than the ones expressed in the original material. If it does not, they may need to be encouraged to use a thesaurus to look for new words to say the same thing. As proficiency advances this step becomes easier to do, and it is worth noting that paraphrasing should be introduced with learners at the intermediate level and worked on as they advance in proficiency. Beginner students simply do not have the vocabulary to put ideas into their own words, and it becomes nothing more than a frustrating and futile process. (If you attempt to introduce paraphrasing at this level, offer the alternate wording, so they can gain some practice selecting words and phrases to use to "say it" another way.)

Paraphrasing is a very important skill for your ELLs to acquire and gives them excellent language practice. Spending time teaching paraphrasing skills while you teach your content is a very worthwhile use of time.

Evaluating Note Taking

Evaluating Students

Note taking, like all skills, is one that students will need to practice and hone. It is important that as you emphasize note-taking skills, students understand they will be held accountable for their work and progress. If students feel that there is no value attached to their note taking, they will simply not participate and will use other students' notes when it comes time to study for a test. It is important that students understand that note taking will be a part of their grade and that the teacher will collect their notes often in order to assess them.

It is important to make sure that students understand that they will be assessed both on their ability to take notes and, perhaps more importantly, their ability to revise those notes. The emphasis is placed on improvement, and kids are encouraged to revise their notes and make sure they are correct, as opposed to simply thinking that taking notes is a one-shot deal. Figure 7.6 is an example of a note-taking rubric.

In addition to creating multiple opportunities for students to revise and edit their notes, it also important to create exams, quizzes, and projects where they are allowed to *use* their notes. These provide students with yet another incentive to improve their note-taking skills and create a direct incentive for taking effective notes: a better grade on their quizzes, tests, and projects. Here are some options for giving kids credit for their notes, showing them that note taking is important:

- Collect and grade notes.
- Create exams and quizzes where students need to use their notes during the exam or quiz.
- Create exams and quizzes that are highly based in the notes, and make part of their grade on the exam or quiz the quality of their notes.
- Create short homework assignments that students need to use their notes to complete. Students turn in their notes with the assignment.

Informing Instruction

It is obviously important to hold students accountable for taking notes and to provide them incentives for doing so correctly, but, as with all forms of assessment, it is equally important to use students' notes to inform your instruction. In evaluating students' notes, pay careful attention to how effective the average ELL student is at taking notes. If many students have large gaps in their notes or seem to be missing key words, it is likely that you need to rethink your strategies, possibly slowing down your speech or making sure to emphasize key points or giving them more scaffolds (word boxes, key phrases on the board) as they take notes. Essentially, viewing ELL students' notes can provide great insight into how much your students are grasping your instruction and how much they are missing— evaluating students notes is just as much about evaluating yourself as it is about evaluating your ELL students.

Conclusion

Teaching note taking to ELLs is a complex yet extremely important task. As educators, our goal is to prepare our students for either postsecondary education or life beyond high school, and in both cases being able to take useful notes matters. When teaching note taking, keep "Eight Strategies You Should Make Sure You Are Doing to Teach Note Taking" nearby to remind yourself of the key actions you, as the teacher, can take to help better facilitate the note-taking process.

FIGURE 7.6 Note-taking rubric

Criteria	4 Exceeds Proficiency	3 Meets Proficiency	2 Approaching Proficiency	1 Substantially Below Proficient	Comments
Structure and Notation Format Do you have all the right headings and titles on your notes? Do you put your notes in the appropriate notation format?	You have *every* title and heading that you need, and the notes are in the correct notation format.	You have *most of the* titles and headings that you need but are missing a few, and the notes are in the correct notation format.	You have *some of the* titles and headings that you need but are missing a few, and the notes are not in the correct notation format.	You have *almost none of* the titles and headings that you need, and the notes are not in the correct notation format.	
Content Do you have all the important information?	You have written down *nearly every* important point and have *no large gaps* in your information.	You have written down *most of the* important points and have only *small gaps* in your information.	You have written down *some of the* important points and still have *some large gaps* in your information.	You have *very few* important points and *many large gaps* in your information.	
Abbreviations Do you include abbreviations whenever possible?	You *always* use abbreviations, using the abbreviation list provided and your own abbreviations that follow the structures taught in class.	You *almost always* use abbreviations, using the abbreviation list provided and your own abbreviations that follow the structures taught in class.	You *sometimes* use abbreviations, using the abbreviation list provided and your own abbreviations that follow the structures taught in class.	You *almost never* use abbreviations, using the abbreviation list provided and your own abbreviations that follow the structures taught in class.	
Signal Words Do you include signal words when appropriate? Do you appropriately interpret signal words?	You *always* include signal words where appropriate, and you *always* demonstrate an understanding of the meaning of signal words.	You *almost always* include signal words where appropriate and you *almost always* demonstrate an understanding of the meaning of the signal words.	You *sometimes* include signal words where appropriate, and you *sometimes* demonstrate an understanding of the meaning of signal words.	You *almost never* include signal words where appropriate, and you *almost never* demonstrate an understanding of the meaning of signal words.	
Revision Have you used all the resources available (teacher's notes, students' notes, abbreviation lists, etc.) to revise your notes?	You have used *all* available resources and have *completely* corrected and completed your notes.	You have used *almost all* available resources and have *almost* completely corrected and completed your notes, still leaving a few errors.	You have used *some of* the available resources and have *partially* corrected and completed your notes.	You have used *almost none* of the available resources and have *barely* corrected and completed your notes.	

Checklist

Eight Strategies You Should Make Sure You Are Doing to Teach Note Taking

☐ I have my students participate in listening activities before asking them to engage in note taking.

☐ I provide visual aids to help my students understand the information being expressed orally.

☐ I alter my speech in terms of clarity, speed, and word choice.

☐ I explicitly teach students how to take notes, including lessons on abbreviations and signal words.

☐ I provide my students with partially completed notes and multiple note-taking formats.

☐ I provide students with opportunities to revise their notes.

☐ I provide students with multiple opportunities to earn credit for taking effective notes.

☐ I use students' notes to inform my instruction.

CHAPTER 8

Writing in a Second Language

Elizabeth, Liberia and Ms. Leininger

> Writing is both a "marker" of high-skill, high-wage, professional work and a "gatekeeper" with clear equity implications. People unable to express themselves clearly in writing limit their opportunities for professional, salaried employment.
> Bob Kerrey, President of New School University in New York and Chairman of the National Commission on Writing

Guiding Questions

- What are the factors that play a role in writing proficiency in secondary classrooms, and what are the additional challenges that English language learners face in developing writing proficiency?
- How can we adapt the writing process for English language learners?
- How do we scaffold the traditional writing genres and use graphic organizers, checklists, and rubrics to instruct English language learners to write effectively in the different academic writing forms?
- What are the recommended writing genres and assignments for English language learners at different proficiency levels?
- What are the best practices for instructing and correcting grammar and mechanics in writing?
- How can we help students develop writing fluency?
- What are the best practices for assessing students' writing proficiency?

Challenges for ELLs

Whether you are a content teacher or a language teacher, tackling academic writing with English language learners (ELLs) can at times feel like an insurmountable challenge. Yet, if ELLs are to graduate from high school today, they must be able to meet the same rigorous writing standards as secondary students for whom English is a first language. The following list presents the major challenges ELLs face when writing in English:

- Understanding and meeting *high expectations* such as state *writing standards*
- *Expressing themselves* in a new language

- Acquiring basic *writing fluency and ease* (writing without having to stop and translate words, and writing in an uninhibited way, without worrying about making mistakes)
- Learning English *sound-spelling correspondence*

Whether you are a content teacher or a language teacher, it is important to understand the special challenges ELLs face as they attempt to write in their second language, so the next section will explore and describe the challenges of writing in a second language. Following that, we will give you strategies and teaching resources to strengthen your writing instruction, as you work collaboratively with other teachers to create a more comprehensive writing curriculum for second-language writers.

Understanding and Meeting High Expectations

In order for students to be successful in secondary school, and later in college, they need to be able to write clearly and proficiently. For this reason, all states have set high expectations for students' writing performance. Certainly it is our job to prepare ELLs to be successful writers who are able to meet the demands of secondary classrooms and beyond—helping them progress toward writing proficiency as they use writing on a daily basis to develop their critical thinking skills. Our learners are experimenting with new words, phrases, and expressions, but at the same time they need to work toward meeting rigorous standards for writing quantity and quality if they are to be successful in both secondary school and the world beyond.

Even though ELLs are new to the language and often new to the country, they are held to the same writing standards as native English speakers. We believe that holding all students accountable for their learning is essential. That said, we also recognize that expecting newly arrived adolescent ELLs to perform as well as their native English-speaking counterparts on the writing portion of standardized tests is not appropriate, given the fact that they have been identified as still in the process of learning English (Cech, 2009). Although we hold firm in our beliefs, we recognize that, nationally, this is a contentious issue that has yet to be resolved. Yet, no matter the resolution, it is our responsibility to provide our learners with a working knowledge of secondary writing standards to use as a road map on their way to developing full writing proficiency in English. Certainly secondary writing standards are helpful to teachers so that they can pinpoint where their learners are in terms of gaining the skills that are necessary to become proficient writers in their new language.

Expressing Oneself in a New Language

Adolescence is a time when all students, regardless of where they are from, are learning a lot about who they are and how they want to express themselves to the world. This challenge—of trying to, at once, know yourself, and properly and adequately express yourself—is further complicated for ELLs. For adolescent ELLs, the native language represents a huge part of their persona—within it are their cultural and linguistic identities that have been formed since childhood. Adolescent ELLs have already begun to build a solid foundation for the person they will become, and this person exists primarily in the language of their native tongue. It can be an extremely difficult and often painful process for ELLs to transition from a familiar culture and language to a completely new language and culture. Personal expression in English is affected by all of this as ELLs struggle and learn to find the words to express their innermost thoughts. Because ELLs are attempting to express themselves in a language they are newly learning, they will often feel frustrated by their inability to share information about themselves and express their dreams, views, and opinions in a way that is meaningful and satisfying.

At the same time, adolescent ELLs are also learning to express themselves academically through writing, a much more cognitively demanding task than expressing personal thoughts, emotions, and opinions. The struggle of self-expression through academic writing is one most of us can identify with, but it can create even more frustration and difficulty for ELLs. These students struggle with being properly understood, being able to convey personal style, communicating humor or sarcasm if desired, and of course expressing complex ideas with a limited vocabulary and developing grammar system.

With the advent of online translators, many adolescents are tempted to use the Internet to translate large chunks of text to help them express complex ideas in a new language. They hope that the translators can serve the function of circumventing their struggle to communicate the way they desire. Use of the internet for this purpose may range from the translation of large quantities of text within an assignment to entire assignments. It is quite obvious when students use this strategy because their writing will either drastically improve because of a higher level of vocabulary or not make any sense.

As helpful as online translators can be for looking up one word at a time, it is usually impossible for a computer to interpret a writer's intended meaning accurately. This misinterpretation often results in a slew of mistranslated multiple-meaning words that ultimately leads to incomprehensible text. Because we know this easy-to-use tool is tempting for our students, it is helpful to teach about the benefits and pitfalls of electronic translation, and also to be on the lookout for instances of overuse and abuse. Oftentimes, students do not even realize that using such online and handheld translators results in mistaken or inappropriate translations, making such instances wonderful opportunities for teachable moments. Certainly, given the enormity of the task at hand—learning how to write effectively at high levels in a new language—you will want to also reassure your students that, while there are no shortcuts, with exposure and practice their writing skills will improve. You should also stress that, as their teacher, you will support them every step of the way.

Writing Fluency and Ease

One of the biggest challenges for ELLs is developing writing fluency in English. This task is especially challenging for students at a beginner or low-intermediate level. Lack of fluency is the result of students struggling to successfully manage many linguistic skills at once: translating in their minds what they want to write on paper; figuring out how to use new systems of syntax, text structure, and mechanics; correctly conjugating verb tenses; painstakingly looking up key words or phrases; and applying rules of spelling correctly, or at least close to correctly, so as to effectively convey meaning. Some adolescent ELLs lack writing fluency because they lack practice in the exercise of writing, whether in their native language or English. Help your students build writing fluency by getting them to write *every day*. Suggestions for daily writing activities to build fluency, as well as strategies for helping students develop their writing skills, are detailed in a later section of this chapter, "Helping ELLs Overcome Writing Challenges."

Learning to Spell Sounds in English

One of the reasons why the English language is viewed as such a complicated and difficult language to learn is the variety of ways the same sound can be spelled in English. There are rules that govern spelling and pronunciation, but there are numerous rules and many exceptions. For example, there are only five vowel letters (if you do not include the variant *y* for *i*), yet these five vowel letters can be used to produce fifteen vowel sounds—six short, seven long, and two reduced vowels (D. Freeman & Freeman, 2007), and each sound can often be expressed through more than one spelling combination. For example, the short *o* sound can be expressed with a single *o* as in "pot" or by the combination *ou* as in "bought."

The ability to develop proficient spelling has a strong connection to the way readers judge a student's writing proficiency. But more importantly, ELL students' ability to spell well affects their fluency and confidence. Constantly questioning how to spell a word is both time-consuming and frustrating, and often leads to students sticking to words they do know how to spell, thus limiting their ability to fully express themselves. Research shows that, on the whole, poor spellers write at a lower quantity and quality (Joshi, Treiman, Carreker, & Moats, 2008–9, p. 9).

As we saw in Chapter 5, when students are proficient in another language upon entering school, and especially when they have been educated in that language, are literate, and share an alphabet, they draw on that knowledge to produce English in terms of how to represent speech sounds graphically. As a result, some of the spelling "errors" we will see are actually evidence of encoding rules drawn from the native language that yield incorrect spelling in English. As an example, the letter *i* in Spanish is always pronounced "ee," so if a Spanish speaker wrote *sit* for *seat*, this representation of the word could be showing knowledge of native language spelling rules rather than incorrect word choice. For more on the types of cross-lingual inventive spelling to expect across the various languages, see Swan and Smith (2001).

Because spelling is a common frustration for ELLs, it needs to be taught systematically. Since the topic is quite detailed, we recommend teachers access comprehensive teaching resources explicitly designed to guide spelling instruction, such as Bear, Helman, Templeton, Invernizzi, and Johnston (2007) and Joshi and colleagues (2008–9). However, as a general rule, when working on spelling, be sure to limit your focus to one pattern (consonant-vowel-consonant-*e* rule as in "cake"), one "spelling demon" (e.g., "dough"), or one difference in spelling across languages (vowels in English compared to vowels in Spanish) at a time, allowing students to see how words function according to the many rules that govern word encoding in English.

Helping ELLs Overcome Writing Challenges

In this section and those that follow we will explore some of the strategies and tools that language and content teachers can use to help their ELLs advance in

Principles

- Create a safe, supportive learning environment where it is okay to make mistakes, ask questions, and ask for help. Use peer support and have plenty of resources in your classroom to aid students (such as ESL student dictionaries, electronic translators, children's/students' thesauri).

- Within your discipline, provide experience with different writing forms and purposes to ensure students gain experience with each.

- Provide real-world writing experiences (memoir, biography, op-ed, newspaper article) to give students access to writing as it occurs beyond the classroom.

- Provide needed scaffolding (checklists, graphic organizers, prompts) and modeling, so students can use their developing writing skills in a supported context.

- Provide clear expectations for writing assignments to ensure that students feel confident about how to approach writing activities and assignments.

- Provide tools (rubrics, checklists) for editing so students can check their own work. Match the checklists and tools to difficulties students are experiencing (using -*ed* on regular past tense verbs to express actions in the past tense; stating the main idea in a clear topic sentence, etc.).

- Provide focused, constructive feedback about content and form through frequent conferencing to allow students to absorb information and apply it to future writing experiences.

their writing proficiency and overcome some of the challenges detailed in the previous section. Before detailing our strategies, we are going to provide some principles that should guide your important work in instructing ELLs in writing.

Tailoring the Writing Process to the Needs of ELLs

As most teachers are well aware, the writing process essentially consists of five stages:

1. *Prewriting:* gathering ideas by brainstorming, outlining, journaling, or otherwise investigating a topic.

2. *Drafting:* writing about the topic, getting ideas on paper, and forming a loose organizational structure.

3. *Revising:* continuing to develop the content (plot, argument, support), clarifying ideas, and solidifying the organizational structure.

4. *Editing:* rereading and correcting for grammar, spelling, and other mechanical errors.

5. *Publishing:* displaying or sharing the "final" piece with others.

Some teachers who use the workshop model of writing may explicitly add a conferencing stage, which consists of a student-teacher conference in which the student asks questions and gets feedback during the drafting stage. Whatever the practices in your district are, keep in mind that the stages of the writing process are flexible and fluid; students may be simultaneously engaged in prewriting and drafting, or be editing while revising. Likewise, there is by no means a fixed amount of time students must spend in each stage, or anything wrong with revisiting stages multiple times. The writing process is just that: a process. Let students go with the flow of their ideas and support them as they work in whatever way fits best with them. Whether you are a content or language teacher, if you engage your ELLs in the writing process to help them produce and refine writing pieces, you will want to use the ELL-friendly strategies we provide in this chapter.

Modifying the Writing Process for ELLs

It is important to expose adolescent ELLs to the writing process as early as possible. Incorporating the steps and language of the writing process in your writing instruction will help students start to understand the crucial concept that all writing is a process and will begin to prepare ELLs for mainstream English courses and standardized testing. At the same time, the writing process must be modified for ELLs, especially for those at lower English proficiency levels. Here are four ways to modify the writing process for ELLs of all levels:

More Time

It may seem obvious that students who are learning a new language *while simultaneously* engaging in the stages of the writing process would need more time to complete an assignment or project than their English-dominant peers. However, the idea of giving ELLs more time cannot be overstated. Writing takes time; good writing takes a long time; and good writing in a second language takes even longer. This generalization is especially true for students who are perfectionists about their work or who are extremely eager and motivated to excel in English. Many ELLs will need more time in each stage of the writing process, though it is in the drafting and revising stages that most ELLs will benefit from the gift of time. This means more time to work on and conference about assignments in the classroom and more time to revise and edit. Because working in a new language can sometimes feel exhausting or be exasperating, it is enormously helpful to provide students with the encouragement they will need to persist. When we give students the support and time they need to adequately work through the various stages of the writing process, they are able to produce their best quality writing.

More Models

Just as the idea of extra time cannot be overstated when embarking on the writing process with ELLs, neither can the use of models. Use as many models as you can possibly find and vary them by proficiency level. Do not limit your use of models to those that match the current proficiency level of the student, using only simple models with beginner students and more complex models with more advanced students. All students' writing greatly benefits when they are shown models of varying proficiency levels, within an appropriate range of difficulty. Use of a range of models gives students a broader yet clearer idea of what they are being asked to write, and it will serve to relieve anxiety students may have around needing to create something that looks exactly like one model or exemplar. We recommend using teacher-created models, textbook examples, professional models, and peer models.

More Focused Editing

In terms of editing ELLs' writing, teachers should initially focus only on improving the content of the writing. Only in the last draft should teachers concern themselves with sentence-level grammatical errors. If you spend too much time focusing on every mistake that students commit as they draft their essays, your students will get frustrated and may shut down—not fully benefiting from all stages of the writing process. The revision process for ELLs begins with an emphasis on how to expand and clarify their writing, and later emphasizes editing and refining.

When working on writing with ELLs you always need to determine how many things to focus on at one time, depending on both the writing proficiency level of your students and their personalities. If you choose to use peer editing in your classroom, it must be a very structured activity. For example, students can review a peer's writing piece and look for one element on which to give feedback—such as subject-verb agreement. Even then though, providing lists of verbs and their conjugations may be helpful. In addition, peer feedback should be positive. Instruct students on how to give positive feedback by teaching them starter sentences or phrases they can use, or by using symbols such as smiley faces or stars to signal important feedback. Bear in mind that, for some students, receiving peer feedback is a new experience, and they may not be satisfied with peer feedback alone since, during their past schooling experiences they have always been given feedback from adults. If you know that your students have this kind of background, try to introduce peer editing carefully, combining it with teacher feedback to aid in this transition.

More Welcoming, Flexible Publication

"Publication" is key to establishing the importance of, and learner's sense of accomplishment in, completing a writing piece, especially one that has been through multiple drafts and revisions. Recognizing individual and group achievement with a celebration instills a sense of pride in student authors and often serves to motivate them to work harder, more skillfully, and more knowledgably on their next piece. It also serves to empower and legitimize them, as they move from students simply doing their homework to authors publishing their work.

The idea of publication is to celebrate writing and at the same time force students to use their other language skills– reading, listening, and speaking. Depending on the proficiency levels of students in your class, publication techniques and practices will differ. Students may share a "Golden Line," a favorite passage or paragraph, or their entire piece. Sharing may be done out loud or silently. It may take place in pairs, in groups, or as a whole class. Regardless of how your students choose to structure the publication, it is important that students get a taste of what it is like to be on both the presenting and receiving ends of peer publication. Sharing one's work can be intimidating at first, but it can be rewarding both during the process and afterward. Students learn to overcome their fears and get to know their classmates on a more personal and academic level, and this is an excellent way to build community in the classroom.

Getting Ideas Out in English

While breaking down and scaffolding the writing process for your students, you are simultaneously teaching and encouraging them to communicate their ideas in a way that maintains their creative integrity and matches their proficiency level. Teach students how to "talk around" an idea using simpler vocabulary and syntax, rather than the more complex words and phrasing they may be accustomed to in their native language. Students will feel empowered as they work to develop greater English proficiency, rather than feel silenced or frustrated that they cannot express themselves because they do not yet know the specific word they want to use in English. Since most adolescent ELLs are critical thinkers with complex reasoning to share, help them talk around an idea using words, phrases, and expressions they know and feel comfortable with to effectively communicate their ideas to others. Always encourage your students to try talking around something first, rather than going straight for a dictionary or online translation service. The idea is to stay in the target language as much as possible so that English can become a viable medium in which to express their thoughts over time.

One final way teachers can help students develop and expand their language skills is to show them how to use descriptive words and sensory imagery (sight, sound, touch, etc.), different literary devices (similes, metaphors, etc.), and literary elements (parallelism and point of view in content writing; characterization, dialogue, and foreshadowing in literary texts; etc.). With clear, consistent instruction, and plenty of modeling and practice, students will begin to master and eventually become comfortable using all these things in their writing. Not only will practice make students better writers in general, but it will also do wonders with regard to preparing them for mainstream English in either a high school or college setting.

Modeling

As mentioned earlier, one of the most important ways you can help your ELLs improve their writing skills, especially their academic writing, is by using models. Models allow you to show examples of *what to do* and, just as importantly, *what not to do*. They can serve as reference points, guides, or motivational tools that inspire ELLs to try to write in English, because it can be frightening and confusing to start a writing project without having a model for what the final product should look like. Models are especially important for students with low literacy skills. Students with higher literacy abilities have had greater exposure to a larger quantity and variety of texts, and are more generally familiar with written text. Students with low literacy skills lack such exposure, and so we need to be responsible for providing them with that exposure through models.

What types of models should you use? First, be sure to use a range of models that match the range of your students' proficiencies. Second, it is essential to provide many models. Just one or two models used in one or two class periods will not suffice. Students need to be frequently exposed to different models, from those of published writers, to teacher-created models, to mainstream student and peer models.

Using models from students within the same class or in a different period (though admittedly time-consuming to collect, make anonymous, copy, and redistribute) often engages students on a more personal level than models from unknown sources. Be sure to keep the names of the students whose work you use confidential (though oftentimes they themselves will reveal their identity because they are proud their work is being highlighted). Using current students' work as models also ensures that you are addressing the current writing issues of the students in your class, and it is a perfect way to use student work as a way to drive instruction.

The Fluency Challenge: Developing Writing Fluency Using Daily Writing

In order for students to become fluent writers, they must engage in the act of writing every day and practice various forms of writing using a variety of formats. Developing writing fluency also means experimenting with the new vocabulary students learn through other classroom activities. As a result, you need to give them many opportunities to practice their writing skills on a daily basis. The following subsections contain suggestions for incorporating daily writing activities into your classroom.

Do Now

"Do Now" is a strategy for getting students into the routine of writing in class every single day. A "Do Now" is a short 5–10-minute activity assigned at the very beginning of class. "Do Nows" serve to focus students by getting them to think and work immediately upon entering class; they also allow you to take attendance or pass out any necessary paper or supplies students need for that day's lesson. A "Do Now" activity may be used to review a recently taught concept, assess students' understanding of a topic, or introduce a new idea or topic to the class. The trick to having a successful "Do Now" is that it must be something that students can easily understand and do independently of the teacher. For example, English/ESL teachers may ask students to practice using a specific grammatical feature in writing (telling about a past experience); science teachers may ask students to compare species or chemical elements by characteristics; social studies teachers may ask students to describe what they know about a historical figure; and math teachers may ask students to explain a recently taught skill or concept. With "Do Nows," a student's writing does not need to be grammatically or mechanically correct; rather, the purpose is writing practice—the focus is on content and not grammar. "Do Nows" provide students the opportunity to get the pen to the page through expressing simple ideas or opinions, or writing short responses to questions or prompts.

Captions

Captions are a quick and easy way to get students writing. Choose any picture—it can be from current media, from a current text selection, a drawing that students create themselves, or a mystery image—and tell students to write a caption for that image. Encourage students to use humor, insight, and creativity to express their knowledge and personality through their writing. Writing captions will help students develop flexibility and agility with language as they learn to express ideas succinctly. Creating engaging captions is training in becoming more creative and sophisticated writers, and is especially helpful in developing specific vocabulary.

Journal Writing

Journal writing can be a rewarding activity, both academically and emotionally. It is also a great way to get students comfortable with the physical act of writing. Encourage your students to journal write about anything they want. In this way, you remove all potential obstacles related to understanding the topic, as well as avoiding a lack of interest in responding to a prompt or question, by opening up the assignment completely. Although it is always good to start by giving students' choice, you may find that beginning writers need a little prompting to get them started. To solve this problem you can offer up some general suggestions, such as describing a person you care about, a conversation you recently had with a friend or stranger, or even writing the lyrics to a favorite song. General suggestions will be helpful for many students; other students will benefit most from more personalized attention. Approach students individually for a short conference where you ask the student probing questions that may help identify topics that interest the student. A variation on one-on-one conferencing is a dialogue learning log for content teachers—students write what they are learning, note continuing questions, and express their wonderings about a topic. You then read these learning logs on your own time and respond to your students, inviting further reflection and exploration of the topic.

Exit Tickets

Exit tickets are a great way to end class with a quick writing activity. Exit tickets can be used to gauge student comprehension of a topic by asking students to answer a question related to the focus of that class, make a short list of what was learned, or write a one-sentence summary of a topic studied. Exit tickets can also be used to introduce a topic or concept for the following day or to set learning goals for the homework or a longer unit of study.

To use the exit ticket strategy, reserve the last 10–15 minutes of class to explain the purpose and procedure of exit tickets, and allow students enough time to complete the task. Ask students to use a half sheet of paper to complete an exit ticket, such as stating whether they agree or disagree with the actions taken by a governor, president, or ruler. This strategy should not be used as a writing evaluation; the purpose is to encourage an expression of understanding through writing. The purpose is not to assess students' English. Be sure to explain that this is their ticket out of class, but that they should not worry about spelling and grammar for this assignment. As students exit class, collect their tickets as they walk out the door.

If this exercise is done on a daily basis or multiple times a week, many students' exit ticket responses may become repetitive, incorporating the same wording and phrasing. Exit tickets are a good way to encourage the development of writing fluency, but it is important to remember that ELLs are still working with a limited knowledge of vocabulary and syntax. To help students break out of a writing rut, provide them with examples of how to vary what they say: show them different sentence structures, teach synonyms and idioms to vary the vocabulary, and share the exit tickets of peers to expose students to alternative ways of expressing themselves.

TABLE 8.1   Writing Communicative Functions/Performance Indicators

Language Domain	Beginner	Intermediate	Advanced
Writing in English language arts, social studies, and science	Write simple descriptions of an event using visuals and demonstrating understanding of capitalization and present progressive tense.	Summarize a sequence of events . . . *ELA:* in narrative text using present tense. *Social Studies:* in historical text using learned vocabulary, regular/irregular past tense.	*ELA:* Develop and begin drafting a dramatization, including dialogue, of the chosen text for current time and location. *Social studies:* Produce contrastive summaries of historical periods using graphic organizers. *Science:* Summarize, in paragraph form, scientific research data presented in text and tables.

Communicative Functions/Performance Indicators

As introduced and discussed in Chapter 5, a communicative function/performance indicator is essentially the purpose, or function, that communication serves. "Performance indicators" describe the performances that can be used to indicate a student's ability to successfully communicate, in this case through writing. English language learners want to communicate their understanding of key academic concepts, but the amount and sophistication of a learner's writing skill will vary depending on his or her language proficiency.

Table 8.1 shows the types of writing language functions students can be expected to perform in an English language arts, social studies, or science class (the *performance indicators*) in order to demonstrate their knowledge and understanding at each proficiency level.

Teachers will want to start small and assign writing assignments that match their learners' proficiency levels, while promoting writing development in their classrooms.

Guiding ELLs to Write Expository Text in English

There is greater variation and flexibility in paragraphs of creative writing than in those of informational or expository writing, and students should be made aware of this difference. Usually, creative writing is not where our ELLs typically have the most writing difficulties. It is in understanding and using the expository form of writing that is often most challenging for writers new to English. Expository writing requires the writer to follow a specific format in order to convey cognitively challenging ideas or concepts and to engage in analysis, persuasion, and well-structured comparisons and contrasts (styles of writing that will be discussed more thoroughly later on in this chapter). Students may have learned to write expository texts differently in their countries of origin, following different protocols and working toward slightly different ends. Therefore, we need to help students get their bearings when writing expository text in English, by being clear about the structure of the standard expository paragraph as it is commonly taught in English-speaking countries.

For beginner students, you should provide numerous models and scaffolds, and build in repeated practice to help them understand and learn the expository paragraph writing structure. Appropriate beginner-level themes for practicing standard paragraphs are personal descriptions and preferences, as well as other such topics about which they already know a great deal. This way, the instructional writing focus is on format rather than content. Allow students sufficient time for the standard expository paragraph format to sink in and become part of their academic writing repertoire. This process requires extensive exposure and practice—reading and writing many versions of the same basic format.

For intermediate students, begin to transition from personal themes to hot-button or high-interest topics popular with adolescents such as love, relationships, independence, responsibilities, fairness and equality, social networking, and technology. For advanced students, the focus should be on more complex, academic topics. At the advanced level, students are better able to represent more cognitively demanding tasks such as use of logic, analysis, and synthesis to support complex reasoning in English.

Once students know how to write expository or informational paragraphs, they are ready to use this skill in varied writing tasks required of them in middle and high school classrooms. In the next section we present some common writing genres required in secondary classrooms. For each, we present a short explanation, some typical challenges and difficulties for ELLs, and some tools that may be useful to teachers (graphic organizers and checklists).

Teaching and Modifying Genres for ELLs

Differentiating Genres by Proficiency Level

The following section will discuss different ways of teaching and modifying the different writing genres for ELLs. Before we present this information, however, we want to provide Table 8.2, which suggests which genres are appropriate for the different proficiency levels of your students—which genres are easier for beginner ELLs to understand and learn, and which should be used primarily with more advanced learners. We use the genre organizational structure presented by D. Freeman and Freeman (2009) and based on Schleppegrell (2004).

Becoming proficient in writing means learning the various writing genres and being able to skillfully communicate one's ideas through those genres. For this reason, we next discuss the characteristics of personal writing, factual writing, and analytic writing, and we provide tools and strategies for how to best guide ELLs toward writing proficiently in each genre. As we provide examples of each, we outline common challenges or difficulties ELLs face, as well as helpful modifications. You will also find graphic organizers, checklists, and rubrics that correspond to each. We begin with examples of personal, factual, and analytic writing that are easier for ELLs to access (in terms of time intensity and length of assignment). These might be used as informal or formative assessments, assigned as class work, or completed as homework. Then we will talk about writing assign-

TABLE 8.2   Appropriate Writing Genres for Different Proficiency Levels

Beginner	Intermediate and Advanced
Personal:	*Personal:*
• Recount	• More extensive narratives
• Simple narrative	• Reflective essays
• Reader response	
• Short memoir	
Factual:	*Factual:*
• Procedure	• Complex procedures
• Directions	• Detailed research reports
• Retelling (i.e., of historic events)	
• Summary (basic facts as a single report)	
Analytic:	*Analytic:*
• Simple explanations	• Account
• Comparisons	• Explanation
	• Exposition
	• Persuasive essay

Derived from: Freeman and Freeman, 2009 and Schleppegrell, 2004.

ments that are more difficult for ELLs to access. These are more demanding and lengthy genres that are often used in formal assessments or assigned as final or culminating projects in secondary classrooms.

Personal Writing

Reader Response

Reader response is an early-acquired writing activity typically used to get students writing as they read a text or after they have read it. It is a good idea to introduce this activity to ELLs by using reader response stems such as those in the box titled "Reader Response Stems." The purpose of this type of writing is for readers to respond in a personal way to a text. Readers can make connections, express an insight or misunderstanding, ask a question, or express an opinion. Another adaptation for using reader response with ELLs is to focus on one type of response—say, for example, making a connection using the stem "This reminds me of . . . ." By asking students to make a connection—between the text they are reading and their own lives, the lives of friends or family, a television show or movie, prior learning, or another text—students personalize their reading and writing experience, and also avoid making the common mistake of simply restating the text in their own words (which is a summary, not reader response). As stated in Chapter 1, personalization of instruction is the hallmark of secondary reform efforts and needs to manifest a strong presence in our curriculum and instruction. (See Figure 8.1 for instruction guidelines.)

One difficulty ELLs may have with successfully writing a reader response is that explicitly stating a personal opinion and a connection to a text is not a skill necessarily valued in all cultures. Instead, sometimes the emphasis is placed on remembering or understanding the author's words or the factual information in a text, rather than a learner's reaction to the author or the information provided (Flaitz, 2006). Teach your students that making a personal connection to a text will

Reader Response Do's

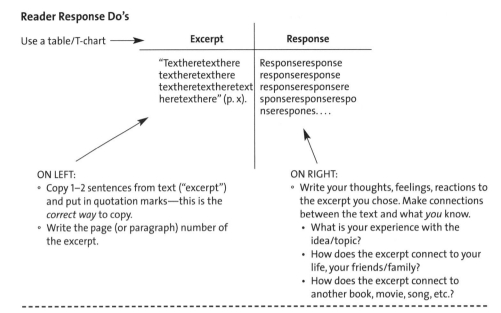

Use a table/T-chart ⟶

Excerpt	Response
"Textheretexthere textheretexthere textheretextheretext heretexthere" (p. x).	Responseresponse responseresponse responseresponsere sponseresponserespo nseresponses....

ON LEFT:
- Copy 1–2 sentences from text ("excerpt") and put in quotation marks—this is the *correct way* to copy.
- Write the page (or paragraph) number of the excerpt.

ON RIGHT:
- Write your thoughts, feelings, reactions to the excerpt you chose. Make connections between the text and what *you* know.
  - What is your experience with the idea/topic?
  - How does the excerpt connect to your life, your friends/family?
  - How does the excerpt connect to another book, movie, song, etc.?

Reader Response Don'ts

- Do not summarize or rewrite excerpt in your words.
- Do not ask a question to which you know the answer.
- Do not give general examples, or talk about the general "you" or "people" or "they."
  - "It is hard if you don't know the language," or, "Many people have these problems."

FIGURE 8.1   Reader response do's and don'ts

strengthen their understanding and long-term retention of information. Show your students that their thoughts and opinions matter, and that learning to clearly and eloquently express those thoughts and opinions through writing will help them communicate better in all aspects of their lives in the United States. Teach them that this behavior is valued and expected in their new culture, while still attempting to respect their culture's values.

Memoir

Memoir is a great writing assignment for ELLs. Memoir is a formal writing genre, so there is an abundance of resources and models available that can be used with students of all proficiency levels. The secret to supporting ELLs in writing meaningful memoirs is to tap into their deep reservoir of experience. Students are full of stories, including those as natives in their own country and many from their current lives as immigrants to the United States. These experiences are rich fodder for storytelling and expression. More often than not, students see their own lives and personal interactions as mundane or irrelevant; they may not immediately recognize the significance or impact of events in their life, and they often feel stuck when asked to write about an important experience in their life. It is for this reason that models are so crucial in helping students develop their own voice: students read examples of how other authors have transformed personal experience into a memoir, and they are inspired and motivated to tell their own tale.

Reader Response Stems

- I think . . .
- I wonder . . .
- I was surprised by . . .
- I'm not sure about . . .
- I didn't realize . . .
- This reminds me of . . .
- I can see . . .
- This is different from . . .
- This part is hard to understand because . . .

- In the next part, I predict . . .
- I wonder why the author . . .
- I think this means . . .
- It is important to remember . . .
- I was confused by . . .
- If I were the author I would . . .
- What if . . .
- This makes sense now because . . .
- At first I thought . . . But now I think . . .

Adapted from: Beers, K. (2002). *When kids can't read: what teachers can do: a guide for teachers 6–12.* (p. 108) Portsmith, NH: Heinemann.

By exposing students to a variety of models—published authors, teacher memoirs, and past or current student pieces—students begin to form ideas about events from their own lives that they may be able to turn into a captivating memoir.

The three main ingredients for memoir are a focus on a brief period of time or series of related events; first-person point of view—"I," "me," "my" voice—including many thoughts and emotions of the author; and how the events described resulted in a lesson learned by the author. Aside from these three specifications, memoirs read more or less like a narrative: an author tells his or her story of the past. (See Figure 8.2 for memoir criteria and assessment guidelines.)

Narrative/Short Story

There are many ways to go about teaching narrative, or short story. It is a big leap from writing about oneself to creating an original story. However, short stories are often based in reality or taken from other texts. To help students generate ideas and a plot for their own short story, encourage them to think about stories told in their families, stories they know from other texts, television, or movies, and stories they hear from their friends or in the halls of school. Counsel students to start with these stories and add to them, build upon them, expand them—in essence, personalize them.

Begin by teaching the idea of plot line, then emphasize and return to this idea throughout your writing instruction. Keep coming back to plot line and pushing students to look at their developing piece as it relates to the plot line checklist (which follows this paragraph) and graphic (Figure 8.3). Does *their* story have all the checklist ingredients? Is *their* story laid out in a proportion similar to that of the plot line graphic? It is important to remember that when instructing students, especially ELLs, how to write in a new genre such as short story, the primary focus is on helping them understand and follow the structure and ingredients of that genre; the quality of the plot itself and any stylistic devices is a secondary focus.

FIGURE 8.2 Memoir rubric

Criteria (Standards)	4 Exceeds Proficiency	3 Meets Proficiency	2 Approaching Proficiency	1 Substantially Below Proficient	Comments
Plot Includes the following: • First-person point of view • Relevant personal information or history that provides a context for the event(s) of the story • A focus on a brief period of time or series of related events	Author tells a very clear, organized, focused story; includes enough personal history and context to clearly show how the events are important and meaningful to the author.	Author tells a clear, organized, focused story; includes some personal history and context to show how the events of the memoir are important and meaningful to the author.	Memoir includes 2 of the 3 plot points (first-person POV, personal history to give context, focus on a brief event) —story lacks focus and/or importance.	Memoir includes 1 of the 3 plot points (first-person POV, personal history to give context, focus on a brief event) —story is incomprehensible and/or incomplete.	
Setting Includes the following: • A place, location where the events happen • A specific time when the event(s) happen	Time and place are clearly described—author includes descriptive imagery/literary devices; the importance of the specific time and place is very easy to understand.	Time and place are described; author includes some descriptive imagery/literary devices; the importance of the time and place is easy to understand.	Time or place is not described or is confusing; very few details; setting is not very important to the story.	Time *and* place are not described or confusing; no details; setting is not important to the story at all.	

Character Includes the following: • Author as main character (may include others) • Thoughts, emotions, actions, words, and rationales of author • There is a consistent point of view	Author's unique perspective, actions, thoughts, emotions and words are very clear, consistent, and descriptive in all parts of the story; other characters' words and actions are original, detailed, and clearly important to the story.	Author's perspective, actions, thoughts, emotions and words are clear and consistent in all parts of the story; other characters' words and actions are described and important to the story.	Author's perspective includes some thoughts, emotions, actions and words; story is not fully developed; other characters' words and actions are described.	Author's perspective is inconsistent or unclear; not enough information about author or other characters to understand the story.
Lesson • There is a personal lesson, realization, transformation or discovery about self or life	Author clearly shows how the events resulted in an important lesson, realization, discovery about self or life.	Author tells how the focused events resulted in a lesson, realization, transformation or discovery about self or life.	The lesson is unclear, or unclearly related to the focused events of the story.	The memoir does not demonstrate any lesson, realization, or discovery.

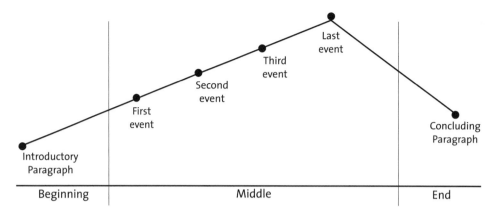

FIGURE 8.3 Plot line graphic

Remind students that they must first learn the conventions of the genre and then engage in repeated practice of its basic structure in order to improve their writing and work toward mastery. (See Figure 8.4 for instruction and assessment ideas.)

Narrative/Short Story Checklist

1. Plot
    - There is a character(s) and a problem situation or conflict.
    - There are a series of events (two or more) related to the problem or conflict.
    - The events lead toward suspense and anticipation for the reader.
    - There is a climax or turning point for the main character.
    - There is a conclusion of events.
2. Setting
    - There is a place, location where the events happen.
    - There is time (may be general or specific) when the events happen.
3. Characters
    - There is one or more main characters—living things.
    - Characters think, act, and talk to move the story.
    - There is a consistent point of view.
4. Theme
    - There is a point or meaning to the story.

Poetry/Imitation Writing

A relatively easy way to get students writing, and introduce them to poetry at the same time, is through imitation writing. In imitation writing, students use an author's piece and particular style as a model to create their own individual pieces of prose or poetry. Imitation writing can be used with any genre, though it usually works better with creative genres. Choose pieces with a lot of sensory imagery and literary devices or pieces with a strong pattern that students can pick up on, adapt, and make their own.

FIGURE 8.4 Narrative/short story rubric

Criteria (Standards)	4 Exceeds Proficiency	3 Meets Proficiency	2 Approaching Proficiency	1 Substantially Below Proficient	Comments
Plot Includes the following: • Character(s) and a problem situation or conflict • A series of events related to the problem or conflict and leading toward suspense and anticipation • A climax or turning point for the main character • A conclusion of events	Story follows an original, believable, clear, and easy-to-understand plot line that includes well-developed characters, a series of events, suspenseful climax, and credible conclusion.	Story follows a believable, clear, and easy-to-understand plot line that includes developed characters, a series of events, a climax, and a conclusion.	Story includes *most of* the plot points—one or more plot points (characters, events, climax, conclusion) are confusing or missing.	Story includes only a couple of the plot points—two or more plot points (characters, events, climax, conclusion) are confusing or missing.	
Setting Includes the following: • A place, location where the events happen • A time (may be general or specific) when the events happen	Time and place are clear, original, well described, and appropriate to the plot; includes some descriptive, sensory imagery.	Time and place are clear and fit the plot, and are described in the story; attempts at descriptive, sensory imagery.	Either time or place is confusing or hard to understand or lacking enough detail to be known.	Time and place are confusing or hard to understand or lacking enough detail to be known.	

continued

FIGURE 8.4 *(continued)*

Criteria (Standards)	4 Exceeds Proficiency	3 Meets Proficiency	2 Approaching Proficiency	1 Substantially Below Proficient	Comments
Character Includes the following: • There is one or more main characters—living things • Characters think, act, and talk to move the story • There is a consistent point of view	Characters are original and believable, are well developed through thoughts, actions, and dialogue, and clearly move the story; point of view is fitting and consistent.	Characters are believable, developed through thoughts, actions, and dialogue, and move the story; point of view is clear and consistent.	Characters are developed with two of the three characteristics (thoughts, actions, speech) and move the story; POV is inconsistent.	Characters are developed with one of the three characteristics (thoughts, actions, speech); purpose of characters and/or POV is confusing or unclear.	
Theme • Includes a point, meaning, or purpose	The point or meaning of the story is original and very clear (though not necessarily explicitly explained).	The point or meaning of the story is clear (though not necessarily explicitly explained).	There is a vague point or meaning of the story.	The point or meaning of the story is confusing or incomplete.	

188

Vignette: Elizabeth Uses Models to Improve Writing

Elizabeth, a young freshman from Liberia, was a student in my intermediate ESL class. It was the first quarter of the year, and already Elizabeth was expressing her dislike of writing. After looking at some of Elizabeth's writing samples and engaging her in class, it was clear that a least some of her anxiety over writing had to do with her low literacy level. Although English is Elizabeth's native language, the form of English spoken in Liberia differs greatly in accent and cadence from that spoken in the United States. Because of these differences, as well as gaps in her early education and limited familiarity with sound-spelling correspondences, Elizabeth struggled to write more than a couple of words without stopping to ask how to spell a word or express an idea. In addition, her penmanship was poor, but comprehensible, and very slow. Much to Elizabeth's credit, she asked to use the computer to do her work whenever possible to somewhat speed up her fluency and get spell check assistance. And so, when the time came to explain the first-quarter mini-memoir book writing assignment that followed our study of selections from Sandra Cisneros's *The House on Mango Street,* I was already anticipating the complaints and resistance I believed would come from Elizabeth. Sure enough, she was not excited about the project, as many other students were when told they were going to write about themselves and their lives. However, as I began to work with Elizabeth more closely, suggesting she try and model Cisneros's style, Elizabeth began to take a greater interest in, and show more dedication to, her work. She began writing about how she and her mother had to move a few times over the past year and describing her experiences living in the different apartments, each with different characteristics, different environments, and different landlords. Elizabeth was able to recognize some of Cisneros's stylistic devices and imitate them, substituting her own experiences and details. Though she still struggled with spelling and fluency, she was engaged and motivated, and in the end, proud of herself and her accomplishment. Since then I have seen Elizabeth take a greater interest in writing and work hard on her writing skills, pushing herself to revise and improve her work until she is satisfied.

Erin Leininger

Factual Writing: Procedures, Instructions, and Directions

Procedural writing describes a step-by-step process that one must take to arrive at a final answer or product. On the one hand, procedural writing can be a good genre to use with beginning ELLs because it is very formulaic; but on the other hand, you must be sure to choose a topic, or help students choose topics, that do not involve an overwhelming amount of new or very specific vocabulary words.

If your purpose is to help students learn a specific set of vocabulary associated with a particular procedure, such as cooking utensils used in the making of a dessert, procedural writing is a good way to approach such instruction. However, it you only want your students to be introduced to procedural writing and gain practice with it, using topics that are familiar to students will work better and will not complicate the task with new vocabulary learning.

Procedural Writing Topics

- How to use mapquest
- How to get a driver's license
- How to put on makeup
- How to ask someone on a date
- How to play soccer
- How to become a better writer
- How to open a locker

- How to comparison shop
- How to take great photographs
- How to use a microscope
- How to use a cell phone
- How to use an index
- How to open a bank account
- How to get a part-time job

Procedural Writing Checklist

1. Introduction
   - You introduce the topic.
   - You explain your authority on the topic.
   - You list the tools, resources, items needed.
   - You address any safety precautions or procedures necessary.
2. Body
   - Steps are listed in sequential order.
   - All necessary steps, no matter how small, are included.
   - You use transitions to move from step to step.
   - You use appropriate language for your audience.
3. Conclusion
   - You include a way to check if the procedure was correctly completed.
   - You provide a closing sentence/statement.

Lab Reports

Depending on the specific science course in which students are asked to write factual reports, lab reports may differ slightly. The lab report format, checklist, and rubric presented here encompass the standard components, though they certainly can be added to or altered when necessary. Typically, lab reports contain a title, stated purpose, hypothesis, list of materials, step-by-step procedure, results, analysis, and conclusion. (See Figure 8.5 for instruction and assessment ideas.)

Lab Report Checklist

1. *Title* of lab.
2. State the *purpose/problem.*
   - Why are you doing the lab?
   - What questions are you trying to answer?
3. State your *hypothesis.*
   - What do you think the results will be?

FIGURE 8.5 Lab report rubric

Criteria (Standards)	4 Exceeds Proficiency	3 Meets Proficiency	2 Approaching Proficiency	1 Substantially Below Proficient	Comments
Introduction • Title • Purpose/problem • Hypothesis • Materials	All Introduction requirements are included, relevant, and clearly stated.	All Introduction requirements are included.	One or more Introduction requirements are missing or incomprehensible.	Two or more Introduction requirements are missing or incomprehensible.	
Procedure • The process, step by step • Numbered	The lab procedure is clearly detailed and numbered in a step-by-step list or description.	The lab procedure is numbered in a step-by-step list or description.	Some steps in the procedure are missing or confusing.	Many steps in the procedure are missing or confusing; not numbered.	
Results • Data, facts collected • Charts, graphs, diagrams	All data are clearly and correctly recorded; charts, graphs, and or diagrams are correctly used.	All data are clearly and correctly recorded; charts, graphs, or diagrams may be used.	Some data are missing or incorrectly recorded; graphic organizers are not used correctly.	Incomplete or incorrect data and results.	

continued

FIGURE 8.5 (*continued*)

Criteria (Standards)	4 Exceeds Proficiency	3 Meets Proficiency	2 Approaching Proficiency	1 Substantially Below Proficient	Comments
Analysis • A narrative description and analysis of the results (data and graphic organizers)	Very detailed and complete narrative of the results and any graphic organizers.	Clear, complete narrative of the results and any graphic organizers.	Partially incomplete or unclear narrative of the results and any graphic organizers.	Very unclear or missing narrative of the results and any graphic organizers.	
Conclusion • Restate the basics of the lab (purpose, hypothesis, materials, procedure) • What you learned	Clear, complete restatement of all lab basics; thoughtful, reflective statement of what you learned.	Clear, complete restatement of all lab basics; statement of what you learned.	One or more lab basics missing in restatement; statement of learning is unclear or incomplete.	Two or more lab basics missing in restatement; statement of learning is irrelevant or missing.	
Organization • Follows the lab report model from checklist	Perfectly and clearly follows the lab report model.	Clearly follows the lab report model.	Some errors in the lab report model.	Many errors or missing parts in format.	

4. List *all* the *materials* you use.
5. Describe the *procedure* step by step.
   - Steps are numbered *1, 2, 3,* or *First, Second, Third* . . .
6. Present the *results* of the lab.
   - What are the data, the facts, you collected?
   - Use charts, graphs, diagrams to show data.
7. *Analyze* the results.
   - Explain your results in complete sentences, paragraphs.
8. *Conclusion.*
   - Restate the *purpose.*
   - Briefly describe the *procedure.*
   - Was your *hypothesis* correct or incorrect?
   - What did you *learn?*

Factual Retelling

Retelling, though often used as an oral strategy, can also be very effectively used as a writing activity. Retelling typically works best in English language arts and history classes where the content is based more on story and events, rather than in science or math classes where the content is based more on facts and procedure. Retelling is slightly easier than summary (to be described later) because in retelling the writer does not have to pick and choose which pieces of information to include or decide how best to organize the information; rather, a retelling—or rewriting—must include all the same information, and be organized in the same manner, as the source.

TABLE 8.3   Retelling Guides by Content Area

English	History	Science	Math
Tell the setting of the novel (time period and location).	Choose a historical event.	Retell the story of a scientific discovery.	Retell the sequence in a mathematical procedure.
Name the main characters and their relationships to one another.	Describe the events that led up to this moment in history.	What scientists were involved? Give details about all the scientists who contributed to the discovery.	Define the problem and the variables involved.
Summarize the events that take place in each chapter.	Name the countries/regions of the world involved.	Describe the problems that led to the discovery.	Tell the steps involved in solving the problem. If it applies, give alternate ways of solving the problem.
Describe how the novel ends.	Give details about the actual event—where it took place, how long it lasted, etc. Give all key details.	Narrate the sequence of events that took place, eventually leading to the discovery.	Confirm the outcome or outcomes of applying the procedure.
	How did the historical event end (whether a conflict, civilization, exploration, etc.)?	How did their findings impact future scientific discoveries?	

Source: Adapted from Tennessee State Education, "Reading in the Content Areas." 2009. See Tennessee Department of Education Content Area Reading Course 3081 Syllabus at http://www.tennessee.gov/education/ci/reading/grades_9–12 .pdf for an example of how to incorporate retelling in content area instruction.

The purpose of retelling/rewriting is to allow writers to practice using their own words and language to express their understanding. Therefore, you may want to introduce retelling ahead of summary, and you certainly will want to choose texts or sources that are appropriate for the English proficiency levels of your students. For beginner students, it will be necessary to start with very short texts and support students by providing a lot of scaffolding strategies. For example, you could give the students prewritten sentences that retell the event but that are out of order. Then you can have students put the sentences in the correct order and write them out in paragraph form. For intermediate students, short to medium-length texts will be appropriate, and you can experiment with less scaffolding. For advanced students, introduce retelling with short to medium-length texts, provide some modeling and scaffolding, and gradually move students toward using longer texts and encouraging them to use scaffolding guides as needed. Using lists like the one in Table 8.3 is very helpful for your ELLs.

Helpful Writing Formats to Use with ELLs That Can Cross Personal and Factual Genres

Letter Writing

Letter writing can be a nonthreatening way to help students approach writing. Most students are aware of the letter format, as many have sent and received some form of letter, from a traditional snail-mail letter to a more casual e-mail letter. Because letters are a familiar form of communication, students are less likely to be intimidated by a letter-writing assignment. You can start with personal letters that recount or narrate life experiences. You can also write simple business letters to report problems (factual writing). Thus it is the purpose of the letter that determines the genre, with letter being the format in which the genre expresses itself.

Although letters follow specific writing structures and formats, they can also be used as a way to begin analytic writing. Students can write letters to peers or teachers describing what they are learning in a content area classes, for example, thus explaining what they have learned. Letters can also be a way for students to write expository or persuasive essays—for example, engaging in character analysis or analysis of historical events or persuading others not to start smoking or to drive responsibly.

Analytic Writing

Summary

Summary is a widely used writing genre in the educational world. Summaries can be used to assess students' understanding of information taken from any source and content area, be it fiction or informational text, media, or oral discourse. Conceptually, summaries seem simple—the main ideas, important points, basic plot line, and so on. But in reality, writing a summary is a complex, analytic task. First, students must have a firm understanding of what it is they are to summarize. Second, students must be able to determine which pieces of information are the main points, which pieces of information may provide support or detail, and just as importantly, which points do not need to be included in the summary. Finally, students must be able to organize the information into a clear, well-organized summary. The following checklist can help learners to do all these things.

Checklist

Summary Do's and Don'ts

Summary Do's

- ☐ I included the title of the text.
- ☐ I included the names of the main characters, ideas, and concepts.
- ☐ I wrote 1–2 short sentences or paragraphs about the beginning of the text.
- ☐ I wrote 1–2 short sentences or paragraphs about the middle of the text.
- ☐ I wrote 1–2 short sentences or paragraphs about the end of the text.
- ☐ I used present tense.

Summary Don'ts

- ☐ Do not write, "I think . . . ," "I feel . . . ," or "In my opinion . . . ."
- ☐ Do not use entire phrases, sentences, paragraphs copied from text.
- ☐ Do not use unnecessary details such as
  - Lots of dates.
  - Processes or steps in a process.
  - Long descriptions.
  - Dialogues between characters.

To illustrate the difference between reader response and summary, it is helpful to teach these genres together. Point out the contrast between the two genres to help students better understand the distinct characteristics of summary and reader response. (Use Figure 8.1 in conjunction with the "Summary Do's and Don'ts" to help students differentiate between reader response and summary.)

Essays

Teaching the five-paragraph essay may be one of the most important skills you teach your students regarding academic writing. Nearly all academic content classes in secondary school, all standardized tests, and most classes in college require that students write essays, so it is crucial for the writing success of your students to start early and practice often. No matter their proficiency level, students can begin learning and practicing the five-paragraph essay structure. Because the five-paragraph essay can be used in any subject area and for any essay topic (Figure 8.6 can help guide students to produce a successful five-paragraph essay).

Persuasive Essay

The purpose of a persuasive essay is for a writer to present an argument and convince, or persuade, the reader of the argument's validity. In order to write a good persuasive essay, a writer must

- Choose a specific, narrow topic that can be debated (more than one side).
- Be knowledgeable about all sides of the topic, not just the writer's side.
- Successfully argue the writer's side in the context of the opposing side.

FIGURE 8.6 Five-paragraph essay rubric

Criteria (Standards)	4 Exceeds Proficiency	3 Meets Proficiency	2 Approaching Proficiency	1 Substantially Below Proficient	Comments
Introduction • Introduce the topic, question, or issue • Thesis statement • Three or more supporting reasons	The topic, question, issue is clearly introduced and leads to the thesis statement with three clear supporting reasons.	The topic, question, issue is introduced; there is a thesis statement with three clear supporting reasons.	The topic, question, issue is introduced; thesis is incomplete or confusing.	The topic, question, issue is unclear; thesis is incomplete, confusing, or irrelevant.	

Body/Argument
• Topic sentence
• Specific evidence:
  ◦ Examples
  ◦ Facts
  ◦ Quotations
  ◦ Statistics
• Transitions between reasons and evidence
	Three or more supporting reasons are very strong; reasons are clearly introduced in a topic sentence and well supported with specific evidence, examples, facts; transitions skillfully used between evidence and reasons.	Three supporting reasons are clearly introduced in a topic sentence and well supported with specific evidence, examples, facts; transitions used between evidence and reasons.	Fewer than three supporting reasons; one or more reasons and/or supporting evidence are unclear or missing; few transitions.	Supporting reasons and evidence are unclear, confusing, or missing; no transitions.	

Conclusion • Restate thesis • Closing, universal statement	Thesis is skillfully restated; a clear, universal statement concludes the essay.	Thesis is clearly restated; a universal statement concludes the essay.	Thesis restatement and concluding sentence is weak or unclear.	Thesis and conclusion are missing or irrelevant.	
Organization • Follows the five-paragraph model (intro paragraph, three body paragraphs, conclusion paragraph) • Transitions between supporting evidence and paragraphs	Perfectly follows the five-paragraph essay model, and effectively uses a variety of transitions throughout essay.	Follows the five-paragraph essay model and uses transitions when necessary.	Some errors in the five-paragraph essay model; some missing or incorrectly used transitions.	No organizational structure; no use of transitions.	

Basic Persuasive Topics

- The school lunch menu needs to change
- Lengthening/shortening the school day
- Someone in my family deserves an award
- Classrooms need more technology
- School uniforms are a good idea

- Sports and other after school activities deserve financial support by taxpayers
- People worry too much about . . .
- It's more fun to be a kid than an adult
- It's better to be an only child/one of many siblings

Since one key component to a successful essay is knowing the topic well from all sides, help students choose topics with which they are very familiar and with which they may have personal experience. The topic of school uniforms is one that teachers frequently use when first teaching about persuasive essays, and this topic translates well for many ELLs who themselves may have worn school uniforms in their native country. Likewise, topics that relate to school or the home are also good to use when introducing students of all language levels to persuasive essay. As students become more familiar with persuasive writing and as their academic language skills improve, you may experiment with using topics that center more around current events such as global warming, substance abuse, and the juvenile justice system.

One piece of advice to convey to students is that they do not necessarily have to *agree* with the position they are arguing for in their persuasive essay. The purpose of a persuasive essay is not necessarily to share your beliefs and opinions, though that may, at times, be the case. Rather, the purpose is to convincingly present an argument and support it with relevant facts and details. It is often difficult, but excellent practice, for students to try and understand and support a side of an issue that they may not personally agree with. Assure students that they are not "married" to their topic and that writing development is about learning to express ideas and perspectives, even though they may not represent their own views. (See the following "Persuasive Essay Checklist" and Figure 8.7 for instruction and assessment ideas.)

Persuasive Essay Checklist

1. Introductory Paragraph
   - Introduce controversial topic.
   - State your position on the topic.
   - State your three supporting reasons.
2. Body Paragraphs
   - Topic sentence introduces a supporting reason.
   - Reason is supported with specific evidence, examples, facts, and/or statistics.

FIGURE 8.7 Persuasive essay rubric

Criteria (Standards)	4 Exceeds Proficiency	3 Meets Proficiency	2 Approaching Proficiency	1 Substantially Below Proficient	Comments
Topic Is • Clear • Controversial • A statement of position • Stated in introductory paragraph and restated in concluding paragraph	The topic and position are clearly introduced and explained in the introductory paragraph.	The topic and position are clearly introduced and somewhat explained in the introductory paragraph.	The topic or its controversy is unclear or not in the introductory paragraph.	Topic is never stated.	
Supporting Reasons • Intro paragraph: three clear reasons • Body paragraphs: Each reason is supported by specific evidence, examples, facts, statistics	Three supporting reasons are very strong and clear, and well supported with specific evidence, examples, facts, and/or statistics.	Three supporting reasons are clear and supported with specific evidence, examples, facts, and/or statistics.	Fewer than three supporting reasons; one or more reasons and/or supporting evidence are unclear or missing.	Supporting reasons and evidence are unclear, confusing, or missing.	
Opposing Argument • Opposing position is considered, presented, and refuted	All possible opposing positions are carefully considered, clearly presented, and skillfully refuted.	Many possible opposing positions are considered, presented, and refuted.	Some possible opposing positions are presented and argued against.	Opposing positions are not considered or presented.	

Language • Strong, persuasive voice • Natural language • Clear, varied words	Language used is strong, clear, and persuasive; natural for the writer; varied words	Language is clear and persuasive; some variety of words is used.	Language is dull, weak, repetitive, and/or unnatural for the writer.	Language is unconvincing or confusing; essay is incomprehensible.
Organization • Follows the five-paragraph model (intro paragraph, three body paragraphss, conclusion paragraph) • Transitions between supporting evidence and paragraphs	Perfectly follows the five-paragraph essay model, and effectively uses a variety of transitions throughout essay.	Follows the five-paragraph essay model and uses transitions when necessary.	Some errors in the five-paragraph essay model; some missing or incorrectly used transitions.	No organizational structure; no use of transitions.

- Transition to the next paragraphs, presenting two additional reasons.
- Opposing position is considered, presented, and refuted.
3. Concluding Paragraph
   - Restate the topic, your position, and supporting reasons.
   - Closing statement.

Comparison/Contrast Essay

The intention of a comparison/contrast essay is to analyze and then highlight the similarities and differences between two subjects. Comparison/contrast essays can be written using two different, easy-to-follow formats: divided or alternating (see "Compare/Contrast Essay Checklist" for details). Beginner-level topics may include seasons, cars, schools, rooms in a house, and foods. Intermediate-level topics may include musical groups, countries, restaurants, short texts, a movie based on a text, or different lifestyles. Advanced topics may include very specific topics related to historical events or persons; scientific processes, discoveries, or persons; and mathematics equations, theories, or persons.

Compare/Contrast Essay Checklist

1. Introduction
   - There is a lead into the topics.
   - There is a thesis about the topics.
2. Body Paragraphs—Divided or Alternating
   Divided
   - Topic 1 is fully described and analyzed in one to three paragraphs.
   - Topic 2 is fully described and analyzed in one to three paragraphs.
   - Topics 1 and 2 are *compared* and *contrasted* in one to three paragraphs.
   Alternating
   - Topics 1 and 2 are fully described, analyzed, and *compared* in one to three paragraphs.
   - Topics 1 and 2 are fully described, analyzed, and *contrasted* in one to three paragraphs.
3. Concluding Paragraph
   - Restate the topics and thesis.
   - Closing statement proving the thesis.

Historical Essay

What makes a historical essay distinct is that it includes an analytic response to a historically based question. Inherent in a historical essay is the use of past tense, which is not a defining characteristic of all essays. Indeed most essays—literary analysis, the presentation of scientific information—are written in present tense. But historical essays have characteristics in common with other essays: presenting a thesis and supporting it with evidence and fact.

Using Assessment to Guide Instruction

The best way to assess where your students are in terms of writing proficiency is by simply having them perform some of the short in-class writing activities described in this chapter. Just by looking at a few of these writing samples, you can determine a lot about your students' writing skills. Simple, obvious criteria teachers look for when assessing student writing are characteristics such as penmanship, capitalization and punctuation, and paragraph formation. But these are surface features. Remember to also look at organizational strategies, ideas, voice, and word choice. These skills matter much more, and their development should be monitored.

Another way to assess students' writing proficiency to guide instruction is through homework. Using homework as a writing assessment tool works best when paired with in-class writing assessments. This way you can compare the quality and proficiency of students' work in the classroom, under more or less fixed conditions, with the work they complete outside of class, which is subject to various factors. Make sure students understand the importance of doing the work alone, so you can monitor their development and support them well, rather than believing they are more advanced because they get assistance. You may also choose to intentionally focus a particular homework assignment on one writing skill in order to assess individual students or the whole class's proficiency with that particular skill.

Use more formal assessments when you have come to the point where there has been extensive instruction, modeling, and practice of a particular genre and when you are ready to assess whether or not students have learned the specific skills. These final projects, or culminating assignments, are long-term assignments students have worked on, conferenced about, and revised as a final draft. These assignments may also come in the form of end-of-course and standardized tests. When doing formal assessments, it is important to tell students the criteria by which they will be assessed ahead of time. Providing students with a checklist and rubric tells them what content they need to include and which standards they need to address in their assessment. Clear expectations tell students what to do and what is expected, and make it easier for students to succeed.

Language Form versus Content

When conducting assessments, our first focus is always the content expressed. But as evidenced previously, it is also necessary to focus on language form if ELLs are to advance their writing abilities. Looking at language form consists of focusing on grammar, syntax, and mechanics, such as punctuation, capitalization, and paragraph formation. If language form is your focus, it is important to

- Limit your focus to one or two specific language forms (proper capitalization for beginners; past tense for intermediates; subject/verb agreement and use of embedded clauses for advanced students).
- Instruct students beforehand on the language form that will be assessed and allow them multiple opportunities to practice using the form(s) prior to the assessment.

Limiting your mechanics instruction to one or two language forms at a time will be more effective for you and your students. With a limited instructional focus, teachers can make fewer corrections on student work, and students will not be overwhelmed by the quantity of their mistakes. Students will be more likely to learn from those mistakes and thus less likely to make them again, or as often, in the future. Give students time to experiment with the different mechanical forms and make mistakes they can learn from, so that they are prepared when it comes time for an assessment.

Mechanics and Editing

While the primary purpose of writing is communication, we know that mechanical errors can sometimes impede the intended message of communication. Getting students to write is a great accomplishment; but just words on a page are not enough to prepare students for mainstream high school and college courses. Students must have a solid understanding of how to correctly format titles and paragraphs and use capitalization and punctuation. They must know how to write and use dialogue, citations, footnotes, and references. Teach these skills well, and teach them often. Mechanics are the details to which our students do not often pay attention; our ELLs are busy translating in their head, looking up words in the dictionary, or simply trying to finish an assignment that, in their first language, may take them mere minutes, but in English takes them hours. However, it is important to remember that mechanics are crucial for comprehension, and these are specific skills that students must continue to work on as they improve their overall writing. This is the final step—the editing—that students need to do with every piece, and they need strategies to help them do so.

Conclusion

This chapter tackles a major challenge of secondary ELLs—learning to write proficiently in a new language. In order for language and content teachers to help adolescent ELLs meet the writing demands of secondary school, certainly they need to understand the challenges that stand in the way of their learners. Most importantly, teachers must individually and collaboratively teach their ELLs to write effectively for personal and school purposes using proven strategies. This chapter was written to help you do just that. The following checklist can help you analyze what you are already doing well and what you might want to strengthen in your efforts to promote secondary ELLs' writing abilities in your classroom.

Checklist

- ☐ I provide plenty of resources to aid students in my classroom (such as ESL student dictionaries, children's/students' thesauri).

- ☐ I provide experience with different writing forms, as well as purposes, specific to my content area, to ensure students gain experience with each.

- ☐ I expose students to real-world writing (memoir, biography, op-ed, newspaper article) to give students access to writing as it occurs beyond the classroom.

- ☐ I support students with needed scaffolding (checklists, graphic organizers, prompts) and modeling, so students can feel comfortable and confident in developing their writing skills at a pace that works for them.

- ☐ I provide clear expectations for writing assignments to ensure that students can independently and knowledgably approach writing activities and assignments.

- ☐ I teach students to use tools (rubrics, checklists) for editing so they can check their own work.

- ☐ I give focused, constructive feedback about content and form through frequent conferencing to allow students to absorb information and apply it to future writing experiences.

Matthew, Liberia

CHAPTER 9

Supporting English Language Learners in Mainstream English Classes

> Hey Miss, this kid's cool—he likes chess and soccer just like me!
>
> Axel, after interviewing ELL Gilmar

Guiding Questions

- Who are the English language learners in mainstream English language arts classes?
- What are the challenges for English language learners in mainstream English language arts classes?
- What can we do to help English language learners make a successful transition from English as a second language to English language arts classes?
- How can we shape and adapt the English language arts curriculum to support English language learners' learning?
- How can we monitor the ongoing progress of English language learners to see what they are struggling with?

After experiencing a substantial transition from their native culture to American school culture, English language learners (ELLs) placed in mainstream English language arts (ELA) classes now make another difficult transition from the sheltered, supportive environment of the English as a second language (ESL) classroom to what is essentially a whole new program for them: different teachers, different peers, different classroom expectations, and more demanding academic English. (Even in schools where students take ESL and ELA classes concurrently, ELLs may feel more at ease and at home in their ESL classes than in the ELA classroom.) This chapter will focus on how mainstream ELA teachers can learn about and support our ELLs in the classroom, while ensuring that they gain the knowledge of English language arts and literature, as well as the skills, they will need to be successful in and beyond secondary school.

The placement of ELLs in English language arts classes occurs either as ELLs make the successful transition out of ESL classes or as they enter English classes for the purpose of meeting graduation requirements. It is important to remember, however, that ELLs are still continuing to learn English, their second language, as they cross these classroom boundaries. This chapter is written to help in that all-important transition. After we explore some basic information about who ELLs are in mainstream classes and the challenges they face, we will then offer strategies for

- Building a supportive classroom community.
- Providing opportunities to extend speaking and performance skills.
- Developing critical reading and writing skills around literature.
- Teaching students to write in multiple genres.

These strategies will contribute to building students' practice, accuracy, and confidence in reading, writing, speaking, and thinking in English—in short, to their capacity to perform in the English language arts class and beyond.

Who Are the ELLs in Our Classrooms?

First, we have to know who our students are. There are three types of ELLs whom secondary English language arts teachers can expect to see in our classrooms:

1. *Exited ELLs*: These students have completed and tested out of ESL classes, categorized as "proficient" in English by their language proficiency test results. Many such students are still being monitored, as is required, to ensure continued success once exited from ESL services.

2. *Transitioning ELLs*: These students attend some mainstream classes to earn needed English credits, but are also still enrolled in ESL classes. These students may include both "high intermediate/advanced" and "proficient" ELLs, by language proficiency categories (see Chapter 4 for proficiency descriptors), but in schools with concurrent ESL and ELA classes for ELLs, these students may have lower English proficiency levels.

3. *Out-of-program ELLs*: These are students whose parents have waived ESL classes for their children. Parents may opt out of ESL supports for a variety of reasons. They may fear that ESL classes will somehow hold their children back academically, stigmatize them in some way, or inhibit their chances of going on to college (in many states ESL courses are not counted as Carnegie units on high school transcripts). Regardless, we have to be aware that these students exist and may need more support from us than do exited or transitioning ELLs.

Just knowing that ELLs have exited ESL classes does not provide us with enough information about their academic needs and strengths in reading, writing, listening and speaking. It is useful then to find out the results of our ELL students' language proficiency tests, which should be available either from the ESL coordinator at your school or the guidance office. These tests measure the level and quality of students' English language output (speaking and writing) and language input (listening and reading). Knowing our students' strengths and weaknesses in each of these areas can help us to design class presentations, activities, and assignments in ways that build on students' strengths and appropriately address their weaknesses. In addition, you may have other data such as the results from reading and writing assessments conducted in your district or school.

Who Are Your ELLs?

- Are your ELLs exited, are they transitioning, or have they waived ESL classes? If exited, how recently? An ELL may have exited ESL before leaving elementary or middle school, but may not have a strong academic knowledge base in his or her home language. This limitation will affect their ability to acquire new academic knowledge in English.

- Do you know if your ELLs are literate in their native language? A lack of competence in the first language will also affect literacy and oral capacity in the second language (Cummins, 1981, 2006). (See Chapters 2 and 3.)

- Have they had continuous schooling, or have there been gaps? The answer to this question will have a bearing on whether or not the student has a foundation in academic language in his or her first language, which will impact the speed at which the student may grasp content and academic habits of mind in English.

- How confident are your ELLs? Are they risk takers or risk avoiders? Student personalities affect how much they are willing to risk making mistakes in front of others. Risk avoiders may prefer to hide their needs rather than expose them. (See the box below.)

- Do your ELLs have opportunities to hear and practice English outside the classroom? Language acquisition is a determinedly social process, and a student's motivation to learn English will certainly be influenced by existing social supports.

- Are your ELLs involved in after-school activities? Engagement in extracurricular activities helps ELLs to feel an integral part of the life of the school in ways that increase their investment in learning English.

By answering these questions, you will better understand the strengths and needs of your students to help you know how much support they will need in the ELA classroom. If they need a lot of support, you will want to search Chapters 5, 6, 7, and 8 for specialized strategies to support your learners, in addition to those provided in this chapter. As you will see in the next section, the demands are substantial in mainstream ELA classes, and you will want to have as many supportive strategies as possible to aid your learners in meeting those demands. Regardless of where our students are coming from, transitioning and exited ELLs still have needs that may not be apparent to us at first.

Eduardo, 16, traveled back and forth between the United States and Guatemala during his early schooling. He speaks English with an American accent, and he is bright, articulate, a good critical thinker, and an excellent participant in textual discussions in class because he is such a capable listener and interpreter of what he hears. Yet this is his first year in mainstream English, in part because he struggles so much to read and write, whether in English or in Spanish. When asked to take notes in class, he reassures his teacher that he doesn't need to write things down because "it's all in my head, Miss." Over time it becomes clear that Eduardo is avoiding writing in all of his classes.

Adolescent ELLs mask their needs in many ways: not asking questions, nodding and indicating understanding when they do not understand at all, doing their best to be invisible in the classroom so as not to be called upon or otherwise singled out, and, most importantly, using their fluency in basic interpersonal language to mask a lack of academic English. Be on the lookout for students like Eduardo in your classes. As we will discuss later in this chapter, using informal and formative assessments provides a helpful check on student understanding.

The Challenges of English Language Arts

As English teachers, we have a lot on our plates: teaching students critical reading and thinking skills, text-based discussion, vocabulary, grammar, and how to write in multiple genres from personal writing (memoir, poetry) to informational writing (reports, procedures, brochures) to analytical writing (persuasive essays, literary critiques); and we must do all this through and between teaching set literary texts each year. English language arts is not so much a language learning class, then, as it is a content-area class, just like math, science, and history. The time we ELA teachers spend on building language skills usually falls solely within the context of teaching required authors and texts, not directly on language learning and practice as is provided in ESL classes. For ELLs, this shift of emphasis from a language-focused English class to a literature-focused English class can be very difficult.

Moreover, the literature curriculum—requiring set texts in many districts—tends to center on building cultural capital in students rather than on piquing students' passion for reading or building habits of reading for pleasure. The effect of required texts in the secondary classroom, sometimes, is that we focus instruction on specific literary forms and content, and away from more practical language and literacy skills. Many high school ELA curricula, for example, require the teaching of a Shakespeare play each year—not with the goal that students will become proficient in Elizabethan English, but that they will become familiar with the works of a great playwright.

The content focus of ELA, moreover, may leave less time to create individually meaningful learning experiences for ELLs, or learning opportunities that take into account their specific interests or needs. So these are our major challenges as ELA teachers of ELLs.

We have to imagine ourselves as the bridge builders between, on one shore, the set curriculum (and more recently, state and regional tests), and on the other shore, what our students want and need to learn. For ELLs, the river is especially wide: the gap between their lives, needs, and interests on one side and the content of what we teach on the other side is even larger than that for native speakers. So how do we build those bridges?

Motivating ELLs to Achieve in the Mainstream ELA Classroom

Factors affecting motivation are called the *affective filter* and entail a student's level of confidence, family support, social support, and sense of personal identity. Stephen Krashen posited that once students reach an intermediate level of lan-

Jorge, 16, lives with his father and siblings; his mother still lives in Colombia, and he has not seen her for three years. He is a bright young man with good work habits, but the transition from ESL classes to the mainstream ELA class has been hard on his ego: after years of being well known, well liked, and a top performer in his ESL classes, he now feels like a stranger in his English class, where he often feels too embarrassed to raise his hand to ask questions or volunteer answers. To compensate, he has shifted the focus of his efforts from school to two other endeavors: he is a superstar on the high school soccer team (where many of his teammates also speak Spanish), and he has started a job outside of school, where he earns money to help out his family. He has found two feel-good environments—soccer and work, which give him the social payoffs he needs to feel motivated to succeed—and has abandoned the "feel-bad" environment of the classroom. His grades drop as his academic efforts diminish.

guage understanding, the two key factors in further language development are comprehensible input and a low affective filter and that, next to these two factors, traditional classroom instruction is relatively inconsequential (Krashen, 1982).

So what does it mean for teachers to provide comprehensible input? We need to focus energy on finding ways to make high-level literature comprehensible for ELLs—not by "dumbing it down," as some would say, but by supplementing it with more comprehensible texts on similar themes. For example, while studying *Night* in the classroom, students can read young adult novels about the Holocaust at home and see excerpts from films and documentaries on the Holocaust so that they can match images to the words they are reading. Likewise, there are modern English translations of many of Shakespeare's plays that ELLs could use to supplement their study of the original.

Facilitating a low affective filter essentially means lowering the defensive walls that many ELLs may build around themselves—an attitude of not caring or shifting a focus on academic success to a focus on social success—when they feel frustrated by the difficulties of fitting in to a mainstream ELA classroom. Because learning does not take place in a sociocultural vacuum, we need to know who our students are apart from their test scores, and ELLs in particular, for the following reasons. Because ESL programs in secondary schools may isolate ELL students from mainstream students, exiting ELLs can experience some separation anxiety from their ESL classes and classmates. For all intents and purposes, mainstreamed ELLs are entering an unfamiliar secondary school population, and it is important that we not underestimate how powerfully feelings of social isolation can affect academic performance and motivation. Before we can teach ELLs, then, we have to help them to forge social connections with their classmates and get to know who they are as young adults, with minds of their own and lives outside the classroom. Considering the anxiety that ELLs may feel coming into a class where there are no familiar faces, how well we create a welcoming classroom environment for ELLs may be pivotal to their decision to succeed or to fail, to stay in school or drop out, to learn or deliberately to "not-learn" (Valdés, 2001; Kohl, 1991). Creating a classroom space in which students know and trust one another, and can find some commonalities with their peers, is essential.

Building Community

In order to build a sense of community in your ELA classroom, some get-to-know-you activities are discussed in the following subsections, in order from least to most linguistically demanding. Teachers will have their own favorites, but the important thing is to take time to build and sustain classroom community, as this lowers all students' affective filters and allows them to take the risks they need to take to advance their English abilities. To ensure that students know what to do, be sure to scaffold each activity and model it thoroughly with a willing student volunteer, repeating instructions and answering questions, before beginning.

Human Scavenger Hunt

Give students a list of characteristics that they must match to other students in the classroom but that are not visible—for, example, owns a dog, plays a musical instrument, plays soccer, has lived in another country, speaks more than one language, babysits for younger siblings, has sung in public, has traveled out of state, has reached the one-star-general level in Halo (Table 9.1). Students have to write down the name of the student who fits each criterion and ask a follow-up question for each—for example, What kind of dog? What instrument? For which team do you play soccer? In which other country have you lived?

The winner is the student who has the largest number of student names, spelled correctly, and follow-up questions answered. (Why "spelled correctly"? Because ELL students' names may not be familiar to native speakers of English, and we as teachers must reinforce the idea that our names are important to us and should be spelled and pronounced as we wish them to be—out of respect—and not arbitrarily anglicized to "make it easier" for others.) The questions about language and country will increase the likelihood that native speakers of English in the class will interact with non-native speakers. The purpose of the follow-up questions is to provide entry points for conversation ("Oh, you have a dog from the shelter? Me, too! What's its name?") that may continue outside of the classroom.

"I Come from . . ." Poems

A poem-writing exercise, from Linda Christenson's wonderful *Reading, Writing and Rising Up* (2000), provides another format for students to affirm their cultural, family, and other identities. Students begin by quick-writing lists on various topics—favorite foods, favorite music, things your mother says, languages you speak, places you've lived, things you might smell in your neighborhood. Next, they transform each list into a free-form "stanza" of their poem, along the lines of "I am from black-eyed peas and green tomato relish, . . . I am from bayou country and 'Don't eat your meat like it's a popsicle!'" See Melissa's poem on the following page.

TABLE 9.1 Human Scavenger Hunt Question Sheet

Characteristic	Student	Follow-up Question	Answer
Has a dog	*Gina*	*What kind of dog?*	*chihuahua*
Speaks more than one language	*Yersin*	*What other languages?*	*Spanish and some Portuguese*

Where I Am From

I am from cervezas and merengue
on Saturday nights.
Loud laughter and voices
joyfully saying, "Dímelo, loco."

I am from daddy saying, "THAT OUTFIT IS TOO TIGHT!"
and mommy saying, "LIVE YOUR LIFE!"

I am from the school of hard knocks,
trying to prove statistics wrong.
People being ashamed of where they're from
while others hold their heads high
with a gun.

Take a good look at my life
and you will see
pain and sorrow around,
but only happiness in me.

Encourage students to include details from their lives that may seem untranslatable into the English language or American culture—like Melissa's "cervezas," "merengue," and "Dímelo loco"; these are the details that will provide a foundation for teaching students about voice in their writing later.

"Language and You" Survey

In addition to our function of helping ELLs and native speakers to find social commonalities, it is important that we also highlight the special academic skills and talents of ELLs, so that the class views ELLs as a resource in the classroom rather than (as ELLs, sadly, can sometimes feel) a drag on the flow of classroom activity. This survey activity leads to classroom discussions that can effectively open native speakers' eyes to the special knowledge and skills of the ELLs in the classroom.

After students complete the survey (Table 9.2), pair students for one-on-one sharing, ensuring that ELLs are paired with students who are especially good at drawing others out; for ELLs, sharing their experience aloud with students who empathize with, or take an interest in, their language issues will help them to have the courage to share that experience with native speakers who may be baffled at the seeming redundancy of the survey's questions. The native speakers who complete the survey will likely discuss the questions more than the answers ("Who *doesn't* dream in their own language?"); this kind of response in itself can turn on a few light bulbs.

List of Life Goals

A list of life goals is another useful tool for helping students get to know one another, find commonalities, and begin conversations across established social groups. The assignment is for students to write a list of 10 to 20 goals that they have for their life, no matter how outrageous, and to continue to add to this list throughout the year. First, model a list of your own on the board. Modeling this exercise provides an entry point for celebrating language diversity, for demonstrating to ELLs the welcoming, diversity-celebrating tone of our classrooms. For example, a teacher's list might include "I would like to learn to speak Spanish fluently" or "I would like to visit Africa to see the places where some of my students

TABLE 9.2 "Language and You" Survey

What languages can you speak?

What languages can you understand when someone speaks to you?

What kinds of things do you read in English?

What kinds of things do you read in other languages?

What kinds of things do you write in English?

What kinds of things do you write in other languages?

When you do math, what language do you use to count or add or subtract?

What languages do the people you live with speak?

When you have breakfast or dinner with someone at home, what language or languages do you speak?

When you watch television, what are the languages of the programs you like?

When you go home from school (walk or take the bus) with someone, what languages do you speak?

Do you listen to music in more than one language? If so which languages?

When you look up something on the Internet, do you always use one language or more than one? What language or languages do you use?

What language or languages do you dream in?

When you are angry or sad, what language do you usually use to express how you feel?

When you talk on the telephone, what language or languages do you like to use?

Do you ever travel to another country? What language or languages do you speak when you are there?

Do you keep a diary or journal? If so, what language or languages do you write in?

Do you have a friend who speaks a language that is not English?

Do you have a relative who speaks a language that is not English? If yes, what language does your relative or friend speak?

Do you have a neighbor who speaks a language that is not English? If so, what language does your neighbor speak?

Do you have one or more favorite songs? If so, what are they?

Do you have one or more favorite books? If so, what are they?

Do you have one or more favorite movies? If so, what are they?

Do you have one or more favorite TV shows or channels? If so, what are they?

Do you have a favorite place? If so, where is it?

Do you have a hero, or someone you admire very much? If so, who is it?

Source: Adapted from Language and you, The Education Alliance, Brown University, 2008.

were born" or "I would like to walk along the Great Wall in China." Sneaking in these references to the countries of origin of ELLs provides these students with an entry point for sharing their expertise with the class. "Miss, I could teach you some Spanish words." "Would you visit Liberia? That's where I'm from." "Do you speak any Chinese?"

In addition to bringing ELLs into the classroom, these lists of goals are useful to revisit throughout the year to motivate *all* students when they are disconnecting from some of the more challenging assignments of the class. ("Do you remember that one of your goals is to be a lawyer? Writing and speaking persuasively is what lawyers do all the time, so these rhetorical strategies could come in handy later.") Connecting class learning goals to students' personal goals leverages interest, personalizes class work, and can be highly motivational. As with all writing assignments, have students stop and share after the first five or ten minutes of writing so that they can borrow ideas—or language, in the case of ELLs—from their classmates.

Letters

While the introduction of e-mail has made personal letter writing sometimes seem re-dundant, teaching students how to write a formal letter remains a critical skill in the business sector, as well as for satisfied or disgruntled consumers, citizens petitioning their congressional representatives, or concerned readers or viewers of the local news.

Writing a friendly letter to your students early in the school year introduces you to your students in ways that help to build trust and mutual interest upon which to build those critical student-teacher relationships. Having students write back provides early feedback on students' confidence and skills as writers; it also provides another opportunity to tap into the particular needs, talents, and inter-ests of ELLs. (These letters can also be used later as models for comparing the tone and organization of a friendly letter to that of a business letter.) The goals-list ac-tivity (which precedes this one) and the interviews activity (which follows) can be used as the starting point for a mind map (alternatively called a web or brain-storm) on content for the letters.

Since the letter has more sophisticated language and formatting requirements than the previous exercises, scaffolding is especially important. First, provide stu-dents with a model for writing a description of themselves. This can be a letter from a previous student, a letter from you, or an excerpt from a student-friendly text. (In Sharon Draper's young adult novel *Romiette and Julio* (2001), the character Romi journals about her likes and dislikes, her family and friends, her hopes and dreams, in a passage that lends itself to this exercise as well as to modeling how to create single-topic paragraphs each with a clear topic sentence. The web shown in Figure 9.1 is generated from those pages.)

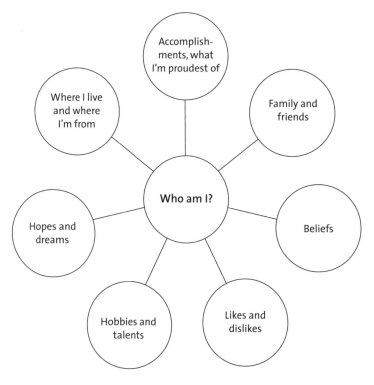

FIGURE 9.1   Web (or brainstorm) for introductory letter

My name
My address

November 8, 2011

Dear Ms. Jones,
    Thank you for your letter. As a new student of yours in the __th grade, I look forward to getting to know you, too. Allow me to tell you something about myself.
    I come from . . .
    My family . . .
    My best friend is . . .
    I like to . . .
    I also like . . .
    Things I dislike include . . .
    My favorite things to do on the weekend are . . .
    In addition to   , I also enjoy . . .
    While I don't like to boast, I have several talents, including . . .
    My hopes and dreams for my life include . . .
    I am looking forward to a great year in this class.

Sincerely,

My signature

My name

Have students note the topic of each paragraph in the model you provide, and ask them to draw a web matching the writer's thought process, then add to it as a class.

The next step is for students to write a letter that includes a paragraph on each of the topic bubbles in the brainstorm.

Another scaffolding tool is a letter template like the one above, providing a list of sentence starters. This is especially helpful for ELLs, as it models some of the formulaic language of a formal letter, with which they may be familiar only in their own language—or not at all.

Providing students with these sentence starters not only gives them a sample structure for the letter, but also provides ELLs with samples of polite, formal English, which may differ markedly from the language they hear in the school hallways. It also provides the appropriate register for the language of commerce and citizenship, the realms that our students enter as soon as they leave the classroom.

Following are excerpts from two student letters:

I'm writing this letter to let you know more about me. Well I just turn 15 this summer Agust 2 I had a sweet 15 like the tradition in Mexico. Every time in mexico when a young gurl is goin to be 15 they celebrate a big party because for us turning 15 means your an adult now, we dress up like a princess with a crown too.

I was born in the U.S but with parents that where born in Mexico wich makes me a Chicana, American/Mexican. One of the things I like about Mexico is their religion their so much to learnd every day. I'm the kind of person that likes to eat alot, I love food and I especially like when my mom cooks mexican food I eat so much that I can't stop, it got that spicy flavor that makes your mouth burn and I like it.

My name is Malinda... I am Cambodian but I don't really like speaking Khmer that much because It's kind of complicated learning how to speak my language. I believe in buddah. I am nice and quiet girl. I don't really talk that much around people I don't know. I have a best friend name Ashley . . . and she is a nice friend we always talk together on the phone non-stop. She is a really cool person once you get to know her more she always make person laugh even when their sad. . . . Everytime when I'm mad or quiet she always ask me what's wrong and then I tell her what happen and she always get what I'm saying because she go through the same thing I'm going through. The things that bother me so much is when someone check through my backpack and take stuff out without asking permission.

The letters reveal a tremendous amount about the students, their language, culture, and beliefs. They also reveal a considerable amount about students' affect—whether shy or confident, happy or depressed, a risk taker or risk averse, socially engaged or isolated—which can provide insight into how best to motivate ELLs or how best to approach them about class work. All this provides fodder for building relationships with other students in the classroom and for finding topics for later writing assignments, for essays, descriptive writing, and reports, for example: "Describe how to make your favorite Cape Verdian dish." Or "Describe a quinceañera to an American girl." Finally, these letters provide early indicators of language issues, such as subject-verb agreement and capitalization, that can be addressed later in the classroom through mini-lessons and personal corrections lists.

Student Interviews

The student interview is a reliable exercise that has the double benefit of gauging students' oral competency and confidence, and also of providing ELLs with a social contact in the classroom. Moreover, the language demands of this activity are fairly repetitive and embedded in a social context, which helps to further meaningful language learning (Vygotsky, 1978). Here are some ideas for scaffolding the assignment:

- First, activate prior knowledge: Ask students if they have ever interviewed anyone or seen or read an interview with someone famous. Use their responses as a jumping-off point for listing some "getting-to-know-you" questions on the board, generating at least 20 or so. Ask them to focus on questions that generate more than one-word answers. When suggestions slow down, be sure to add at least a few questions that may pertain particularly to ELLs, such as "Which languages do you speak other than English?" and "Where were you born?" (In addition to finding commonalities, after all, we want to find and share what is special about our ELLs.)

- Ask students what a journalist would do when interviewing someone for the newspaper to elicit such responses as "Know your questions in advance of the interview" and "Take notes during the interview."

- Show students a clip of an accomplished interviewer such as Maria Hinajosa, Katie Couric, or Tavis Smiley, telling them to write down the professional interviewer's questions and what else they noticed about the interviewer—for example, eye contact, head nodding, phatic noises ("Hmmm," "Uh-huh"), and follow-up or clarifying questions.

- With a willing student, model an in-class interview, taking notes on the board or an overhead so that students can see how taking notes does not require recording every word. So in answer to "What is your favorite thing to do on the weekends?" you note your interviewee's answer as "Play b/ball w/friends + sleep late." (See Chapter 7 for more on teaching note taking.)

Now assign partners to each student, ensuring that ELLs work with friendly, receptive classmates who are native speakers of English. Each student will write down ten questions to ask their partner, at least five from the list generated by the class, and up to five of their own. It is important that students know who their partners are beforehand so that they can choose questions according to what they may or may not know already about their partners. Before partners begin their interviews, announce that after the interviews each of them will introduce their partner to the class, using the information they have gathered from the interview. English language learners may be especially intimidated by public speaking. Assure them that you will help them through the process of writing up their interview results before they have to present to the class, and that they may read from their page if they need to.

After the interviews are completed, circulate to assist students in their interview write-ups, focusing special attention on ELLs who may be shy about asking for help. Some may need help on how to translate from a first-person answer, "I like playing baseball," to a third-person description, "She likes playing baseball." Also, ask ELLs if they would like to practice their presentations on you before they read it to others.

The next step is for partners to read what they have written to each other, correcting and elaborating on information where necessary. Finally, when students present to the class, have partners stand together, so that ELLs do not feel the singular glare of the spotlight. Ultimately, you may wish to post these interview paragraphs in the classroom or publish them with photographs in a class facebook.

Scaffolding Learning for ELLs in the ELA Classroom

Throughout the exercises described in this chapter, you will notice we have incorporated several practices for scaffolding student learning. The purpose of scaffolding is simply to build up the confidence of ELLs (and other learners) as they learn the steps for constructing knowledge on their own.

- *Activating prior knowledge* (APK) is asking students what they already know about a subject. Besides providing a point of connection for new knowledge, APK is helpful to ELLs on two counts: it makes them aware of what is (and is not) common knowledge among their native-speaker peers; it also offers ELLs opportunities to share expertise on a subject about which their native-speaker peers may know little, again emphasizing their role as a resource to the classroom.

- *Brainstorming* and recording the brainstorm as a class, both on the board and in students' notebooks, helps ELLs to see a written record of thinking and speaking in the classroom. The open-ended and collage/*bricolage* nature of brainstorming, too, diminishes the inhibitions that ELLs may feel against speaking in complete sentences or thoughts.

- *Frontloading* provides students with key knowledge before they encounter a text or fully enter an academic unit. An example is the anticipation/reaction guide on *Romeo and Juliet* (see Table 9.4), which hooks students into the major themes of the play. Frontloading can also include key words that students will need to recognize and understand before reading a text—for example, "tesseract" and "telepathy" before reading *A Wrinkle in Time*. This strategy alerts ELLs to the reality that certain words and concepts are new to *everyone* in the classroom, not just to them.

- *Modeling* what students are being asked to do provides visual clues for ELLs who may have trouble contextualizing strictly verbal instructions. For writing assignments, we can provide models that we ourselves have created, and seasoned teachers will have a collection of student writing to use as models. We can also role-play, with the aid of willing students, what we wish for students to do in pair or group activities.

- *Think-pair-share* engages students in practicing a new skill or venturing an answer, first on their own and then with a partner, before having to share with the whole class. For example, students write down their response to a question (e.g., "What is one example of symbolism?"), then discuss it with a partner before being asked to share with the class; this exercise gives ELLs an opportunity to fine-tune their responses with a native-speaking classmate or fellow ELL before being in the spotlight.

- *Graphic organizers* provide a visual guide for organizing parts of an assignment—for example, a Venn diagram for a compare-and-contrast essay. (See Figures 9.1 and 9.7.)

- *Rehearsing or practicing* with a sympathetic audience is an essential part of any required classroom performance. Think-pair-share accomplishes this purpose on a small scale; the student interview activity provides an example of a more extended rehearsal for a more formal presentation.

- *Ongoing informal feedback* helps students to see assessment not as a final judgment but as a stepping-stone to improve their performance. This is especially important for ELLs who are coming from countries where schools emphasize high-stakes national exams as a measure of whether a student should be on a college or a vocational track. (See "Formative Assessment," later in this chapter.)

- *Presenting, posting, or publishing* is an essential final step in the writing process because it perpetuates the idea that we write for an *audience*; it is not an exercise in a vacuum. Moreover, public exhibition of students' work gives ELLs an opportunity to gauge how they are progressing compared to their peer set.

All these scaffolding strategies are represented or implied in the following sections on facilitating reading, writing, speaking, and vocabulary development.

Providing Opportunities to Extend ELLs' Speaking and Performance Skills

An important part of language development is learning to formulate language in the moment, in conversation and social interactions. One way to build the confidence of ELLs in hearing their own voices speak English is to provide opportunities for public speaking and performance in the ELA classroom. Oral language is used in presenting reports, performing short dramatic scenes, text-based discussion, poetry slams, debates, and mock trials, among other formats. In this section, we will look briefly at other ways to support ELLs' oral language development.

Quotation of the Day

Mike Rose (1990) found, in teaching adults to read and to discuss readings, that brief, pithy texts—such as you would find in a book of quotations—could be used effectively for teaching vocabulary as well as for provoking high-interest classroom discussion. Adolescents are developing a sense of identity, and the kinds of motivational or philosophical witticisms found in such collections often stick with them as firmly as favorite song lyrics. For example, dissecting on the overhead projector Thoreau's "Beware all enterprises that require new clothes" provides an opportunity to build on the always-popular adolescent preoccupation with clothing to address issues of selfhood, individuality, and conformity. It also provides an opportunity to define "enterprises" as well as to point out how commands in English imply, rather than state, their subject pronoun ("*You* beware . . ."). Chapter 5 lists a number of essential class discussion tools, including sentence starters and lists of transition words, that can be put to good use here.

Other short, pithy texts include proverbs or sayings—in Spanish, *dichos*—which provide not only vocabulary and discussion fodder, but also the kind of Anglo-American cultural background knowledge that ELLs may not have if they have spent most of their early years in another country or culture. What does it mean to be a "dog in the manger," for example, or to be "the early bird"? The sharing of English sayings can be complemented by ELLs sharing the sayings of their own language and culture, providing a cross-cultural exchange of folk wisdom (For example a Spanish saying like, *Dime con quien andas y te dire quien eres—tell me who you hang out with and I'll tell you who you are*).

Television News Reports

When it comes to individual student presentations and reports—for example, book talks or research project presentations—a television newsmagazine format (á la *The Today Show*) can provide a frame for a series of student presentations. The advantage of this format for ELLs is that despite having to go solo in places, they can feel part of a team of presenters. ("And, now, over to Ying for a word about her favorite inventor, Mr. George Washington Carver. Ying?")

The ubiquity of the television magazine format means that most students will be familiar with its look, rhythm, and sound. After viewing a short segment of a program like this, have students discuss what they noticed about each of the presenters: how they introduce each segment (often with a topical question to hook the viewer, such as "Have you ever wondered what it would be like to travel back in time?"); how they stayed focused on a single topic; preparatory research they did; their use of visual aids; and how they concluded each segment (often with a lesson learned, e.g., "And that, ladies and gentlemen, is how you become an astronaut"). Students will also notice good presenters' habits—speaking clearly, not fidgeting, making eye contact with the host or looking into the camera, not turning their back on the audience/camera.

Students can then be responsible for creating their own "program segments" based on your required assignment. Knowing that they will be on camera ratchets up the seriousness with which students take their presentations. In a reality–television, cell phone–camera world, the mere presence of a video camera, whether or not it is in use, can turn students "on," ready to inhabit the persona of a television star, imitating their enunciation, their intonation, their gestures. For ELLs, in particular, the feeling of imitating someone on television can take the burden off of feeling, "This is *me* talking"; putting on the hat of a performer creates a protective shield such that constructive criticism feels more focused on the performance than on the performer.

Most important for ELLs who are making class presentations is the use of visual aids. Posters, PowerPoint slide shows, presentation boards, and props provide a security blanket for presenters who feel uncertain about their capacity to use language alone to convey their message. To assist ELLs in making presentations, teachers can have ELLs choose images or artifacts they plan to share and start by having them write a description of each item. "This is the kind of diary that Anne Frank used. Here is a photograph of her own handwriting in her diary; as you can see, it's not in English, but in Dutch, because she lived in the Netherlands. On this map, you can see that the Netherlands is a country in northern Europe."

Finally, for all rehearsals, speeches, readings, and presentations of any kind, it is essential that we teach students to applaud at the end. The applause is not a measure of how well the performer did, but a recognition that the performer got up and performed at all. For nonnative speakers of English, the applause may be what gets them out in front of the class the next time.

Debates and Mock Trials

One central purpose of public education in the United States is to prepare students to be active participants in a democracy. Many immigrants arrive in the United States with no experience of the roles and responsibilities of citizens in a democracy. Teaching students to speak persuasively—through debate and mock trials—is an essential responsibility for teachers, and it also provides students with a basic knowledge of their civil rights.

With mock trials, we can once again use to our advantage our students' familiarity with the plethora of courtroom dramas on television—from *Law and Order* to *Judge Judy*. English language learners have ready access to these shows. Many teenagers enjoy adopting the formal postures of judge, jury, witnesses, and attorneys in mock trials, which can explore important themes in the books our students read in class. For example, *Holes* by Louis Sachar can be used to explore the juve-

Albalis, 14, loves to debate. She has a knack for grasping the overarching themes of high-level texts and separating the big ideas from the little details, but her mind works faster than her language skills allow her to express. Her social studies teacher has told her that she would make a good lawyer, considering how much she likes to argue. This idea has taken hold in her mind and leverages her motivation in other classes.

nile justice system—whether it should be focused on punishment or rehabilitation—by putting on trial the wardens at the juvenile detention camp. *Speak* by Laurie Halse Anderson can be used to try the date-rapist, but also to explore the conspiracy of silence among teenagers around issues of sexual violence. While more verbally adept students will tend to opt for the roles of the attorneys, mock trials offer many opportunities for speaking: witnesses to the "crime" in question can provide well-supported roles for ELLs. Since the characters' behaviors and words are all available directly from the book, there is no need for improvisation. Similarly, officers of the court, such as the bailiff and the judge, use formulaic language ("All rise for the right honorable Judge Carlos Santana." "Order in the court." "Call for the defense.") that can be scripted and practiced in advance of the performance. (For a list of frequently used courtroom vocabulary, see http://courts.michigan.gov/plc/day-in-court/vocabulary.htm.)

Within the format of the mock trial performance, the skills and protocols of debate—stating a thesis and supporting it with evidence, taking turns, rebuttals—can be practiced in ways that can be recalled in other debates later in class. Preparing for debates follows preparation for persuasive writing. (See "Scaffolding for a Persuasive Essay.")

Developing Critical
Reading and Writing Skills around Literature

If you remember what it was like the first time you tried to read a novel in another language—not the foreign language textbooks with carefully selected vocabulary and syntax calibrated to your reading level, but a real piece of literature, fraught with incomprehensible idioms and unfamiliar verb tenses, not to mention baffling literary and historical allusions—you may understand what it is like for ELLs transitioning from ESL readings to the ELA literature curriculum. It is not unlike the way a newborn, bombarded with sensory information, must take it all in, though still unsure which bits of information are going to help her survive and which bits are of no consequence to her.

Helping our ELLs to conquer their fears of reading requires that we provide them with the tools to make it accessible, manageable. The starting point for reading will always be a reading journal, in which students take notes, write down passages from the text, and jot down questions. For the strategies mentioned in the following subsections, assume that students will be writing in a designated reading journal.

Introducing a Book

We often jump right into the text of a book before we have given our students a chance to "shake hands" with it. A helpful strategy for introducing a new text to students is to give them a few minutes to look at the cover, flip through the pages, and jot down their observations and predictions about it. Have students share their observations first, then ask what their predictions are about the book's content, theme, characters, setting. This type of anticipatory exercise helps ELLs in particular to move past the newborn's sensory overload situation.

Set a Purpose for Reading

"What is the teacher going to ask me about this?" No student, but especially no ELL, should ever be asking himself this question while reading. Reading unfamiliar and challenging texts is a complex and mind-boggling activity for anyone, since we are trying to determine genre, point of view, context, and purpose in addition to topic and meaning. And ELLs must undertake this task while simultaneously decoding individual words, idioms, and cultural or historical references with which they may not be familiar. Understanding is enhanced dramatically when teachers provide a focus for the reading (Tovani, 2000)—for example, "Look for information about the main character" or "Jot down details that tell you about the setting of the story."

To provide a sense of cohesion for a complex reading that might take ELLs in many different directions of thought, it is important that the purpose we set for reading should lead to discussion and writing that is related to a unit's central theme or question. To prepare students for writing assignments based on texts, setting a purpose for reading can be organized in chart form, so that students can take notes relevant to their purpose. For example, for the essay topic "Who is the real Jay Gatsby?" students created a chart with three headings for taking notes on their reading (Table 9.3).

Anticipation/Reaction Guides

Anticipation/reaction guides are questionnaires structured to anticipate the themes of a text; they can be revisited throughout the reading to record passages relevant to each statement, leading up to a final written assignment. For example, an anticipation/reaction guide for reading *Romeo and Juliet* (or *Romiette and Julio*) might look something like Table 9.4.

These guides not only help students to "preview" the story, but also provide them with talking points throughout the reading, including those that bring up differences between mainstream American culture and the cultures of ELLs' home countries (not to mention the culture of a book's author!).

Coding the Text; Stop and Jot

Many schools use Houghton Mifflin's *Interactive Reader*, (McDougal Littell, 2000) a series of literature anthologies incorporating exercises on theme, style, imagery,

TABLE 9.3   Purposeful Reading Note-Taking Chart

What do people say about Gatsby?	What does Gatsby say about himself?	What's the truth?

TABLE 9.4 Anticipation/Reaction Guide for *Romeo and Juliet*

Text: *Romeo and Juliet*			Name:		
Author: William Shakespeare			Date:		
Before Reading			After Reading		
Agree	Disagree	Statements	Agree	Disagree	Where you see it in the text (Act.Scene.Lines)
		I believe in love at first sight.			
		If my family didn't like my boyfriend or girlfriend, I know that sooner or later I would drop that person.			
		I would never date someone of a different race, culture, or language background from me.			
		I would be willing to die for someone I truly love.			
		I believe there is one and only one person out there who is right for me, my "soul mate."			
		I would never try to hide from my parents the fact that I was dating someone.			
		Fifteen-year-olds are too young to be in serious relationships.			

vocabulary, and other aspects of literature in which students are invited to circle, underline, and otherwise code text as they are reading: a check mark shows where something is made clear; a question mark shows where something in the text is confusing; an exclamation point shows an interesting or surprising passage; and so on. There are periodic "Pause and Reflect" breaks, at which point students answer analytical and evaluative questions, jot notes in the margins, notice patterns, and make self-to-text connections. At the beginning of a memoir by Rudolfo Anaya on his grandfather, for example, the instructions in the text ask students to "circle examples of what Anaya admires about his grandfather."

The principles of the *Interactive Reader* can be used with any reading we do in class. When giving students the description of an end-of-quarter project, for example, we can instruct students to read through the assignment description and circle the five most important words on the page, then discuss with a partner why they believe those are the most important words. This activity often helps ELLs to zero in on the academic vocabulary with which they may be unfamiliar: "articulate," "discuss," "analyze," "evaluate," "summarize," "memoir," "narrative," "stanza," "first-person narrator," and so on. In the process of reviewing, as a class, the words that students have circled, we are better able to assess which critical vocabulary students recognize and understand, which they may recognize but not understand, and which words they may miss altogether.

While we do not want students to mark up school texts, we can have them use Post-it notes to code the text with the symbols we have mentioned or others, such as a double arrow to show a self-to-text connection. Likewise, instead of a

TABLE 9.5 Reading Journal Chart

Text pages	What I understood	New or difficult vocabulary	Questions I have

"Pause and Reflect," we can have students pause at the end of designated passages to "Stop and Jot" using a prompt you supplied before the reading (e.g., "What can you tell about the person telling the story?") or choosing from a posted set of journal entry starters ("I wonder . . . ," "I notice . . . ," "I was confused by . . . ," "This reminds me of . . ."). As students share their jottings with a partner or a small group, the level of comprehension rises for everyone. Once again, ELLs gain a reality check for their level of comprehension ("Does everyone else understand this? Or am I the only one who is confused?") that helps them to narrow the range of questions they may have about a reading selection.

A structured chart for journaling, like the one in Table 9.5 created by Jodi Reiss (2005), can provide ongoing information to teachers about ELLs' reading comprehension.

Another format for journaling about reading, in Table 9.6, takes students beyond comprehension to interpretation and analysis. It works for ELLs because it breaks down the process of analysis into (1) selecting a passage to analyze, (2) copying the passage, (3) putting the author's words into the student's own words, and then (4) interpreting the passage (the "So what?").

TABLE 9.6 Text Analysis Reading Journal Chart

The author writes . . .	I think this means . . .	This is important because . . .

Read-Arounds

It is useful to require students to read aloud on a regular basis, since we can gather much information about comprehension from how students read—their pronunciation, their inflection, their pace, their recognition of punctuation. Putting desks in a circle provides a visual indicator of the order of readers, which means fewer interruptions to ask, "Who's next?" Most important, though, is setting a tone of respect for read-arounds and setting some ground rules. For example, discourage students from correcting each other—allow every reader a chance to sound out words he does not know—and no "helping" unless the reader specifically asks for it; let long pauses go. As a read-around progresses, we can reinforce this focus on building reading skills rather than on the correctness of the reading itself. For example, at a long pause, we can ask the reader, "Can you sound out the first five letters?" Likewise, we can ignore a mispronunciation until the reader has finished the passage, then insert, "That difficult word there was 'extraneous'—does anyone know what it means?" This tactic reassures the reader that she is not being spotlighted for an error, but rather has made a mistake that anyone in the class could have made.

For ELLs, reading aloud may be an uncomfortable experience, so for read-arounds, it is important to allow students (not just ELLs) to choose how long a passage they will read—as much as a page or as little as a sentence. Many ELLs who start the process deathly afraid of reading aloud can be coaxed into reading over time with continued positive feedback. For example, during a read-around, we can write notes to students who struggle with their reading: "I notice that you read a longer passage today—great job! I'm glad to see you challenging yourself!" or "I notice that you are getting better at sounding out words that you don't know—that's an excellent reading skill!"

Experienced ELA teachers become familiar with the areas of set texts that are most difficult for ELLs (and native speakers) to comprehend; as we become more facile with the instruction of a particular text, we can allow our own focus to shift from the text itself to our students' particular needs and struggles in the act of reading.

Reading in Pairs or Small Groups

All the strategies described in this section can be used with a whole class or, once the routines and protocols have been established, in pairs or small groups. The advantage of the smaller group is that students are more actively engaged for longer periods of time; instead of reading once or twice in a class period, then, they may have to read five or ten times. For ELLs, this provides more sheltered practice, as well as a less intimidating arena in which to ask comprehension questions or to volunteer thoughts.

Visual Aids: Films, Pictures, Charts, Tableaux

Visual aids are critical for ELLs' understanding of texts; an author may be brilliantly descriptive, but if students do not possess the vocabulary to decode the description, they need to see what is being described to make sense of it. Here are some ideas for using visual aids:

- When showing films in class, turn on the English subtitles so that students can connect the written word to its use in context. Regardless of a film's sound quality, there will always be dialogue that is missed without the subtitles. Students viewing *Julius Caesar* were especially tuned in to the speeches they had been required to translate into modern English earlier; and they paid close attention to how Shakespeare's words matched the actors' intonation and gesture.

- Also, when showing films in class, it is important to set a purpose for watching, just as you would set a purpose for reading. ("What are some things that Atticus says to his children that tell you what he believes in?") Also, pause the film at certain points to ensure that students are capturing important plot points, especially when those may pivot on quickly delivered dialogue. ("What did he just say? . . . And what do you think that means?")

- In books featuring families, draw family trees to show how characters are related to one another. For example, when teaching *The Crucible,* you can cut out five house shapes and have students create a family tree for each of the families mentioned in the play. This visual reminder helps students to keep straight the relationships between characters as the plot thickens.

- For literature whose settings may be unfamiliar to students, gather representative images from the Internet and put them in a simple PowerPoint presentation (or just print out the stills and post them or pass them around) with subtitles for key words. For example, when teaching Rudolfo Anaya's *Bless Me, Ultima* (1994), you may find pictures of a *curandera* (healer or medicine woman), of the *llano* (the grassy plains of New Mexico where the story takes place), of a *vaquero* (a cowboy), and of *nopales* (prickly pear cactus). Some Spanish-speaking ELLs may have as little knowledge of these words and images as native English speakers and other ELLs; they may have grown up in urban areas and be unfamiliar with rural life.

- For words that are essential to understanding a book's setting or characters, students can create glossaries or picture dictionaries in their reading journals.

- Engaging students in creating frozen tableaux of important scenes from books is another way of helping ELLs to visualize what they are reading. Small groups can be assigned, or can choose, scenes from the class reading to depict, and the class can vote on which tableau best illustrates its scene.

- Students can create character webs (or brainstorms) by recording quotations that tell them something about each character. The character's name is in a bubble at the center, and spokes spray from this hub to bubbles with quotations from the text about that character.

- Another way of documenting characters is through a chart like the one in Table 9.7, in which the main characters of Zora Neale Hurston's *Their Eyes Were Watching God* (2006) are recorded.

Developing Vocabulary to Support Reading Comprehension and Extend Writing Skills

By the end of high school, American students are expected to have a vocabulary of approximately 40,000 word families (Nagy & Anderson, 1984). English language learners may have significantly fewer words at their disposal. The dictionary and the thesaurus can be helpful tools for decoding text, but there are better tools for

FIGURE 9.7 Character Chart

| Characters | Qualities | | Motivation: Goals and Dreams |
	Appearance	Actions and Attitudes	
Janie Starks	40-ish, long hair, beautiful, wears overalls	independent, free-spirited, though obedient at first, finds beauty in nature	freedom, "pear tree love," wants to be her own person—not a man's property.
Logan Killicks	old, bald, "like a skull head," unattractive	farmer, hard-working	wants Janie to be a loyal, hard-working farmer's wife
Joe Starks	well-dressed, handsome but with a paunch	confident, an entrepre-neur, mayor	wants to build an empire and have a trophy wife
Tea Cake Woods	young, 20-ish, handsome	funny, plays guitar, clever, likes to gamble	wants to be a good husband to Janie, not ambitious

building vocabulary that students will actually need to begin to use. Likewise, the SAT prep strategy of having students memorize lists of related words may work for students who come from homes in which even a few of these words are in use, but many ELLs will not have had the experience of hearing a rich variety of English vocabulary, and so they have too small a foundation to which to connect new lexical knowledge. If a rich English vocabulary is not in regular use in their social interactions, or in what they watch on television or listen to on their iPods, then ELLs will depend entirely on the classroom for exposure to standard American English and academic English.

English language arts teachers must create language-rich environments for all students, as well as provide the critical tools for building vocabulary.

Word Walls

One popular strategy for building key vocabulary in ELA and other classrooms is to create a word wall, upon which teachers post key vocabulary for the current unit pertaining to specific categories that run throughout the quarter. Words can be grouped under categories that will remain constant throughout the year: genre, theme, setting, narrator, and so on. For example, for a unit on Elie Wiesel's *Night* (1960), the word wall might look like Table 9.8.

Word Games

We can enlist the help of native speakers in our classrooms to build ELLs' vocabulary by turning the day's vocabulary lesson into a game. For example, we can offer extra credit for students who correctly use the word or words of the day in the course of classroom discussion. Hearing their peers use the words not only reinforces through repetition, but also rewards the use of new words. Or instead of extra credit, we can institute a classroom ritual such as ringing a bell or doing the wave to recognize and celebrate the use of the word of the day. (Some of you may remember that Peewee Herman of *Peewee's Playhouse* always had a secret word of the day; the television audience was instructed to "Scream real loud!" when they heard the word.)

TABLE 9.8   Word Wall Contents for *Night*

Category	Important Terms
Text	*Night*
Author	Elie Wiesel
Narrator	Elie Wiesel
Genre	Historical memoir
Themes	Father-son relationships
	Religious faith
	Humanity and inhumanity
Historical terms	Holocaust, World War II
Key vocabulary	Rabbi, synagogue, Torah, Talmud, Kabbala
Non-English words	Blockaelteste, "Arbeit Macht Frei"
Setting	Romania—ghettos
	Poland—concentration camps

Daily Vocabulary Log

Another strategy is for students to keep a daily vocabulary log, which may look something like Table 9.9. This format provides space for students to write out the sentence in which they found a word, providing both context and usage. (Note that the first entry line should always show a model of a correct entry.) It also requires students to think about what the word might mean, making use of context clues, before checking the dictionary. Requiring students to copy out an author's entire sentence serves the additional purpose of providing them with models for academic or literary English (see box). It is essential that students not be responsible for recording more than three to five new words per day, however, since a longer list diminishes returns on student effort.

Idiom of the Day

Every language has its quirky constructions; English has no shortage of perplexing idioms. Offering up an idiom of the day helps ELLs to become familiar with the least logical, hardest-to-translate English phrases, such as "Let's cut to the chase" or "It's raining cats and dogs."

TABLE 9.9   Daily Vocabulary Log

WORD (page number and location—top/middle/bottom)	SENTENCE: Write out the sentence in which the word appears.	WHAT YOU *THINK* the word means, using the context clues	• PART OF SPEECH of the word • Dictionary DEFINITION of the word • Other FORMS OF THE WORD (underline the form that appears first in the dictionary)
brimmed (p. 50, bottom)	*"Jack took up a coconut shell that brimmed with fresh water from among a group that was arranged in the shade, and drank."*	*something to do with liquid? full?*	• verb, past tense • <u>brim</u>: fill or be full to the point of overflowing • brim, brimming

Since the advent of the internet, students have tended to copy much less text by hand than in years past; they may cut and paste quotations from web sites into a report, but they do not go through the process of laboriously writing out quotations from books onto note cards, then transferring those into their reports. The result is that even though students may read challenging texts, they rarely reproduce them in ways that require them to imitate a more sophisticated sentence or paragraph than they are yet capable of writing themselves. Comedian George Carlin noted that his father used to write out the plays of Shakespeare by hand, just for the sheer joy of the language. While many may frown on "merely" copying text as less than academic in nature, writing out whole sentences of an accomplished writer provides students with the opportunity to slow down and pay attention to the language, syntax, and meaning in sentences in ways they rarely have the opportunity to do anymore.

Much idiomatic language revolves around the correct use of prepositions, particularly difficult for ELLs. In Spanish, for example, one dreams "with" something, rather than dreaming "of" something. And how do we explain the differences, for example, between "running for office" and "running to the office"? Or between "running to" the door and "running into" the door? One strategy for establishing these differences is to dramatize them or otherwise make them visual for ELLs. Designating the class clown as the "interpreter of idioms" for the class can kill two birds with one stone, providing meaningful, sanctioned activity for the former, and a visual (and comical) frame of reference for the latter.

Semantic Clusters: Connotation, Denotation, Register

A dictionary can be a very precise tool, but it often is more confusing than helpful to ELLs; a thesaurus is often more useful in that it provides semantic clusters of words, but a thesaurus will not tell you the difference between a "shove" and a "nudge," for example. When teaching ELLs the difference between words with the same denotation (e.g., smell) but differing connotations (e.g., scent, perfume, odor, stench), it is helpful to use a graphic such as the one in Figure 9.2, which illustrates the *degree* of "pleasantness" of each of these words for "smell." Another version of this might show differences in *register,* as in Figure 9.3.

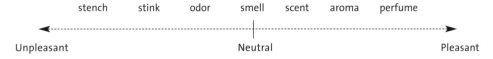

FIGURE 9.2 Word connotations: degrees of pleasantness

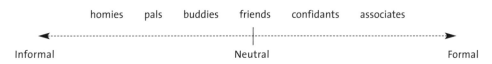

FIGURE 9.3 Word connotations: degrees of formality

Strategies for Supporting ELLs in Writing

Even more intimidating to ELLs than reading in English is writing, the process of accurately recording thought on paper, where there is no immediate audience member to ask, "Do you get what I'm trying to say?" The writing process (described in Chapter 8) is built around the idea that our students have minds and thoughts of their own; that our job as writing teachers is to draw them out, lead them through the process of self-expression. It provides an excellent protocol for working with ELLs on their writing skills, as it begins with scaffolding (prewriting) activities such as brainstorming and modeling, and guides students through the recursive process of drafting and revising until the students' *ideas* are clear, all of which happens before the required fussing over grammar and spelling errors in the editing stage.

Yet, as Lisa Delpit has pointed out (2006), we cannot assume that students will absorb mainstream language and writing forms by osmosis; these need to be taught directly using models, formulaic language, and other scaffolding media.

Teaching Students to Write in Multiple Genres

In the course of their secondary school years, students are required to write in multiple formats—editorials, letters, essays, poems, résumés, memoirs—as well as in multiple genres—namely, personal, factual, and analytical writing. Recent research on systemic functional linguistics (SFL) divides genres into categories based on the linguistic features of each as well as on their purposes and on the roles writers take on (with respect to their readers or audience) for each (Schleppegrell, 2004). For teachers of ELLs, this redefinition of genre is especially helpful, as it makes us more aware of the linguistic challenges of each.

For ELLs, the least language-demanding genre is *factual writing*—for example, reports and instructions—because these require simpler verb tenses (simple present and imperative) and more formulaic sentence structures (using temporal connectives such as "first . . . next . . . then . . ."). *Personal writing* raises the linguistic stakes somewhat because its linguistic features include a variety of past tense verbs and more difficult connectives (e.g., temporal connectives such as "finally," cause/effect connectives such as "even though" and "because," and comparison); there is also more than one actor (not just the writer, but also the other people or characters mentioned), requiring more verb conjugations. *Analytical writing* is the linguistic Everest for ELLs, as its linguistic features include relational processes (verbs such as "indicate," "reflect," "show," "cause," "influence," and "lead to"), sounding authoritative (persuading a reader without expressing explicit feelings or attitudes), and presenting commitment to a proposition by using objective rather than subjective language ("It is clear, likely, possible, usual, certain . . .").

This section of the chapter will discuss one example of personal writing (memoir) and one of analytical writing (persuasive essay), two forms that appear routinely in ELA curricula, though the strategies described for each can be used for other formats and genres. For a rich variety of other prewriting and writing strategies, two recommended resources are: Nancie Atwell's *In the Middle* (1987) and Kelly Gallagher's *Teaching Adolescent Writers* (2006).

Scaffolding for a Persuasive Essay

The best way to prepare ELLs for writing persuasively is to begin with a very simple formula, using a graphic organizer, an accessible topic, and sentence starters; as students master the formula, we can continue to expand its parameters. In Table 9.10, the format that you provide is in bold letters, while the text that students insert is in italics. Complete this chart on the board, with the help of students. Or better yet, enlist two groups of students to complete two versions of the chart, one in favor of cats as pets, and the other in favor of dogs, on opposite sides of a large board.

The next step is to expand the chart to include the evidence supporting each assertion. First, have students copy down one or the other of the charts on the board, leaving a wide margin to the right to add a third column. Then have them share supporting examples of each reason or assertion stated in the first chart. It might end up looking like Table 9.11.

Notice that the bottom right cell of the table provides a prompt for a quotation on the essay's theme, another simple rhetorical flourish. It is easy enough to show ELLs how to use Google and other internet search engines to find quotations on a favorite topic. (This one was found by googling "quotations, cats.")

Read row by row, it is only a short step from this graphic organizer to a five-paragraph essay. Once students master this basic form on an accessible topic such as cats versus dogs, they can try their hand at a more academic topic. For an informational essay, this might include research in the library or on the internet, for example, "Which was the greater inventor, Thomas Edison or Benjamin Franklin?" For an essay responding to literature, the evidence section of the chart might require annotated quotations from the literary text, for example, "Use examples from *The Color of Water* to answer the question, Should parents ever hide their past from their children?"

This chart can be used just as effectively to dissect the reasoning of an accomplished writer or speaker. As students read and dissect other models of persuasive writing, they can expand their essays from the bare-bones versions to more sophisticated variations.

Scaffolding for Memoir

Starting the year off with narrative writing helps students to settle into good writing habits while writing about a topic that fascinates them: themselves. Writing

TABLE 9.10 Graphic Organizer to Prepare for a Persuasive Essay

Topic	*Which makes a better pet — a cat or a dog?*
Statement of Belief (My Argument)	I believe that . . . *cats make better pets than dogs.*
Reasons Supporting My Argument	Here are three reasons to support my belief:
	1. First of all, *cats are cleaner than dogs.*
	2. Second, *cats cost less to keep than dogs.*
	3. and finally, *cats are more independent than dogs.*
Counterargument	Some might argue that . . . *dogs are more fun to play with.*
Rebuttal of Counterargument	However I find that . . . *my cat is just as playful as any dog.*
Conclusion	In conclusion, I restate my belief that . . . *cats make better pets than dogs.*

TABLE 9.11   Completed Graphic Organizer for Persuasive Essay

Topic	Which makes a better pet— a cat or a dog?	Examples
Statement of Belief (My Argument)	I believe that . . . *cats make better pets than dogs.*	
Reasons and Evidence Supporting My Argument	Here are three reasons to support my belief: 1. First of all, *cats are cleaner than dogs.*	For example, *cats bathe themselves, while dogs must be given baths by their owners. Furthermore, cats don't wallow in the mud—or their own feces—as dogs do.*
	2. Second, *cats are more economical than dogs.*	For example, *most cats do not eat nearly as much food as dogs do.* MOREOVER, *they do not require a fenced yard or a special house or bed.*
	3. and finally, *cats are more independent than dogs.*	For example, *if you are going away for an overnight trip, you don't have to find a cat-sitter; just leave out a bowl of food and some water and the cat will be fine. A dog, though, would eat the whole bowlful of food at once, then cry for more in two hours.*
Counterargument	Some might argue that . . . *dogs are more fun to play with.*	For instance, *you can play fetch with a dog.*
Rebuttal of Counter-argument	However, I find that . . . *my cat is just as playful as any dog.*	For example, *my cat can play for hours with a piece of string and a feather, and I've seen some cats that are trained to fetch, too!*
Conclusion	In conclusion, I restate my belief that . . . *cats make better pets than dogs.*	As Helen Powers once said, *"Your cat will never threaten your popularity by barking at three in the morning. He won't attack the mailman or eat the drapes, although he may climb the drapes to see how the room looks from the ceiling."*

stories and memoir requires a different structure from persuasive writing, but one that can lend itself equally well to a graphic organizer. The visual and tangible aspects of this exercise, as well as the scaffolded transition from models to practice, are especially helpful to ELLs. This one was borrowed from the outstanding Arts-Literacy Project at Brown University (http://artslit.org), an excellent resource for ways in which to build literacy through the performing and visual arts.

First, provide students with several memoir excerpts to read and discuss. (Some good ones are "Fish Cheeks" by Amy Tan (2003), "The Indian Dog" by M. Scott Momaday (1998), and "Getups" by Maya Angelou (1994).) In the course of reading the memoir models, undoubtedly there will be students who make self-to-text connections ("Oh, that's just like the time I . . ." or "That happened to me once . . ."). It is useful to let some of these connections play out, as they can provide springboards for the exercise to come.

At the end of each selection, ask students to think about what the most dramatic part of the story was—the climax. Have them fold a blank page, business letter style (two folds, forming three panels). In the center panel, have them illustrate the climax of one story using stick figures, word bubbles, and any other cartoon conventions they know. (It is helpful to have a very simple drawing of your own available to show students so that they realize they do not have to be accomplished artists.) The next step is for students to draw the first and third cells: what happened before the climax and what happened after the climax. In this way, the finished drawing shows how stories have a beginning, middle, and end, also called a story arc.

The next step in this process is for students to create cartoon cells of a memory from their own lives, a memory in which they learned something important. You may wish to choose a focus for the class's memoirs—for example, "early memories from school," "life's lessons learned," or "heroes"—especially if it relates to a particular theme for the unit. Again, students draw the climax first, as that is always the most dramatic and memorable moment of any story, then they draw what happened before in the first cell and what happened afterward (or the lesson learned) in the third cell.

Once students have finished their drawings, they use their cartoons as a prop for telling their story to a partner. The partner is required to listen and ask clarifying questions. The storyteller must record these questions, as she will use them later to flesh out the story in writing. Partners then change roles and repeat the process.

The next stage of the process is for students to write out the complete story, spending as much time and effort on the story's rising action as they do on the climax and falling action. When they get stuck, they can return to the picture. For ELLs, the use of pictures allows them to point and ask a partner or the teacher, "What's the word for this thing?"

Beyond the process itself of writing memoir, the validation of ELLs' life experiences through personal writing is tremendously rewarding, sometimes even life altering. As English teachers we already know that personal writing can be life changing, a clarifying and galvanizing experience. For students who may be separated from family, country, or the warm comfort of a familiar language, personal writing in the form of memoir can provide a security blanket, a soapbox, or just reassurance of their own worth.

Writing Portfolios

All learning—but especially writing—is a work in progress. Portfolios are useful for showing students their concrete progress toward a larger writing goal. Having a record of this progress can be especially helpful with ELLs, who may feel intimidated or overwhelmed by writing assignments. A writing portfolio (which need not be any fancier than a construction paper folder) should contain all the prewriting pieces of an assignment—brainstorms/webs, cartoons, notes, graphic organizers—as well as all drafts of each assignment, with feedback from fellow students or the teacher, and a personal corrections list (Gallagher, 2006), which helps students to take ownership of their errors. (See Table 9.12.)

Formative Assessment

In addition to the writing portfolio, there are many other types of formative assessment available to teachers of ELLs that can provide ongoing feedback on how they are progressing.

TABLE 9.12   Personal Corrections List

Write the sentence where the problem occurs here:	Write a corrected version of the sentence here:	Identify (circle) the problem area in the original sentence from the following list:
Well I just turn 15 this summer Agust 2 I had a sweet 15 like the tradition in Mexico.	*I turned 15 this summer, August 2, and I had a Sweet Fifteen party, a tradition in Mexico.*	grammar word choice run-on clarity spelling punctuation sentence structure verb tense documentation active voice redundancy subject-verb agreement
		grammar word choice run-on clarity spelling punctuation sentence structure verb tense documentation active voice redundancy subject-verb agreement

Source: Adapted from Gallagher (2006).

Entrance and Exit Tickets

Entrance and exit tickets can be index cards or slips of paper on which students may answer any or all of the following questions: What is one thing you learned in class today (or yesterday)? What is one question you have? What is one thing you need to do before the next class? What is one thing you need help with? What was the best or worst part of the homework? It is important that students understand that entrance and exit tickets are not a test, but a source of information for the teacher.

How'm I doing?

Ed Koch, a former mayor of New York City, was famous for asking his audience, "How'm I doing?" at every public forum. One reliable means of getting feedback from ELLs on what they are learning and what they need to learn is to add an extra-credit section to the end of each midterm and end-of-term test in which you pose the following questions: "What have you learned so far this year (or this month or this quarter) in this class?" "What helped you understand or learn these things (whether it is something you did or something your teacher did)?" and "What are some things that you would like to learn, or things that you feel you need to learn or work on to be a better reader, writer, speaker, listener, or thinker?" More points are given for more specific answers. This strategy and the one that follows both have the added benefit of encouraging active learning and helping students to crystallize ideas or knowledge gained through homework or class work before they shift mental gears for the next class.

Rubrics

There is much use and misuse of rubrics these days. Some are so language-dense that for ELLs they may make an assignment seem impenetrable. It is important that we demystify rubrics before students even look at them. The best way to do so follows the format discussed earlier on interviews for building community. For a rubric on poetry, for example ask students:

- "Who is a good poet?" and "What are some good poems?" (Identify models.) Brainstorm their answers on the board.

- "What makes that person a good poet?" and "What does a good poet do?" (Determine personal qualities, habits of mind, work habits, required skills and knowledge.)

- "What makes a poem good?" (Determine criteria for good poems.)

And voilà, students have created a rubric. The lists from this brainstorm can go on the classroom wall and stay there throughout the unit, so that when the official rubric is brought out, they can see that it is merely a formalized version of their own criteria list. It is important to show them that the lists they came up with have simply been translated into academic English.

Conclusion

The strategies presented in this chapter were gathered from many sources to support your work with ELLs, including the proven day-to-day practices of teachers who serve secondary ELLs. You may want to try many of the strategies we have shared, and you may want to share some of your own with the teachers you collaborate with in your school setting.

The key to success with ELLs is not finding a blueprint for what to do in the classroom, but gathering knowledge continually about your ELL students, continually asking yourself and them what works, what helps, what keeps them excited about learning, and what keeps them motivated to learn English so that they can participate fully in our largely English-speaking society.

While at times it can feel as if it is a daunting task to try to meet the language and academic needs of all your ELLs, at the same time these students bring rich cultural and linguistic resources to American classrooms and satisfaction to their teachers. One thing is certain: any efforts that you make for your ELLs—whether academic supports, curricular modifications, community building, or just getting to know their needs and skills better—enrich not only ELLs' education, but also the education of your entire class.

In recognizing the academic talents and addressing the academic needs of

ELLs, we affirm the value of diversity and multiple perspectives in the classroom and of multilingualism in our schools, for it enriches us all. Working with ELLs brings a satisfaction in teaching like no other, because students and families going through the powerful transition into a new language and culture will appreciate your investment in them more than you can ever know.

Checklist

Nine Ways for ELA Teachers to Support ELLs

☐ I know the ESL coordinator or the guidance counselor in charge of ELLs in my school and have acquired from him or her baseline language-proficiency test data for the ELLs in my classes.

☐ I know how recently my ELLs have exited ESL classes or if they have waived or are still in ESL classes.

☐ I have a solid sense of how many opportunities my ELLs have to use English outside the classroom, whether at home, with friends, at jobs, or in after-school activities.

☐ I use community-building activities in my classroom.

☐ I engage students in collaborative learning activities that require them to speak to each other and read aloud.

☐ Each of the ELLs in my classes has at least one native-speaking "work buddy" with whom he or she feels comfortable.

☐ I use several scaffolding strategies for every major assignment or activity.

☐ I use writing portfolios and other forms of formative assessment in my classroom.

☐ I engage all my students in reading, writing, listening, and speaking every day.

Glossary

Academic language The language used in the learning of academic subject matter in formal schooling contexts. It involves aspects of language strongly associated with literacy and academic achievement, including specific academic terms or technical language and speech registers as related to each field of study (e.g., math, science, social studies, language arts) (see *register*).

Acculturation The process in which a person comes in contact with a culture other than his or her own and through this interaction successfully adapts to life in the new culture. The person adopts the values, norms, and practices of the new culture as appropriate, but without denying or rejecting one's own culture or giving up one's primary cultural identity (see *assimilation*).

Additive bilingualism A process by which individuals develop proficiency in a second language subsequent to or simultaneous with the development of proficiency in the primary language, without loss of the primary language (see *subtractive bilingualism*).

Affective filter A kind of mental barrier that can block language that would be otherwise understood from reaching the part of the brain that processes language. Factors that can raise the filter and block input include fatigue, distraction, anxiety, and being in a state of culture shock (see *culture shock*).

Alternative assessment Assessment procedures and techniques that occur as an outgrowth of instruction and that show a student's growth over time. Alternative assessments measure what students can produce rather than what they can recall or reproduce. Alternative assessments include, but are not limited to, student-teacher conferences, work samples evaluated by rubrics, and performance in the classroom (see *authentic assessment*).

Assimilation The process by which a person fully adopts the values, norms, and practices of the new culture and relinquishes his or her home culture. The process may create adjustment problems for individuals if they deny or reject their original cultural identity and their home language in the process (see *acculturation*).

Authentic assessment The multiple forms of assessment that evaluate students' learning and their attitudes and approaches toward learning during instructionally relevant activities—for example, using a rubric to assess students' language use during a social studies lesson. Authentic assessment reflects good instructional practices and the kinds of skills and knowledge useful to students in performing daily life and school activities.

BICS/basic interpersonal communication skills A term coined by Jim Cummins that refers to the type of language proficiency that is acquired through face-to-face communication and that is necessary for social interactions, including those that occur in a classroom. This type of conversational language proficiency is both context embedded (the context makes the meaning clear) and cognitively undemanding (the concept is easily acquired). BICS or conversational language proficiency develops relatively quickly, usually within two years, provided the learner has access to English speakers (see *CALP*).

Bilingual program A program that uses two languages for instruction. In bilingual programs in the United States, English language learners receive content instruction in their native language and English as a second language instruction. There are different types of bilingual education programs, including transitional bilingual education (TBE), developmental bilingual education (DBE), and dual-language or two-way immersion programs (TWI). The differences stem from the length of time students are placed in the program and how dedicated the program is to cultivating lasting knowledge and growth in the primary language. TBE programs use the native language temporarily, and the goal is to transition to English, whereas DBE programs aim to maintain the native language while developing proficiency in English. Like DBE programs, dual-language or two-way immersion programs also seek to promote bilingualism, biliteracy, and biculturalism for all students enrolled. (see *dual–language program*; see *two-way immersion program*).

Bilingualism/multilingualism   The ability to understand and use two (or more) languages in particular contexts and for particular purposes. Bilinguals can have the same levels of proficiency in both languages (e.g., advanced in both) or different levels of proficiency (e.g., advanced in one and beginning or intermediate in the other). Bilinguals do not necessarily have the same level of proficiency in speaking, listening, reading, and writing in the languages they know.

Biliteracy   The ability to read and write in two languages. Usually refers to full proficiency in both languages and the ability to read and write at age-appropriate levels in both languages.

CALP/cognitive academic language proficiency   A term coined by Jim Cummins that refers to the type of language proficiency that is required to achieve academically. CALP is both context reduced (there is little support in the learning context to facilitate understanding) and cognitively demanding (the concepts are challenging for the learner to grasp). Research has shown that it can take four to nine years to acquire CALP (see *BICS*).

Cognate   A word that is related to a word in another language (e.g., *observe* in English to *observar* in Spanish). Cognates have a common origin and thus are similar or identical in meaning and often in spelling.

Culture shock   The anxiety and feelings of disorientation and confusion produced when a person moves to a completely new environment. The physical and emotional discomfort one suffers when coming to live in another country or a place different from the place of origin and is unsure as to what is appropriate and what is not.

Communicative function   The purposes for which language is used. Includes three broad functions: communication (the transmission of information), integration (expression of affiliation and belonging to a particular social group), and expression (the display of individual feelings, ideas, and personality). Examples include asking for or giving information, describing past actions, expressing feelings, and expressing regret.

Conversational fluency/conversational language proficiency   See *BICS*.

Cultural distance   The degree of emotional or psychological closeness felt between members of two cultural groups, usually because their values and ways of doing things are similar. It refers to one's willingness to associate with members of another group because of the degree of affinity felt.

Dialect   A variety of speaking, writing, or signing a language that is distinguished by differences in vocabulary, sentence structure, and pronunciation. English and other languages are composed of many different dialects, often associated with particular regions or groups of speakers.

Dual-language program   An instructional program with the goals of educating all children (both language minority and language majority) to become biliterate and culturally sensitive individuals. In this model there is always instruction in both languages for all children. When successful, all students leave these programs fully functional in two languages, including becoming biliterate (see *two-way immersion program*; see *biliteracy*).

ESL (English as a second language)   A program for English language learners in which English is the medium and goal of instruction. Students are generally placed in classes with students of the same level of academic English proficiency (beginner, intermediate, and advanced) and are given specially tailored instruction that moves them toward full proficiency in English in the areas of reading, writing, speaking, and listening [also referred to as ENL (English as a new language) and ELD (English language development)].

First language   See *native language*.

Formative (informal) assessments   Assessments that are part of the instructional process and that provide information so teachers can adjust teaching and learning in order for learners to achieve greater success. The assessments include but are not limited to teacher observation, conferencing with students, and self- and peer assessments provided that they lead to needed instructional adjustments that enable learners to learn better (see *summative assessments*; see *alternative assessment; see authentic assessment*).

Full inclusion ESL/mainstream ESL   A program model in which English language learners are placed in all mainstream classes with their non-ELL counterparts. This model works on the assumption that when these students are immersed in English they will gain academic proficiency in English. In the best implementation of this model, an ESL-trained teacher would serve as the classroom teacher, providing sheltered instruction to ELLs (see *sheltered instruction*).

Heritage language program   A program designed for students whose home or ancestral language is a language other than English, including Native Americans, immigrants, and those born in the United States whose family or ancestors came from another country and speak a language other than English. The program is designed to develop, maintain, and promote the home or ancestral language of the learners.

Immigrant   A person who makes a decision to relocate to another country with the intention of living there permanently. Because the move is planned and there are conditions for entry, the immigrating persons usually have resources available to them that support their move, both financial and social.

Language minority   A term applied to students who come from a minority group and speak a language other than English, including those whose first language is not English or those who speak a variety of English, as used in a foreign country or U.S. possession, that is so distinct that ELL instruction is necessary (e.g. Liberian English). These students may or may not be proficient in English.

Language proficiency   The ability to use language accurately and appropriately in its oral and written forms in a variety of settings. Proficiency varies as a function of the context, purpose, and content of communication (see *BICS* and *CALP*).

Language loss   A condition in which a person who originally spoke one language (e.g., Navajo) no longer retains any functional proficiency in that language because it was replaced with another language. Language loss can also occur on the community level.

Limited formal schooling (LFS)   The condition of students who enter U.S. schools with little or no schooling in their native language. These students must develop literacy for the first time and acquire the academic content knowledge and skills they have missed. A newcomer program is one that is designed for students who lack prior schooling and must learn to read and write for the first time. These programs generally try to accelerate learning as much as possible to make up for lost time and often do so by extended schooling options (extended day, year) (see *newcomer program*).

Migrant   A student whose parent or guardian is a migratory agricultural worker, including workers in the dairy and fishing industries, and who, in the preceding 36 months, has accompanied a parent or guardian who is engaged in temporary or seasonal employment. Some broaden this definition to include students whose parents must move frequently in order to find any sort of work to support the family, thus frequently interrupting or stopping their education.

National origin minority group (student)   A student whose inability to speak and understand the English language excludes him or her from effective participation in the educational program offered by a school district, generally a student who was born in a country outside the United States or whose family has an ancestry from a country outside the United States and who speaks a language other than English at home.

Native language   The language or languages that children acquire naturally, without instruction, during the preschool years from parents, siblings, and others in their social environment. A child can have more than one primary language if he or she acquires more than one language during the period of primary language development. Learning two languages at the same time is also sometimes referred to as simultaneous bilingual acquisition. (**Native language is** also referred to as **home language, first language,** and **primary language.**)

Native language arts   A class in which students who natively speak a particular language can develop their primary language reading and writing (e.g., Spanish for native speakers). This class often exposes students to read and appreciate the literature produced in their native language and to learn about the lives and work of the major authors that span the cultural groups who share the native language.

Newcomer program   A program model aimed at students who not only have limited proficiency in English, but also have limited literacy skills in their primary language. These students' lack of basic literacy in their first language can usually be attributed to a lack of formal schooling in their home country. Although newcomer programs vary in design, they are all set up to address the unique needs of this special population of students. Newcomer programs, in addition to academic English, may focus on acculturation to the U.S. school system, preparing students for their lives in new communities, and developing a student's primary language. Most newcomer programs share some common features, among which are that the programs are distinct from regular language support programs, that they use instructional strategies aimed at initial literacy development, and that they have courses or activities aimed at orienting students to different aspects of American culture and society.

Performance assessment   Often used as a synonym for alternative or authentic assessment, a form of assessment that requires students to perform a task rather than take a teacher-made or statewide test. In performance assessment, teachers rate an actual student performance according to previously established criteria. Students may either perform a task or create a product and are assessed on both the process and the end result of their work (see *alternative assessment*; see *authentic assessment*).

Performance indicator   A written statement that describes what students must be able to do to indicate their learning of content according to their level of proficiency. In WIDA (World Class Instructional Design and Assessment) Consortium states, a performance indicator consists of a description of the linguistic complexity (amount and quality of speech or writing) for a given situation, the level of vocabulary (specificity of words or phrases for a given context), and the language control a student must exhibit (the comprehensibility of the communication based on the number and type of errors).

Portfolio assessment   A portfolio is a purposeful collection of a student's work that documents his or her efforts, progress, and achievements over time in given areas of learning, either language or subject matter, or both.

Proficiency (level of, stage of)   The ability to use language for both basic communicative tasks and academic purposes. Proficiency definitions usually include aspects pertaining to the amount of language used, the grammatical control or number of errors, and the range of vocabulary the individual is able to use.

Pull-out ESL   In this ESL instructional model, English language learners are enrolled in mainstream classes, but at different points throughout the day are pulled out of those classes for specific ESL instruction.

Push-in ESL   In this ESL instructional model, the English language learners are enrolled in mainstream classes, but an ESL teacher is in class with them providing support, much as inclusion special educators do. In this situation the ESL teacher and the classroom teacher usually work together to support the students and often share common planning time.

Realia   Objects or activities used to relate classroom teaching to real life (e.g., use of actual foods and supermarket circulars to develop the language related to foods, food purchasing, etc.).

Register Characterized by specific features of discourse (talk or text) and associated with specific social contexts. Registers vary depending on the setting, their speaker's relationship to the person to whom they are speaking, and the function of the interaction. Academic registers include the unique terms and expressions, meanings, and sentence structures that occur in talking or writing about a particular discipline (math, science, social studies).

Refugee A person who leaves his or her country involuntarily and usually precipitously. Many refugees leave because they are fearful of being persecuted for reasons of race, religion, nationality, membership in a particular social group, or political opinion. Many situations produce refugees, most typically natural disasters, famine, war, or political upheaval.

Scaffolding A guided learning technique in which teachers modify the language demands placed on students to match the language level of students and add other supports to their verbal instruction (scaffolds) that enhance communication, such as visuals, hands-on learning, and high levels of interaction to insure understanding (see *sheltered instruction*).

Sequential bilingualism The process by which a person becomes bilingual by first learning one language and then learning the other. This situation occurs most naturally when students leave their homes in which a language other than English is commonly spoken or immigrate to another country after being raised and schooled in another language environment (see *simultaneous bilingualism*).

Sheltered (content) instruction Sheltered instruction is an approach in which students develop knowledge in specific subject areas through the medium of their second language. Teachers modify their use of English to teach core subjects (e.g., math, science) in order to ensure that the material is comprehensible to learners and that it promotes their second-language development. They also adjust the language demands of the lesson in many ways, such as by modifying speech rate and tone, simplifying vocabulary and grammar, repeating key words, phrases, or concepts, using context clues and models extensively, relating instruction to students' background knowledge and experience, and using other learning supports (e.g., demonstrations, visuals, graphic organizers, or cooperative work) to make academic instruction understandable to students of different second-language proficiency levels [also referred to as sheltered English instruction (SEI); specially designed academic instruction in English (SDAIE)].

Simultaneous bilingualism The process by which a person becomes bilingual by learning two languages at the same time. This situation occurs most naturally when students are raised in a home and community where two languages are actively spoken. Generally, in order to be considered a simultaneous bilingual, a child must learn both languages prior to the age of three (see *sequential bilingualism*).

Subtractive bilingualism A process in which individuals lose all or some of their primary-language abilities (and possibly culture) as they acquire a new language and culture. This occurs frequently in the case of language minority students who attend schools where no provision is made to maintain and develop their primary language (see *additive bilingualism*).

Summative assessments Assessments that are given periodically to determine what students know and are able to do at the end of instruction. Summative assessments are accountability measures, most typically state assessments, district benchmark assessments, and end-of-unit and end-of-semester examinations (see *formative assessments*).

Two-way immersion (TWI) program A program that serves both language-minority and language-majority students in the same classrooms. These programs use each group of students' first language for academic instruction at certain points during the day or week. They aim for additive bilingualism and biculturalism for both groups of students (see *dual-language program*).

Undocumented students Students who are born outside the United States or Canada and enter the country without the proper documentation; they are not citizens or legal residents.

Waived (waivered) ELL students   Students who qualify for ESL or bilingual services but whose parents exercise their right to reject the services that are offered. These students are ELLs, but they do not participate in any special programming offered; instead, they are placed into mainstream classes without support of any kind.

References

Abedi, J. (2001, Summer). *Assessment and accommodations for English language learners: Issues and recommendations*. Los Angeles: UCLA Center for the Study of Evaluation, National Center for Research on Evaluation, Standards, and Student Testing (CRESST). Available at www.cse.ucla.edu/products/policy/cresst_policy4.pdf.

Achieve, Inc. (2004, December). *The expectations gap: A 50-State review of high school graduation requirements*. Washington, DC: Achieve, Inc. (American Diploma Project Network).

Achieve, Inc. (2007, April). *Closing the expectations gap 2007: An annual 50-state progress report on the alignment of high school policies with the demands of college and work*. Washington, DC: Achieve, Inc. (American Diploma Project Network).

Advocates for Children of New York and the New York Immigration Coalition. (2002, June). *Creating a formula for success: Why English language learner students are dropping out of school, and how to increase graduation rates*. New York: Advocates for Children of New York. Available at http://www.advocatesforchildren.org/reportsbytopic.php.

Alliance for Excellent Education. (2004, May). *How to know a good adolescent literacy program when you see one: Quality criteria to consider* (Issue Brief). Washington, DC: Author.

American Educational Research Association. (2004, Winter). English language learners: Boosting academic achievement. *Research Points: Essential Information for Educational Policy, 2*(1).

American Federation of Teachers. (1999). *Making standards matter*. Washington, DC: American Federation of Teachers.

American School Counselor Association. (2004). *Ethical standards for school counselors*. Retrieved on December 25, 2008, at http://www.schoolcounselor.org/files/ethical%20standards.pdf.

Anaya, R. (1994). *Bless Me Ultima*. New York. Grand Central Publishing.

Anderson, R. C., Wilson, P. T., & Fielding, I. G. (1988). Growth in reading and how children spend their time outside of school. *Reading Research Quarterly, 23*(3), 285–303.

Angelou, M. (1994). Getups. *Wouldn't Take Nothing For My Journey Now* (pp. 51-58). New York: Bantam.

Ardilla, A. (2003). Language representation and working memory with bilinguals. *Journal of Communication Disorders, 36*(2), 233–240.

Association for Supervision and Curriculum Development. (2006). *Legislative agenda—High school reform* (one-page summary). Alexandria, VA: ASCD. Available at www.ascd.org/actioncenter.

Atwell, N. (1987). *In the middle: New understandings about writing, reading, and learning*. Portsmouth, NH: Heinemann.

August, D. (2002). *From Spanish to English: Reading and writing for English language learners*. Pittsburgh, PA: New Standards Project, University of Pittsburgh.

August, D., & Shanahan, T. (Eds.). (2006a). *Developing literacy in second-language learners: Report of the National Literacy Panel on Language-Minority Children and Youth*. Mahwah, NJ: Lawrence Erlbaum Associates.

August, D., & Shanahan, T. (Eds.). (2006b). *Executive summary, Developing literacy in second-language learners: Report of the National Literacy Panel on Language-Minority Children and Youth*. (Full volume published in Mahwah, NJ: Lawrence Erlbaum Associates.) Executive summary available at http://www.cal.org/projects/archive/natlitpanel.html

Baloche, L. A. (1998). *The cooperative classroom: Empowering learning*. Upper Saddle River, NJ: Prentice Hall.

Barton, P. (2005, February). *One-third of a nation: Rising dropout rates and declining opportunities*. Princeton, NJ: Educational Testing Service.

Barton, P. (2006). *High school reform and work: Facing labor market realities*. Princeton, NJ: Educational Testing Service.

Bear, D. R., Helman, L., Templeton, S., Invernizzi, M., & Johnston, F. (2007). *Words their way with English learners: Word study for phonics, vocabulary and spelling instruction*. Upper Saddle River, NJ: Pearson/Merrill Prentice Hall.

Beers, K. (2002). *When kids can't read: What teachers can do: A guide for teachers 6-12*. Portsmith, NH: Heinemann.

Berkeley Unified School District. (2008). *Mission statement*. Retrieved on December 25, 2008, from http://www.berkeley.net/index.php?page=our-mission-and-vision.

Bentley, S., & Bacon, S. E. (1996, Spring). The all-new, state-of-the-art ILA definition of listening: Now that we have it, what do we do with it? *Listening Post (Journal of the International Listening Association), 1*, 5.

Berndt, T. J., Hawkins, J. A., & Ziao, Z. (1999). Influences of friends and friendships on adjustment to junior high school. *Merrill-Palmer Quarterly, 45*(1), 13–41.

Biancarosa, G., & Snow, C. (2004). *Reading next: A vision for action and research in middle and high school literacy—A report to Carnegie Corporation of New York*. Washington, DC: Alliance for Excellent Education.

Blum, R. W. (2005). A case for school connectedness. *Educational Leadership, 62*(7), 16–20.

Boch, F., & Piolat, A. (2005, September). Note taking and learning: A summary of research. *The WAC Journal, 16*. Retrieved January 15, 2008, from http://wac.colostate.edu/journal/vol16/index.htm.

Brown, H. D. (2006). *Principles of language learning and teaching* (5th ed.). White Plains, NY: Pearson/Longman Education.

Bureau of Labor Statistics. (2007). *American time use survey*. Washington, DC: U.S. Department of Labor. Available at http://www.bls.gov/TUS.

Canale, M. & Swain, M. (1980). Theoretical bases of communicative approaches to second language teaching and testing. *Applied Linguistics, 1*(1): 1-47.

Carrell, P. L. (2007). *Notetaking strategies and their relationship to performance on listening comprehension and communicative assessment tasks*. (TOEFL Monograph Series/ETS [Educational Testing Service] Research Report #RR-07-01 [TOEFL-MS-35].)

Carrier, K. A. (2003). Improving high school English language learners' second language listening through strategy instruction. *Bilingual Research Journal, 27*(3) 383–408.

Castañeda v. Pickard, 648 F.2d 989 (1981). Supreme Court of the United States. Retrieved on July 16, 2009 from http://www.stanford.edu/~kenro/LAU/IAPolicy/IA1bCastanedaFullText.htm.

Cech, S. J. (2009, January 8). Testing tension: Weigh proficiency, assess content. *Quality counts: Portrait of a population: How English-language learners are putting schools to the test. Education Week, 28*(17), 35–36.

Center for Applied Linguistics. (2009). *Heritage languages in America*. Retrieved on February 1, 2009, from http://www.cal.org/heritage/about/principles.html.

Center for School and District Improvement. (2004, March). *English language learner (ELL) programs at the secondary level in relation to student performance*. Portland, OR: Northwest Regional Educational Laboratory (www.nwrel.org).

Chall, J. S., & Dale, E. (1995). *Readability revisited: The new Dale-Chall readability formula*. Cambridge, MA. Brookline Books.

Chamot, A. U., & O'Malley, J. M. (1994). *The CALLA handbook: Implementing the cognitive academic language learning approach*. Reading, MA: Addison-Wesley.

Chavkin, N. F., & Gonzalez, D. L. (1995). *Forging partnerships between Mexican American parents and the schools*. (ERIC Document 388 489.) Charleston, WV: ERIC Clearinghouse on Rural Education and Small Schools.

Chimacum Middle School. (no date). *Paraphrase vs. summarize*. Available at http://educatoral.com/paraphrase-vs-summarize.html (Mr. Gonzalez's Web page). Chimacum, WA: Chimacum Middle School.

Christensen, L. (2000). *Reading, writing, and rising up: Teaching about social justice and the power of the written word*. Milwaukee, WI: Rethinking Schools, Ltd.

Cleveland-Marwick, K., Fox, C., Handorf, S., & Stern, K. (Eds.) (2006). *Longman Study Dictionary of American English*. White Plains, NY: Pearson Longman.

Cloud, N. (2002). Culturally and linguistically responsive instructional planning. In A. J. Artiles and A. A. Ortiz (Eds.), *English language learners with special education needs: Identification, assessment, and instruction* (pp. 107–132). Washington, DC: ERIC Clearinghouse on Languages and Linguistics, Center for Applied Linguistics and Delta Systems.

Cloud, N., Genesee, F., & Hamayan, E. (2009). *Literacy instruction for English language learners: A teacher's guide to research-based practices*. Portsmouth, NH: Heinemann.

Coady, J., Magoto, J., Hubbard, P., Graney, J., & Mokhari, K. (1993). High frequency vocabulary and reading proficiency in ESL reading. In T. Huckin, M. Haynes, & J. Coady (Eds.), *Second language reading and vocabulary learning* (pp. 217–228). Norwood, NJ: Ablex.

Coelho, E. (1994). Social integration of immigrant and refugee children. In F. Genesee (Ed.) *Education second language children: The whole child, the whole curriculum, the whole community*. (pp. 301–327). New York: Cambridge University Press.

Coelho, E. (2006, March). Sharing space with English. *Essential Teacher, 3*(1), 28–31.

Coiro, J. (2001). *Using expository text patterns to enhance comprehension.* Available at www.Suite101.com; downloaded September 26, 2006, from www.i5ive.com/print_article.cfm/1411/68477.

Cole, R. W. (1995). *Educating everybody's children: Diverse teaching Strategies for diverse learners.* Alexandria, VA: Association for Supervision and Curriculum Development.

Coltrane, B. (2002). *English language learners and high-stakes tests: An overview of the issues.* (Digest EDO-FL-02-07.) Washington, DC: Center for Applied Linguistics. Available at http://www.cal.org/resources/digest/0207coltrane.html.

Committee on Increasing High School Students' Engagement and Motivation to Learn, National Research Council. (2003). *Engaging schools: Fostering high school students' motivation to learn.* Washington, DC: National Academies Press

Cook, V. (2001). Using the first language in the classroom. *Canadian Modern Language Review, 57*(3), 402–423.

Cooper, D., & Snell, J. L. (2003). Bullying—Not just a kid thing. *Educational Leadership, 60*(6), 22–25.

Coxhead, A. (2000). A new academic word list. *TESOL Quarterly, 34,* 213-238.

Cummins, J. (1981). The role of primary language development in promoting educational success for language minority students. In *Schooling and language minority students: A theoretical framework.* Los Angeles: Dissemination and Assessment Center, California State University.

Cummins, J. (1991). Interdependence of first- and second-language proficiency in bilingual children. In E. Bailystok (Ed.), *Language processing in bilingual children* (pp. 70–89). New York: Cambridge University Press.

Cummins, J. Bismilla,V., Chow, P, Cohen, S., Giampapa, F., Leonia, L., Sandhu, P. & Sastri, P (2005). Affirming identity in multilingual classrooms. *Educational Leadership, 63*(1), 38-43.

Cummins, J. (2006). *Challenges, opportunities and choices in educating minority group students.* Presented at Hedmark Univeristy College, October 27, 2006, Elverum, Norway.

Daniels, E. (2005). On the minds of middle schoolers. *Educational Leadership, 62*(7), 52–54.

DeCapua, A., Smathers, W., & Tang, L. F. (2007, March). Schooling, interrupted. *Educational Leadership, 64*(6), 40–46

Delpit, L. (2006). *Other people's children: Cultural conflict in the classroom.* New York: New Press.

Del Rosario Basterra, M. (1998, Winter–1999, Spring). *Using standardized tests to make high-stake decisions on English-language learners: Dilemmas and critical issues.* Chevy Chase, MD: Mid-Atlantic Equity Center.

Denver Public Schools. (2006). *Introduction: Strategies to support culturally competent instruction.* Retrieved December 25, 2006 from http://curriculum.dpsk12.org/Planning_guides/Literacy/Secondary_Culturally_Competent_Strategies.pdf.

Dickson, S. V., Simmons, D. C., & Kameenui, E. J. (1995). *Text organization and its relation to reading comprehension: A synthesis of the research.* (Technical Report No. 17.) Eugene: University of Oregon, National Center to Improve the Tools of Educators.

Donato, R., & Brooks, F. B. (2004). Literary discussions and advanced speaking functions: Researching the (dis)connection. *Foreign Language Annals, 37,* 183–199.

Draper, S.M. (2001). *Romiette and Julio.* New York: Simon Pulse, a Division of Simon & Shuster.

Dristas, V. M., & Grisenti, G. (1995). *Motivation: Does interest influence reading and speaking proficiency in second language acquisition?* Unpublished manuscript.

Echevarría, J., Vogt, M. E., & Short, D. J. (2008). *Making content comprehensible for English Learners: The SIOP® Model* (3rd ed.). Boston: Pearson/Allyn and Bacon.

Edelsky, C. (1982). Writing in a bilingual program: The relation of L$_1$ and L$_2$ texts. *TESOL Quarterly, 16*(2), 211–228.

ELA/Department for Learning and Educational Achievement. (2008). EXTRA! EXTRA! Learn all about it: Teaching with Colorado's historic newspapers. *Comprehending content: Historical documents through a strategy lens.* Golden,CO: Jefferson County Public Schools. Available through www.cal-webs.org/handouts05/CHNP_4.doc.

ERIC Clearinghouse on Urban Education. (1997). *Urban policies and programs to reduce truancy.* (ERIC/CUE Digest, Number 129.) New York: ERIC Clearinghouse on Urban Education, Institute for Urban and Minority Education.

Espejo, R. (2002). Introduction. *Teen issues: America's youth.* San Diego: Lucent Books.

Espinosa, L. M. (1995). *Hispanic parent involvement in early childhood programs.*

(ERIC Clearinghouse on Elementary and Early Childhood Education No. ED 382 412.) Champaign-Urbana: University of Illinois.

Fairfax County Public Schools. (2008). *ESOL mission statement.* Retrieved on December 25, 2008, from http://www.fcps.edu/DIS/OESOL/index.htm.

Faltis, C. (1986). Initial cross-lingual reading transfer in bilingual second grade classrooms. In E. Garcia & B. Flores (Eds.), *Language and literacy research in bilingual education* (pp. 145–157). Tempe: Arizona State University Press.

Faltis, C. J., & Coulter, C. A. (2008). *Teaching English learners and immigrant students in secondary school.* Upper Saddle River, NJ: Pearson/Merrill Prentice Hall.

Faltis, C., & Hudelson, S. (1998). *Bilingual education in elementary and secondary school communities: Toward understanding and caring.* Boston: Allyn and Bacon.

Fang, Z., & Schleppegrell, M. J. (2008). *Reading in secondary content areas: A language-based pedagogy.* Ann Arbor: University of Michigan Press.

Feger, M. (2006). "I want to read": How culturally relevant texts increase student engagement in reading. *Multicultural Education, 13*(3), 18–19.

Fisher, D., Brozo, W. G., Frey, N., & Ivey, G. (2007). *50 content area strategies for adolescent literacy.* Upper Saddle River, NJ: Pearson/Merrill Prentice Hall.

Fisher, D., & Frey, N. (2004). *Improving adolescent literacy: Strategies at work.* Upper Saddle River, NJ: Pearson/Merrill Prentice Hall.

Flaitz, J. (Ed.). (2003). *Understanding your international students: An educational, cultural and linguistic guide.* Ann Arbor: University of Michigan Press.

Flaitz, J. (2006). *Understanding your refugee and immigrant students. An educational, cultural and linguistic guide.* Ann Arbor: University of Michigan Press.

Flowers, N., Mertens, S., & Mulhall, P. (2000). What makes interdisciplinary teams effective? *Middle School Journal, 31*(4), 53-56.

Freeman, D. E., & Freeman, Y. S. (2004). *Essential linguistics: What you need to know to teach reading, ESL spelling, phonics and grammar.* Portsmouth, NH: Heinemann.

Freeman, D., & Freeman, Y. (2007). *English language learners: The essential guide.* New York: Scholastic.

Freeman, D. E., & Freeman, Y. S. (2009). *Academic language for English language learners and struggling readers: How to help students succeed across content areas.* Portsmouth, NH: Heinemann.

Freeman, Y., & Freeman, D. (1998). *ESL/EFL teaching: Principles for success.* Portsmouth, NH: Heinemann.

Freeman, Y., & Freeman, D. (2002). Keys for success for struggling older English learners. *NABE News, 25*(3), 5–7, 37.

Fry, R. (2007, June 6). How far behind in math and reading are English language learners? *Pew Hispanic Center Report,* Washington, DC.

Gallagher, K. (2006). *Teaching adolescent writers.* Portland, ME: Stenhouse.

Gascoigne, C. (2002). Documenting the initial second language reading experience: The readers speak. *Foreign Language Annals, 35*(5), 554–560.

Gay, G. (2000). *Culturally responsive teaching: Theory, research and practice.* New York: Teachers College Press.

Genesee, F. (Ed.). (1999). *Program alternatives for linguistically diverse students.* Santa Cruz: Center for Research on Education, Diversity and Excellence, University of California, Santa Cruz.

Genesee, F. (2006). Conceptual Framework. In *PreK–12 English language proficiency standards* (pp. 9–19). Alexandria, VA: Teachers of English to Speakers of Other Languages.

Gibbons, P. (1991). *Learning to learn in a second language.* Portsmouth, NH: Heinemann.

Gibson, M., Gándara, P., & Koyama, J. (2004). *School connections: U.S. Mexican youth, peers, and school achievement.* New York: Teachers College Press.

Goldberg, A., Russell, M., & Cook, A. (2003). The effect of computers on student writing: A meta-analysis of studies from 1992 to 2002. *Journal of Technology, Learning and Assessment, 2*(1). Available online at http://escholarship.bc.edu/jtla/vol2/1/.

Goodland, J. (1984). *A place called school: Prospects for the future.* New York: McGraw-Hill.

Gottlieb, M., & Nguyen, D. (2007). *Assessment and accountability in language education programs: A guide for administrators and teachers.* Philadelphia: Caslon.

Graves, M. F. (2006). *The vocabulary book: Learning and instruction.* New York; Newark, DE; and Urbana, IL: Teachers College Press; International Reading Association; and National Council of Teachers of English.

Gordon, T. (2007). *Teaching young children a second language.* Westport, CT: Praeger.

Hadley, A. O. (1993). *Teaching language in context* (2nd ed.). Boston: Heinle and Heinle.

Halliday, M. A. K., & Hasan, R. (1985). *Language, context, and text: Aspects of language in a social-semiotic perspective.* Oxford, UK: Oxford University Press.

Halse, L. H. (1999) *Speak.* New York: Penguin Group (Penguin Putnam Books for Young Readers).

Heller, R., & Greenleaf, C L. (2007) *Literacy instruction in the content areas: Getting to the core of middle and high school improvement.* Washington, DC: Alliance for Excellent Education (AEE).

Henderson, R., & Landesman, E. (1992). *Mathematics and middle school students of Mexican descent: The effects of thematically integrated instruction.* Santa Cruz, CA: National Center for Research on Cultural Diversity and Language Learning.

Hertz-Lazarowitz, R., & Shachar, H. (1990). Teachers verbal behavior in cooperative and whole-class instruction. In S. Sharan (Ed.), *Cooperative learning: Theory and research* (pp. 77–94). New York: Praeger.

Hetzner, A. (2007, December 21). Holiday trips cut into school time: Educators in bilingual facilities say long absences are particularly acute. *Milwaukee Journal Sentinal.* Available at http://www.jsonline.com/story/index.aspx?id=699080.

Heubert, J. P. (2002). *High-stakes testing: opportunities and risks.* Wakefield, MA: National Center on Accessing the General Curriculum. Retrieved July 4, 2009, from http://www.cast.org/publications/ncac/ncac_highstakes.html.

Hill, J. D., & Flynn, K. M. (2006). *Classroom instruction that works with English language learners.* Alexandria, VA: Association for Supervision and Curriculum Development.

Hoffman, D. & Levak, B.A. (2003). Personalizing schools. *Educational Leadership, 61* (1), 30-34.

Hollins, E. (1996). A framework for understanding cultural diversity in the classroom. In *Culture in school learning: Revealing the deeper meaning* (chap. 7, pp. 135–160). Mahwah, NJ: Lawrence Erlbaum.

Hood, L. (2003). *Immigrant students, urban high schools: The challenge continues.* New York: Carnegie Corporation of New York.

Houston Independent School District. (2008). *Bilingual/ESL program.* Retrieved on December 25, 2008, from http://www.houstonisd.org/portal/site/Multilingual/menuitem.be152463474f1aa27300dc10e041f76a/?vgnextoid=271b57ebf04ef010VgnVCM10000028147fa6RCRD&vgnextfmt=default.

Hudelson, S., & Serna, I. (1994). Beginning literacy in English in a whole-language bilingual program. In A. Flurkey & R. Meyer (Eds.), *Under the whole language umbrella: Many cultures, many voices* (pp. 278–294). Urbana, IL: National Council of Teachers of English.

Hult, R. E. (1979). On pedagogical caring. *Educational Theory, 29*(3), 237–243.

Hungerford, T., Jovell, I., & Mayberry, B. (2002). *Precalculus: A graphing approach.* New York: Holt, Rinehart, and Winston.

Hurston, Z.N. (2006). *Their Eyes Were Watching God.* New York: Harper Perennial Modern Classics, a Division of Harper Collins.

Hymes, D.H. (1971). *On communicative competence.* Philadelphia: The University of Pennsylvania Press.

Hymes, D.H. (1996). Two types of linguistic relativity. In W. Bright (Ed.) *Sociolinguistics.* (pp. 114–158). The Hague: Mouton.

Individuals with Disabilities Education Act (November, 2004). 20 U.S.C. §1415 (b) (4); 34 C.F.R. §300.503(c)(1).

Irujo, S. (2004, May/June). Test preparation for English Language Learners: Pros and cons. *The ELL Outlook.* Available at http://www.coursecrafters.com/ELL-Outlook/2004/may_jun/ELLOutlookITIArticle4.htm.

Irvine, J. J., & Armento, B. J. (2001). *Culturally responsive teaching: Lesson planning for elementary and middle grades.* Boston: McGraw Hill.

Ivey, G., & Fisher, D. (2006). *Creating literacy-rich schools for adolescents.* Alexandria, VA: Association for Supervision and Curriculum Development.

Jiménez, R. T. (2005). *Moving beyond the obvious: Examining our thinking about linguistically diverse students.* North Central Regional Educational Laboratory. Naperville, IL: Learning Point Associates. \

Johnson, D.W., Johnson, E., & Holubec, R.T. (1994). *Cooperative learning in the classroom.* Alexandria, VA: Association for Supervision and Curriculum Development.

Johnson, D. W., Johnson, R. T., & Smith, K. A. (1998). *Active learning: Cooperation in the college classroom.* Edina, MN: Interaction.

Joint Committee of the American Educational Research Association, American Psychological Association, and National Council on Measurement in Education. (1999). *Standards for educational and psychological testing.* Washington, DC: American Educational Research Association.

Joshi, R. M., Treiman, R., Carreker, S., & Moats, L. C. (2008-9, Winter). The real magic of spelling: Improved reading and writing. *American Educator, 32*(4), 6–16, 42–43.

Juvonen, J., Le, V., Kaganoff, T, Augustine, C., & Constant, L. (2004). *Focus on the wonder years: Challenges facing the American middle school.* Santa Monica, CA: Rand Corporation.

Kagan, S. (1994). *Cooperative Learning.* San Clemente, California: Kagan Publishing.

Kagan, S. (1995). We can talk: Cooperative learning in the elementary ESL classrooms. *Elementary Education Newsletter, 17*(2), 3–4. (*Online Resource Digest No. EDO-FL-95-08.* Washington, DC: Center for Applied Linguistics. Available at http://www.cal.org/resources/digest/kagan001.html.)

Kerry, B. (2004, September 14). *Writing skills necessary for employment, says big business.* Press Release. New York: The National Commission on Writing for America's Families Schools and Colleges, the College Board.

Kinsella, K. (1999). Expanding literacy across the content areas for ESL readers: A workshop conducted by Kate Kinsella, Ed.D. *Twenty-third annual statewide conference for teachers of linguistically and culturally diverse students,* Oak Brook, IL, December 7, 1999.

Kohl, H. (1991). *I won't learn from you: The role of assent in learning.* Minneapolis: Milkweed Editions.

Krashen, S. D. (1982). *Principles and practice in second language acquisition.* Elmsford, NY: Pergamon Press.

Krashen, S. (1996). *Under attack: The case against bilingual education.* Culver City, CA: Language Education Associates.

Krashen, S. (2004). *The power of reading* (2nd ed.). Portsmouth, NH: Heinemann.

Krashen, S. D., & Terrell, T. D. (1983). *The natural approach: Language acquisition in the classroom.* Hayward, CA: Alemany Press.

Krueger, C. (2006). In-state tuition for undocumented immigrants. *ECS State Notes: Tuition and fees.* Denver: Education Commission of the States. Accessed on December 26, 2008, at www.ecs.org/clearinghouse/61/00/6100.htm.

Ladson-Billings, B. (1992). Reading between the lines and beyond the pages: A culturally relevant approach to literacy teaching. *Theory into Practice, 31*(4), 312–320.

Lightbown, P., & Spada, N. (2006). *How languages are learned* (3rd ed.). New York: Oxford University Press.

Lucas, T. (1996, December). *Promoting secondary school transitions for immigrant adolescents.* (ERIC Digest EDO-FL-97-04.) Washington, DC: Center for Applied Linguistics.

Lyster, R. (2004). Differential effects of prompts and recasts in form-focused instruction. *Studies in Second Language Acquisition, 26,* 399–432.

Marshall, J. (2000). Research on response to literature. In R. L. Kamil, P. B. Mosenthal, P. D. Son, & R. Barr (Eds.), *Handbook of reading research* (vol. 3, pp. 381–402). Mahwah, NJ: Lawrence Erlbaum.

Maxwell, L. A. (2009). Shifting landscape: Immigration transforms communities. *Quality counts* (pp. 10–12). Washington, DC: Education Week.

McCall-Perez, Z. (2000, October). The counselor as an advocate for English language learners: An action research approach. *Professional School Counseling, 4*(1), 13–22.

McDougal Little (2000). InterActive Reader: The Language of Literature. Geneva, IL: Holt McDougal, A Division of Houghton Mifflin.

Menken, K. (2008). English learners left behind: Standardized testing as language policy. Clevedon, England: Multilingual Matters.

Michaels, S., O'Connor, C.)., & Resnick, L.B. (2008). Diliberative discourse idealized and realized: Accountable talk in the classroom and in civic life. *Studies in Philosophy and Education, 27* (4) 283-297.

Minicucci, C. (1996). *Learning science and English: How school reform advances scientific learning for limited English proficient middle school students.* Santa Cruz, CA: National Center for Research on Cultural Diversity and Language Learning.

Momaday, N.S. (1998). Indian Dog. In *Man Made of Words: Essays, Stories, Passages (pp. 172-3).* New York: St. Martin's Press.

Montano-Harmon, M. R. (1999). *Developing English for academic purposes.* Fullerton: California State University. Available at http://www.genconnection.com/English/ap/LanguageRegisters.htm. Retrieved January 22, 2009.

Moore, D. W., Bean, T, W., Birdyshaw, D., & Rycik, J. A. (1999). *Adolescent literacy: A position statement for the Commission on Adolescent Literacy of the International Reading Association.* Newark, DE: International Reading Asssociation.

Moore, H. H. (1994). *The multilingual translator: Words and phrases in 15 languages to help you communicate with students of diverse backgrounds.* New York: Scholastic.

Morley, J. (1999, January/February). Current perspectives on improving aural comprehension. *ESL Magazine, 2*(1), 16–19.

Mota-Altman, N. (2006, Summer). *Academic language: Everyone's "second" language.* California English. 11(4) Retrieved on April 18, 2008, from http://www.nwp.org/cs/public/print/resource/2329?x-print_friendly=1

Nagy, W. E., & Anderson, R. C. (1984) How many words are there in printed school English? *Reading Research Quarterly, 19*(2), 304–330.

Nagy, W. E., García, G. E., Durgunoglu, A. Y., & Hancin-Bhatt, B. (1993). Spanish-English bilingual students' use of cognates in English reading. *Journal of Reading Behavior, 25*(3), 241–259.

Nash, R. (1993). *NTC's dictionary of Spanish cognates: Thematically organized.* New York: McGraw-Hill.

Nation, I.S.P. (2008). *Teaching vocabulary: Strategies and techniques.* Boston: Heinle/Cengage Learning.

Nation, I. S. P. (2001). *Learning vocabulary in another language.* Cambridge, UK: Cambridge University Press.

National Council of Teachers of English. (2006). *English language learners: A policy research brief.* Urbana, IL: NCTE.

National Council of Teachers of English. (2007a). *Adolescent Literacy.* A Policy Brief Produced by the National Council of Teachers of English and Produced by the James R. Quire Office for Policy Research at the University of Michigan. Available at http://www.ncte.org/adlit. Urbana, IL: National Council of Teachers of English.

National Council of Teachers of English. (2007b, November). Twenty-first century literacies: A changing world for literacy teachers. *Council Chronicle. 17*(2), 13–19.

National Endowment for Financial Education. (2007). *High school financial planning program.* Available at http://hsfpp.nefe.org/home/.

National Middle School Association. (2006, February). *Research Summary: Bullying.* Westerville, OH: National Middle School Association. Available at www.nmsa.org.

NCTE ELL Task Force. (2006, April). *NCTE position paper on the role of English teachers in educating English language learners (ELLs).* Retrieved on April 12, 2008, from www.ncte.org/positions/statements/teacherseducatingell.

Noddings, N. (1999). Care, justice and equity. In M. S. Katz, N. Noddings, & K. A. Strike (Eds.), *Justice and caring: The search for common ground in education* (pp. 7–20). New York: Teachers College Press.

Odean, P. M. (1987). Teaching Paraphrasing to ESL Students. *MinneTESOL Journal, 6,* 15-27.

Ontario Ministry of Education. (2005). *Many roots, many voices: Supporting English language learners in every classroom.* Toronto: Queen's Printer for Ontario. Available at http://www.edu.gov.on.ca/eng/document/manyroots/.

Partnership for 21st Century Skills. (2007, November). *Beyond the 3Rs: Voter attitudes toward 21st century schools.* Retrieved on April 18, 2008, from http://www.21stcenturyskills.org/documents/p21_poll report_2pg.pdf.

Passel, J. S. (2003). *Further demographic information relating to the DREAM Act.* Washington, DC: Urban Institute. Retrieved on May 3, 2009, from http://www.nilc.org/immlawpolicy/DREAM/DREAM_Demographics.pdf.

Pedersen, P. B., & Carey, J. C. (Eds.). (2002). *Multicultural counseling in schools: A practical handbook* (2nd ed.). Boston: Allyn & Bacon.

Plyler v. Doe, 457 U.S. 202 (1982). Supreme Court of the United States. Retrieved on December 26, 2008, from http://www.law.cornell.edu/supct/html/historics/USSC_CR_0457_0202_ZO.html.

Ragan, A. (2006, March/April). Using adapted texts in ELL classrooms. *ELL Outlook.* Downloaded on May 21, 2009, at http://www.coursecrafters.com/ELL-Outlook/2006/mar_apr/ELLOutlookITI Article1.htm.

Ramirez, J. A. (2008). Co-constructing a nurturing and culturally relevant academic environment for struggling readers: (Dis)locating crisis and risk through strategic alignment (January 1, 2008). *Electronic Doctoral Dissertations for University of Massachusetts, Amherst.* Paper AAI3325279. Summary available at http://scholarworks.umass.edu/dissertations/AAI3325279.

Reiss, J. (2005). *Teaching content to English language learners: Strategies for secondary school success.* White Plains, NY: Longman/Pearson Education.

Rhode Island Kids Count. (2007). *2007 Rhode Island Kids Count Factbook.* Providence: RI Kids Count. Available at http://www.rikidscount.org/matriarch/MultiPiecePage.asp_Q_PageID_E_655_A_PageName_E_2006Factbook.

Riches, C., & Genesee, F. (2006). Literacy: Crosslinguistic and crossmodal issues. In F. Genesee, K. Lindholm-Leary, W. Saunders, & D. Christian (Eds.), *Educating English language learners: A synthesis of research evidence.* NewYork: Cambridge University Press.

Rivera, C., & Collum, E. (Eds.). (2006). *State assessment policy and practice for English language learners: A national perspective.* Mahwah, NJ: Erlbaum Associates.

Romo, H. (1997). *Ethnic and racial relations in the schools.* Charleston, WV: ERIC Clearinghouse on Rural Education and Small Schools. ERIC Digest No. ED 414 113.

Rose, M. (1990). *Lives on the boundary: A moving account of the struggles and achievements of America's educationally underprepared.* New York: Penguin Books.

Rosenbloom, S. R. (2004). Experiences of discrimination among African American, Asian American, and Latino adolescents in an urban high school. *Youth and Society, 35*(4), 420–451.

Ross, R. (2007, October 22). Bullying, harassment, and children from immigrant families. *Stand up to bullying! Strategies to make Connecticut safe for learning.* A forum held by the Office of the Child Advocate, the Commission on Children, and other partners. Legislative Office Building, Hartford CT.

Rothenberg, C., & Fisher, D. (2007). *Teaching English language learners: A differentiated approach.* Upper Saddle River, NJ: Pearson.

Rubin, J. (1994). A review of second language listening comprehension research. *Modern Language Journal, 78,* 199–221.

Ruiz-de-Velasco, J., & Fix, M. (2000). *Overlooked and underserved: Immigrant students in U.S. secondary schools.* Washington, DC: Urban Institute.

Ruiz-de-Velasco, J., & Fix, M. (2002). Limited English proficient students and high-stakes accountability systems. In D. M. Piche, W. L. Taylor, & R. A. Reed (Eds.), *Rights at risk: Equality in an age of terrorism.* Report of the Citizens' Commission on Civil Rights. Washington, DC: U.S. Commission on Civil Rights. Available at http://www.cccr.org/publications/publication.cfm?id=1.

Sachar, L. (2000). *Holes.* New York: Scholastic

Samway, K. D. (2006). *When English Language learners write: Connecting research to practice, K–8.* Portsmouth, NH: Heinemann.

Schaps, E. (2003). Creating a school community. *Educational Leadership, 60*(6), 31–33.

Schleppegrell, M. J. (2001). Linguistic features of the language of schooling. *Linguistics and Education, 12*(4), 431–459.

Schleppegrell, M. J. (2004). *The language of schooling: A functional linguistics perspective.* Mahwah, NJ: Lawrence Erlbaum.

Schleppegrell, M. J., & Colombi, M. C. (2002). *Developing advanced literacy in first and second languages: Meaning with Power.* Mahwah, NJ: Lawrence Erlbaum.

Scribner, J. D., Young, M. D., & Pedroza, A. (1999). Building collaborative relationships with parents. In P. Reyes, J. D. Scribner, & A. P. Scribner (Eds.), *Lessons from high-performing Hispanic schools: Creating learning communities* (pp. 36–60). New York: Teachers College Press.

Short, D. (2007). *Designing comprehensive course assessment prompts, portfolio tasks and exhibition projects for ELLs.* Paper presented at Secondary ESL Institute, Pawtucket, RI, December 2007.

Short, D. J., & Fitzsimmons, S. (2007). *Double the work: Challenges and solutions to acquiring language and academic literacy for adolescent English language learners.* A report commissioned by the Carnegie Corporation of New York. Washington, DC: Alliance for Excellent Education. Available at http://www.all4ed.org/publication_material/reports/double_work.

Shrum, J., & Glisan, E. (2005). *Teacher's handbook* (3rd ed.). Boston: Heinle and Heinle.

Slavin, R. E., & Cheung, A. (2003). *Effective reading programs for English language learners: A best-evidence synthesis.* (CRESPAR Report No. 66.) Baltimore: Center for Research on the Education of Students Placed at Risk, Johns Hopkins University.

Solórzano, R. W. (2008). High stakes testing: Issues, implications, and remedies for English language learners. *Review of Educational Research, 78*(2), 260–329. Online version available at http://rer.sagepub.com/cgi/content/abstract/78/2/260.

Stipek, D. (2006). Relationships matter. *Educational Leadership, 64*(1), 46–49.

Swan, M., & Smith, B. (2001). *Learner English: A teacher's guide to interference and other problems* (2nd ed.). New York: Cambridge University Press.

Swanson, C. B. (2008, April 1). *Cities in crisis: A special analytic report on high school graduation.* Bethesda, MD: Editorial Projects in Education Research Center.

Swanson, C. H. (1997). *Who's listening in the classroom? A research paradigm.* Paper presented at the Annual Meeting of the International Listening Association, Sacramento, CA. (Available as ERIC Document No. 407 659.)

Tan, A. (2003). Fish Cheeks. *The Opposite of Fate: A book of Musings* (pp. 125-7). New York: Penguin Group.

Taraba, J. (2004). Transitional words and phrases. University of Richmond Writers Web. Richmond: the Writing Center. Available at http://writing2.richmond.edu/writing/wweb/trans1.html.

Teachers of English to Speakers of Other Languages. (2003, March). *Position paper on high-stakes testing for K–12 English language learners in the United States of America.* Alexandria, VA: Author. Available at http://www.tesol.org/s_tesol/seccss.asp?CID=32&DID=37.

Teachers of English to Speakers of Other Languages. (2005, October). *Position paper on assessment and ac-*

countability of English language learners under the No Child Left Behind Act of 2001 (Public Law 107-110). Available at http://www.tesol.org/s_tesol/seccss.asp?CID=32&DID=37.

Teachers of English to Speakers of Other Languages, Inc. (2006). *PreK–12 English language proficiency standards.* Alexandria, VA: Author.

Tennessee State Education Department. (2009). *Reading in the content areas. Tennessee Department of Education Content Area Reading Course Syllabus 3081.* Available at www.tennessee.gov/education/ci/reading/grades_9-12.pdf.

Thornburgh, N. (2006). Dropout nation. *Time, 167*(16), 30–40.

Tovani, C. (2000). *I read it but I don't get it: Comprehension strategies for adolescent readers.* Portland, ME: Stenhouse.

Travieso-Parker, L. (2006). *Policies, pedagogy, and practices: Educational experiences of Latino English Language Learners in Virginia.* Unpublished doctoral dissertation, Virginia Polytechnic Institute and State University, Blacksburg.

U.S. Department of Education. (2008). Family Educational Rights and Privacy Act (FERPA). Retrieved on December 25, 2008, from http://www.ed.gov/policy/gen/guid/fpco/ferpa/index.html.

U.S. Department of Education, National Center for Education Statistics. (2006). *Public elementary and secondary students, staff, schools, and school districts: School year 2003–04* (NCES 2006–307). Retrieved December 21 2008, from http://nces.ed.gov/fastfacts/display.asp?id=96.

U.S. Office for Civil Rights. (2004, June 21). Letter on OCR Case Number 08041022-D from OCR to Dr. Sally Downey, Superintendent, Joint Technical Education District, Mesa, AZ. Downloaded from http://www.ed.gov/about/offices/list/ocr/letters/evit08041022-d.html.

Valdés, G. (2001). *Learning and not learning English: Latino students in American schools.* New York: Teachers College Press.

Ventriglia, L. (1982). *Conversations of Miguel and Maria: How children learn English as a second language.* Reading, MA: Addison-Wesley.

Verplaetse, L. S., & Migliacci, N. (2008). Making mainstream content comprehensible through sheltered instruction. In L. S. Verplaetse & N. Migliacci (Eds.), *Inclusive pedagogy for English language learners* (pp. 127–166). Mahwah, NJ: Lawrence Erlbaum Associates.

Violand-Sánchez, E., & Hainer-Violand, J. (2006). The power of positive identity. *Educational Leadership, 64*(1), 36–40.

Vu, P. (2008, June 24). *States credit foreign language study.* Downloaded July 15, 2008, at http://www.stateline.org/live/details/story?contentid+320478.

Vygotsky, L. S. (1978). *Mind in society: The development of higher psychological processes.* Cambridge, MA: Harvard University Press.

Weinstein, G. (2004). Moving toward learner-centered teaching with accountability. Theme issue (Guest Editor), *CATESOL Journal, 16*(1), 97–110.

Wentzel, K. R., & Caldwell, K. (1997). Friendships, peer acceptance, and group membership: Relations to academic achievement in middle school. *Child Development, 68,* 1198–1209.

West, M. (1953). *A general service list of English words.* London: Longmans, Green, and Company.

WIDA Consortium. (2004). *Performance definitions for the levels of English language proficiency.,* Retrieved on April 12, 2008, from http://www.wida.us/standards/RG_Performance%20Definitions.pdf.

Wiesel, E. (1960). *Night.* New York: Hill & Wang.

Wiggens, G.P., & McTighe, J. (2005). *Understanding by design.* Expanded Second edition. Alexandria, VA: Association for Supervision and Cirriculum Development.

Wilen, D. K. (2004). *English language learners: An introductory guide for educators. Helping children at home and school II: Handouts for families and educators.* Bethesda, MD: National Association of School Psychologists.

Williams, F. C. (2003, October). Concerns of newly arrived immigrant students: Implications for school counselors. *Professional School Counseling, 7*(1), 9–13.

Williams, J. (2001). Classroom conversations: Opportunities to learn for ESL students in mainstream classrooms. *The Reading Teacher, 54*(8), 750–757.

Willingham, D. T. (2007, Summer). Critical thinking: Why is it so hard to teach? *American Educator, 31*(2), 8–19. Available at http://www.aft.org/pubs-reports/american_educator/issues/summer07/Crit_Thinking.pdf.

World-Class Instructional Design and Assessment (WIDA) Consortium. (2007). *WIDA ELP standards and resource guide* (2007 ed.). Madison: Wisconsin Center for Education Research at the School of Education, University of Wisconsin–Madison. Available at http://wida.us.

Wright, W. E. (2006). A catch-22 for language learners. *Educational Leadership, 64*(3), 22-27.

Index